Hurricane

Hurricane

Edward Bishop

Airlife
England

ISBN 0 906393 62 0

First published 1986
by Airlife Publishing Ltd.

Printed in England by Livesey Ltd., Shrewsbury.

Airlife Publishing Ltd.

7 St. John's Hill, Shrewsbury, England.

Contents

Preface

Perhaps it was inevitable that I should write about the Hurricane, although until Alastair Simpson of Airlife suggested the Spitfire's more numerous Battle of Britain companion as a subject I had not considered it. I should have known better. Yet, I hesitated. Publication of my book, *The Battle of Britain,* was as long ago as 1960 to commemorate the 20th anniversary and I thought I had left all that behind me. Very soon, however, I rediscovered the fascination of the period and, of course, the Hurricane's subsequent career.

Sadly, many who had helped me hitherto were no longer here, but since their assistance and support has carried forward into this book I repeat my indebtedness to them all and in particular to Lord Beaverbrook, so generous with his time and hospitality, and to Lord Dowding who so patiently answered my questions.

In some instances continuity has been achieved. Group Captain Tom Gleave, helpful also with a later book, *The Guinea Pig Club,* entertained me at the Royal Air Force Club, bringing with him Robert Wright who was at Dowding's side at Bentley Priory. It was also reassuring to find at least one familiar face at the Air Historical Branch of the Ministry of Defence in the person of Denis Bateman who in 1958 unearthed for *The Wooden Wonder* a picture of the bear which "crewed" a Mosquito in the Far East. Unable to pinpoint photographs of Hurricanes in Russia, I returned to Denis Bateman who redirected me with the negative numbers to the Imperial War Museum — as ever very helpful — but where in this respect I had previously drawn a blank.

My thanks are also due to staff at the Adastral House Library of the Ministry of Defence and to Reg Mack of the Royal Air Force Museum. Assistance with illustrations was also received from Richard Riding, editor of *Aeroplane Monthly* and his colleague, David Moncur of the Quadrant Picture Library which includes the *Flight* and *Aeroplane* collections; and from Mark Skidmore, formerly of British Aerospace, Kingston, where the Hurricane was designed. I value, too, the encouragement of Air Commodore Henry Probert, Head of the Air Historical Branch, two of whose predecessors, Mr. J. C. Nerney and Mr. L. A. Jackets facilitated my research in 1958 and 1959.

I wish to thank also Air Chief Marshal Sir Harry Broadhurst who kindly sent me in handwriting an account of how he acquired his "private" Hurricane.

I am especially indebted to Francis K. Mason for permission to use technical and other material from *The Hawker Hurricane,* his Macdonald monograph of 1962. Publication of the Appendices would not have been possible without this much appreciated assistance. Comprehensive records no longer exist at British Aerospace.

Lastly, it has been a bonus to have two such helpful neighbours as Wing Commander Bryan Winslett who took part in the Turbinlite night fighter trials, employing the Hurricane as satellite to the Havoc, and Major Matthew Oliver who loaned research material.

Edward Bishop

Chapter 1
How it happened

'The name of Hawker deserves to live in the history of aviation' . . . *Flight,* 1921.

Aerospace design teams, dependent upon computers, schoolchildren learning maths with pocket calculators, must marvel that the Hurricane ever happened. The Hawker Hurricane was the product of pencil and paper arithmetic and comparatively unlettered talents. Its solid performance as Britain's predominant fighter aircraft in the opening stages of the Second World War reflected the reliability of its design and production pedigree and the dependable nature of its creators.

In the beginning there was Sopwith, then there were Sigrist, Hawker, Camm, Spriggs and Bulman. Of course, there were others, but these are the principals without whom there would have been no Hawker pedigree; no monoplane eight-gun fighter to precede the Supermarine Spitfire and outnumber it in the Battle of Britain of 1940.

After the First World War the Sopwith Aviation Company had found itself with a production line but little business. Thomas Octavius Murdoch Sopwith, eighth child of a comfortably well-off north of England family, was born in 1888; on schedule for indulging as a young man the novel pleasures of motor racing, competitive flying and driving fast motor-boats. As horsemen employed grooms, Sopwith needed mechanics to service his machines.

In 1910 he employed Fred Sigrist as chauffeur and odd-job man. Sigrist was soon to care for a six-cylinder Napier motor-car, motor-boats and Sopwith's aeroplanes — an Avis monoplane built by Howard Wright, a Wright biplane and a Bleriot monoplane.

When Sigrist needed help, he engaged H. E. Kauper, who had replied to an advertisement for an aeroplane mechanic and a carpenter. Kauper knew that Harry Hawker, an Australian friend, had arrived in England and was looking for work. In June 1912 Sopwith hired Hawker, banking as a deposit the £40 which Hawker had saved for his passage home.

As Hawker joined Sopwith, the aviation company, operating from sheds encircled by the motor-racing track at Brooklands in Surrey, received a Naval order.

In Sigrist, who became works manager; Kauper, foreman, and Hawker, responsible for the flight shed, Sopwith had recruited by instinct the nucleus of an 'engineering' staff.

Sopwith hired Harry Hawker in June, 1912, and by September the young Australian had a pilot's licence. *(British Aerospace)*

Sopwith and his sister May with Howard Wright biplane. *(Flight)*

A factory was established at a disused roller-skating rink some seven miles down river at Kingston-on-Thames.

Chalk outlines appeared on the walls as though cavemen had been busy. A plan view was on the floor. There were no detailed drawings or stress diagrams; not even slide rules. Conditions were rudimentary at the work place which, within 22 years, was to give birth to the Hawker Hurricane.

Harry Hawker, son of a Cornish blacksmith and Scottish mother, had run away from school in Australia at the age of 12 and found work at five shillings a week with a motor-car business. He had saved £100 and sailed for England with Kauper. Taking a series of humble jobs, he spent any spare time at Brooklands, watching the flying.

Sopwith had hired Hawker by hunch and shortly afterwards he taught him to fly. By September 1912 Hawker possessed a pilot's certificate. Within a year he held the British air records for speed, altitude and endurance; a grand slam of successes rendered the more remarkable because he was by no means robust, and suffered from air sickness and back trouble. An almost statutory Australian irreverence cockily expressed by his preference for perching a flat cap back-to-front on his curly head and a reputation as Constance Babington-Smith writes in *Testing Time,* for being 'quick as a wink and sparking with fun', camouflaged his physical weaknesses.

Very soon he was Sopwith's test pilot. He was intimately involved with each new aeroplane from design to modifications until he was killed in a crash on 12 July 1921. But he had survived long enough to give his name to the company which created the Hurricane and to help establish the Hawker Hurricane's strong and healthy pedigree.

From the Tabloid fighter of the First World War, Sopwith, and subsequently Hawker aircraft, were full of Harry Hawker's ideas. They evolved from hard and dangerous experience as a test pilot and from one sensational international exploit.

On 18 May 1919, partnered by Commander Kenneth Mackenzie Grieve of the Royal Navy as navigator in a single-engined Sopwith biplane, Hawker attempted a first west-east trans-Atlantic non-stop flight from Newfoundland to Ireland. The machine, carrying 350 gallons of fuel for an estimated 22 hours' duration, was confronted by northerly gale force winds. Less than half way, with 180 gallons expended and the engine over-heating, Hawker put down in the sea. The pair were presumed lost and King George V sent a telegram of condolence to Mrs Hawker, but the *Mary,* a small Danish freighter on the Mexico run, had sighted the wreckage and after only 30 minutes in the sea Hawker and Mackenzie Grieve were rescued. (Captain John Alcock and Arthur Whitten Brown achieved the first Atlantic crossing from Newfoundland in a Vickers Vimy on 15 June 1919, and were knighted).

The dramatic nature of their failure established Hawker and his partner as popular heroes and unusually for a civilian, Hawker was awarded the Air Force Cross.

But before long Harry Hawker would be as much out of work as so many less fortunate servicemen survivors of the First World War. In September 1920, in the absence of government orders, Sopwith put the company into voluntary liquidation while it remained solvent. Within two months the H. G. Hawker Engineering Company was registered as a private company with capital of £20,000 in £1 shares 'to acquire from F. I. Bennett all the patents, rights etc, relating to the manufacture of motor-cycles . . .'. It was hoped to make aeroplanes and after the motor-cycle venture had evaporated, Sigrist said to Sopwith and Hawker: 'Let's make aeroplanes again'.

Sigrist, who had prospered on a royalty from each Sopwith aeroplane, joined Sopwith and Hawker as an investor. Frank Spriggs, whom Sopwith, to free himself from ledgers, had promoted from office boy to costing bookkeeper, completed the team.

In less than a year Hawker was dead. He crashed while testing his Nieuport Goshawk entry at Hendon four days before the 16 July 1921 aerial Derby.

From his airfield two miles away at Stag Lane, Captain Geoffrey de Havilland watched the aeroplane climb steeply and fall out of control. An inquest revealed that Hawker ought not to have been flying. A tubercular spine had reduced his vertebrae to a shell. A haemorrhage was thought to have paralysed his legs in flight. But crash details released years later suggest fire had caused loss of control. Harry Hawker had gone at the early age of 31, this 'great and restless spirit', as his near contemporary test pilot Harald Penrose was to describe him.

Flight commented: 'The name of Hawker deserves to live in the history of aviation, not for the performances associated with the name, but for his contributions to the increase of aeronautical knowledge. He decided to build better aeroplanes than anyone has built'.

Since the absorption of the Hawker aircraft companies by the impersonal British Aerospace, Hawker's name has been dissociated from present-day aviation. But it lives on, coupled with the company's historically most celebrated aeroplane, the Hawker Hurricane. Hawker-Siddeley is no longer in aviation.

Sidney Camm, who was to design the Hurricane, joined the company in 1923 as senior draughtsman, too late to have worked with Harry Hawker. His qualifications were academically scrappy, but he was rich in practice and in experience in this young industry. He was a carpenter whose hobby interest in model gliders as a member — later secretary — of the Windsor Model Aeroplane Club, had impelled him to night school and flying machines.

Sydney Camm brought to Hawkers credentials earned at Martinsydes after being employed there in 1912 as a woodworker. When Martinsydes ceased production in 1921 Camm had progressed from craftsman to

Now will she start? Sopwith and Howard Wright machine. *(Flight)*

mechanic, draughtsman and senior draughtsman.

As with Sigrist, Hawker and Spriggs, Sopwith warmed instinctively to Camm who in 1925 at the age of 32 was appointed chief designer. Sopwith has said that he recognised Camm as a genius, though other colleagues disputed this assessment, rating him a designer of skill and ability.

Certainly, it was Camm's skill and ability that established the line of piston-engined aeroplanes which was to peak in the Hawker Hurricane, Tempest and Typhoon and extend into the Hunter and Harrier, influencing even the Hawk and Tornado.

From Camm's drawing board in swift succession over the next nine years came, among others, the Hart, Fury, Hornet, Audax and Hotspur; an apprenticeship for the Hurricane. The method of construction of the Hurricane differed only in details and size from its predecessors.

In these years the Hawker team and its biplanes matured. Sopwith, now greying, reflected how well his instinct had served him and stood back as Camm sped from one design to the next. He admired Camm's dedication, but privately sympathised with members of the staff who suffered this thrusting, impossible-to-satisfy chief designer.

As Camm dominated the design department at Kingston, Spriggs, immaculately suited and unsuspected by an increasing workforce as the general dogsbody he once was, drove a managerial desk.

Sigrist was here, there and everywhere, 'an absolute whirlwind of energy and activity', Harald Penrose remembers. The H. G. Hawker Engineering Company had learned to live without Harry Hawker.

An aircraft manufacturer with a declining order book is very soon no company at all, as Sopwith had found in 1919. In the 1920s and early 1930s, after the war-to-end-wars, a company dependent upon military spending was particularly vulnerable. Once an aeroplane was on the drawing board it was prudent to look ahead to the next . . . and the next . . . and the next for fear that competitors would beat you to the Air Ministry door. Sydney Camm (26,000 aeroplanes were built from his 52 designs) never neglected the trail from Kingston-on-Thames to Adastral House in Holborn where Royal Air Force requirements were planned. Camm wooed his Service customer and paid careful attention to the reports and recommendations of the Hawker and Service test pilots upon which the company's welfare depended.

Towards the end of the Hart and Fury stream Camm was conscious that biplane fighter performance could not be much improved. It seemed to have peaked in his design of a Fury to fulfil an order for the Yugoslav Air Force.

In 1933 he began to consider the design of what was at first known as the Fury monoplane. The concept of a monoplane fighter superseding the biplane was not exclusive to Camm and Hawkers. At Supermarine, a Vickers Aviation subsidiary since November 1928, R. J. Mitchell, designer of the renowned seaplane series culminating in the SB6B monoplane winner of the Schneider Trophy in 1931, nursed similar ambitions.

At much the same time Adolf Hitler and his National Socialist Party came to power in Germany (30 January 1933), pledged to rearm, and the British Air Marshals began to shed their suspicions of the monoplane. Together these events conspired to encourage private venture design and production which would result in the Hurricane — and the Spitfire.

The emphasis in the ventures remained much on the 'private'. As the 1930s progressed, Winston Churchill, a back-bench Member of Parliament in the wilderness, warned of the perils of German rearmament. His efforts were not, however, assisted by the participation of the National Government (under Labour's Ramsay MacDonald from November 1931 to June 1935) in the Disarmament Conference at Geneva until it was adjourned indefinitely in June 1934. Nor, as will become evident, did the appointment by Lord Londonderry, the Air Minister, of

Air Chief Marshal Sir Edward Ellington as Chief of the Air Staff after the untimely death in 1933 of Air Chief Marshal Sir Geoffrey Salmond, help the fighters. Londonderry has been much criticised, but there were positive results of his term at the Air Ministry. Despite Geneva, he managed to retain an air force and he established the committee under Mr. H. T. Tizard which fostered radar and promoted the concept of monoplane fighter design, leading to the Hurricane and the Spitfire.

Camm had been convinced that the monoplane would supersede the biplane from the time of his appointment in 1925 as chief designer at Hawkers. Before embarking on his biplane series he had visualised a small monoplane fighter to be armed with two Vickers machine-guns and engined by a Bristol Jupiter. He was ahead of his contemporaries, but Air Ministry attitudes were still conditioned by the disintegration in 1912 of two monoplanes, after which Royal Flying Corps pilots had been ordered not to fly Service monoplanes.

On a hot day in the holiday month of August 1933, Camm called at Adastral House by appointment on Major Buchanan, Deputy

But for Sir Thomas Sopwith there would have been no Hawkers to build the Hurricane. He employed Sigrist, Hawker and Spriggs. *(British Aerospace)*

Sopwith's oddjob man Fred Sigrist (second left) had faith in Hawker after the First World War and backed his venture. *(Flight)*

Director of Research and Development. He knew that the air staff was disappointed by the failure of the manufacturers to push up the speeds of fighters. In the air exercises of 1930 no fighter managed to catch his own light bomber, the Hart. A bomber had outpaced fighters. The implications were serious.

Since then, the advent of the Demon, Camm's two-seater fighter variant of the Hart and the Fury in 1931, had produced marginal superiority and this was subsequently improved by the Gloster Gladiator, ordered in 1935 as the last of the RAF's biplane fighters. But the Gladiator's top speed of 253 mph was not considered good enough.

In Buchanan's office on that August day Camm presented the concept of his monoplane fighter. Buchanan said he would see what he could do, warning that 'in these days of disarmament' the cost and revolutionary proposal of a monoplane were against him.

Camm was not alone in receiving this rebuff. R. J. Mitchell, who was to design the Spitfire, had failed in the F 7/30 specification competition with his Goshawk-powered Supermarine Type 224 monoplane, as had the Bristol Aeroplane Company and Westland with their proposals. But in the autumn of 1933 the idea of a monoplane fighter, offering the promise of increased speed, became more acceptable. On 4 October 1933 Germany's withdrawal from the Disarmament Conference and the League of Nations helped to shock the doubters into accepting the monoplane as the fighter of the future.

After the First World War the Hawkers were familiar figures at air displays. *(Flight)*

Even so, Hawkers had to finance its Fury monoplane as a private venture. Similarly, Rolls-Royce was to develop a private venture engine, the PV 12 or Merlin. When the new engine replaced the Goshawk in the Hawker design, the name Fury was dropped and it became simply the Interceptor Monoplane.

There were design alterations to accommodate the Merlin but the steel tubular structure, fabric covering and overall strength of Camm's designs, which had served Hawkers so faithfully, remained. The main differences were that a 'greenhouse' was built round the pilot in the cockpit because of the expected faster speeds; leading and trailing edges of the wings were slightly tapered; and a large radiator was situated under their centre. The undercarriage was fixed as in the Fury biplane and armament restricted to four machine-guns. Only after Camm had moved the radiator 18 inches aft, because the Merlin was heavier than the Goshawk, was room available for a retractable undercarriage.

At Hawkers, outward appearances gave no hint that the company was burying the biplane and fixed undercarriage past of Sopwith and Hawker. There was an almost Dickensian atmosphere as the ranks of more than 70 draughtsmen quietly manoeuvred their set squares on oak drawings-boards in the long design office. In their midst, Camm, whose pencil had established the transition from Fury biplane to Hurricane monoplane, presided over his draughtsmen's labours from a glass box. Each man knew that at any moment he might be subject to the scrutiny of Sydney Camm, tall, bent and hook-nosed, observing him and his work like some latter-day beadle. Although he was a good family man, at work Camm could be, a colleague noted, 'cruel and quite unreasonable', and 'thoroughly obstructive to the introduction of essential modifications unless he originated

Unrecognisable as Sopwith's office boy, Sir Frank Spriggs (right) was the driving force behind Hurricane production and Hawker's commercial success. *(British Aerospace)*

them'. He also tended to tick off senior staff in front of visitors. An encouraging pat on the back would have been out of character, even for 'his little-known assistant', Roy Chaplin, whom Harald Penrose noted as 'a sound engineer and administrator who was very loyal to Camm, though Camm never gave him his due'.

The fact was that the creator of the Hurricane was a hard taskmaster, of whom Sopwith remarked that he wondered why the men put up with him. The reality lay in the depression years and the unemployment of the early 1930s before rearmament provided more opportunities in the aircraft industry.

Camm paced among the drawing-board as though keeping a schoolroom class up to its work. Outside, the gloomy and somewhat dingy design office, suburban trains of Southern Electric rattled past on the nearby Waterloo line. It was an uninspiring birthplace for the revolutionary eight-gun fighter which was predominantly responsible for the defeat of the Luftwaffe in 1940.

Camm, his team, and all at Hawkers, were engaged in a great act of faith. Whatever personal solace Buchanan and some serving officers at the Air Ministry might offer, the Interceptor Monoplane continued to face formidable official opposition, not least of which was the obduracy of Air Chief Marshal Sir Edward Ellington, Chief of the Air Staff in the critical years between 1933 and 1937. The current rearmament programme was planned for completion in 1942 and Ellington had convinced himself that there would be no war until that year. He also believed that the bomber would remain the dominant weapon in the air and should, therefore, receive priority over fighter development; an opinion to which Stanley Baldwin, the Conservative politician, who replaced Ramsay MacDonald as Prime Minister in June 1935, gave voice in the phrase: 'The bomber will always get through'. Baldwin was conditioned to some extent by the thinking of Air Marshals who had fought as young pilots in the Royal Flying Corps and who had yet to accept fully the speed and armament potentialities of a monoplane fighter.

Fortunately, however, there was a young squadron leader in the Operational

Requirements Branch of the Air Ministry who launched a persistent one-man campaign to win them over. Ralph Sorley believed that monoplane fighters would produce speeds so fast that their pilots would not be able to hold an enemy in their sights for more than two seconds. Consequently eight guns would be needed to achieve the necessary concentrated fire-power. He supported his argument for a monoplane eight-gun fighter with the results of experiments carried out by Captain F. W. Hill, senior ballistics officer at the Aeroplane and Armament Establishment at Martlesham Heath in Suffolk. On 19 July 1934 Captain Hill presented them at an Air Ministry conference on armament.

By now Camm, because of the advent of the Merlin, was designing as a private venture an air interceptor monoplane much advanced on the monoplane version of the Fury. Sorley called at Kingston to press the incorporation of eight guns, encouraging Camm that strong Hawker wings would provide an incomparable mounting for eight Brownings.

It was a courageous initiative on the part of a young squadron leader in the face of formidable opposition, including that of Air Chief Marshal Sir Robert Brooke-Popham, Commander-in-Chief, Air Defence of Great Britain, who thought 'eight guns was going a bit far'. Early next year, 1935, when the Air Ministry at last issued a specification (F5/34) for a monoplane fighter giving 275 mph at 15,000 feet, eight guns were called for.

To Camm, as also to Mitchell at Supermarine, the specification was academic. He was already confident of bettering it. The Air Ministry issued a revised Specification F36/34 in terms of what Hawkers were already doing.

Meanwhile the Government remained convinced that the bomber should take priority until as late as 21 May 1935. On that day the Cabinet considered a report from a recently appointed Air Parity Sub-Committee, chaired by Sir Philip Cunliffe-Lister, President of the Board of Trade, who, as Viscount Swinton, was to become Air Minister on 7 June. The very phrasing of the report emphasises how private were the company ventures. It read: 'The firms of Hawker and Supermarine are, we are informed, designing low-wing monoplanes with retractable undercarriages, flaps for slow landing, and an estimated speed of 300 mph. Prototypes may be expected in July and October, 1935, respectively'.

While Hawkers and Supermarine were going it alone courageously, production of medium and heavy bombers had been ordered off the drawing-board. Ellington, Chief of the Air Staff, had frustrated similar action on the new fighters. The best that could be achieved for the future Hurricane and Spitfire were orders for prototypes and these were sanctioned only after the personal insistence of the Air Member for Research and Development. Little known to the public, the then Air Marshal Sir Hugh Dowding had rendered his first great service towards saving Britain from invasion in 1940. But there was still no production order for either monoplane fighter.

Despite the report of the Air Parity Sub-Committee, the policy of priority for the Bomber Command of the RAF would not be reversed until the Inskip Report of 1937, the basis of the Empire's preparation for war, awarded priority to Fighter Command. The Air Staff did not like this, regarding expansion of Fighter Command in defence against any attempted knock-out blow as risky in the extreme. It still favoured the deterrence of a strong bomber force, a policy vigorously pushed by a certain Group Captain Arthur Harris, Ellington's Deputy Director of Plans, who believed the bomber to be the decisive weapon.

The appointment in 1936 of Sir Thomas Inskip to the new post of Minister for the Co-ordination of Defence was described by Winston Churchill as 'the most astonishing appointment since Caligula made his horse a Consul'. In the House of Commons, Lieutenant-Commander R. T. H. Fletcher heaped further opprobrium, portraying this chubby Bristol lawyer as a 'barrage balloon — cumbrous and not of any proven worth'. Inskip knew nothing about defence when he took office, but flying in the face of the Air

Sir Sidney Camm, designer of the Hurricane and creator of a long Hawker pedigree, H. K. Jones also of Hawkers, and P. W. S. 'George' Bulman. *(Flight)*

Staff he assured a future for the Hurricane and the Spitfire.

A year earlier, Baldwin, after taking Ramsay MacDonald's place as Prime Minister, had in some measure soothed Churchill's hurt in the wilderness by inviting him to join the newly formed Committee of Imperial Defence on Air Defence Research. For all his initial sarcasm over Inskip, Churchill subsequently provided him with information and suggestions, some of which promoted the cause of the monoplane fighters.

The obstacles encountered by Camm (and Mitchell) have long since been overlaid by the operational success stories of their aircraft. At Kingston, Camm, the former woodworker, contended with the unknown. The constructional pedigree existed, but the overall performance demands of a monoplane, not to say wing flaps and a retractable undercarriage, called for innovations, particularly new hydraulic control systems. Camm had also to consider blind-flying instrument panels and more sophisticated radio and oxygen supply requirements. He supervised work on a multitude of detail while the monoplane took general shape, first as a series of scale models and then as a wooden mock-up.

Camm presented the mock-up to visitors from the Air Ministry on 10 January 1935. Although the design did not accommodate more than four guns at this stage, Air Commodore L. A. Pattinson from Armaments Research and Wing Commander C. N. Lowe from Air Defence of Great Britain were not unduly concerned. Licence to manufacture the Browning in Britain had not yet been obtained from the Colt Patent Firearms Company in the United States. It was July before the contracts were awarded to the Birmingham Small Arms Company and Vickers, the .300 inch Browning being adapted to fire British .303 rimmed ammunition.

Unrelenting, Camm drove on his draughtsmen in the long room at Kingston's Canonbury Park Road and on 21 February 1935 he sent provisional performance figures to the Royal Air Force. The Air Marshals were surprised. Camm's estimates exceeded their expectations after they had conceded Sorley's case for an eight-gun fighter. Maximum level speed at 15,000 feet had increased from the specification's 275 mph to 330 mph. It so happened that it was on this very day that Hawkers received a firm order

The somewhat gloomy surroundings in which the Hurricane was designed at Hawker's Canonbury Park Road, Kingston-upon-Thames works. *(British Aerospace)*

for one prototype of the fighter which Pattinson had seen in mock-up. Henceforth the embryo Hurricane would be honoured with a registration number — K5083.

Now, as the private venture began to be paid for, the company was better placed to consider expansion. Rearmament, gradually and grudgingly accepted at Westminster, had started to improve its prospects in the preceding two years. In 1933, when Adolf Hitler was proclaimed Chancellor of Germany, the H. G. Hawker Engineering Company gave way to Hawker Aircraft, a public company, in a financial arrangement which allowed for expansion.

Sopwith, Spriggs and Sigrist, who had joined Harry Hawker in his enterprise after the First World War, recognised the need to fortify the business financially and provide space for expanding production. Capacity at Kingston was limited because much of the shop floor had been leased to the Leyland Motor Company in the thin times of the late 1920s. So Hawkers bought the Gloster Aircraft Company at Brockworth. Although this brought no immediate relief, as Glosters were heavily engaged with the Gauntlet biplane, the RAF's last open-cockpit fighter and predecessor of the Gladiator, it was a far-sighted acquisition, providing additional capacity for future Hurricane production. Spriggs was appointed chairman at Glosters. Camm and P. W. S. 'George' Bulman, chief test pilot, joined the Hawker board amid developments engendering confidence and a sense of company and personal achievement, which could only enhance the prospects of the new monoplane fighter.

As the fuselage took shape and the hole in the hump, so characteristic of a Sydney Camm design, became more obviously a cockpit, George Bulman was a frequent visitor to the shop floor. Hawker's chief test pilot was impatient to familiarise himself with the controls. The appointments of Bulman and Camm as directors, in June 1935, were unusual distinctions for a chief designer and chief test pilot. Other than Harry Hawker, no British test pilot had sat on an aircraft manufacturer's board.

Camm did not take kindly to being told his business, but he listened to Bulman with whom he had worked amicably for ten years. He always acknowledged that the success of his aircraft owed much to Bulman and his fellow test pilots.

When K5083's cockpit was ready the chief test pilot climbed in. Operationally the Hurricane was to accommodate 'the long and the short and the tall'. Not all would find it as roomy as Bulman. He was a small man and his light physique facilitated quick and easy access. He felt very much at home.

Chapter 2
Bulman takes her up

'Another winner, I think . . .' George Bulman, 6 November 1935

The airframe of the prototype was finished in August and in September the Merlin was installed. On 23 October 1935, the fuselage and two wings were transported by lorry to Brooklands. It seemed entirely right that the first Hawker Hurricane should fly from the field where in 1912 Sopwith had hired Hawker.

Bulman, who would take her up when she was ready, watched keenly as the fabric-covered wings were slotted into the centre section. He was reputed to put in more hours of preparation on the ground than in the air, ensuring that his recommendations were carried out. In previous weeks he had attended undercarriage retraction tests.

A tight tarpaulin concealed the dismembered prototype as it arrived in the conspiratorial first light of that late autumn day. Larger than any load normally received at Brooklands, it halted while the gates were removed. Then, against the sombre backdrop of Surrey pines and the steep concrete banking of the race-track's mountain circuit, the lorry moved to the Hawker assembly hangar on the airfield. Bill Bailey, the foreman, and Bert Hayward, the rigger, removed the wraps.

Bulman's homework for the maiden flight of K5083 was characteristically painstaking. Shortly before the outbreak in August 1914 of the First World War he had worked at the

Hawker sheds at Brooklands. *(Flight)*

Bank of England as a junior clerk. He joined the Royal Flying Corps and qualified as a pilot. At Hawkers he brought the fastidiousness of Threadneedle Street to his paperwork and the experience of a fighter pilot to his test flying.

When the prototype was ready he noted that, ballasted for guns and ammunition and fuelled, the aircraft showed an all-up weight of 5,416 pounds. Centre of gravity had shifted a mere half-inch from Camm's estimate.

Bulman taxied K5083, accustoming himself to the field of vision from the cockpit and the greenhouse effect of the canopy. An open-cockpit aviator he had some sympathy with Brooke-Popham's reservations about putting the pilot indoors, although he accepted that future speeds would require it.

For all his experience Bulman was facing the unknown. He could draw upon his war years in the Royal Flying Corps, post-war service in the Royal Air Force as chief test pilot at the Royal Aircraft Establishment and subsequent years at Hawkers, but after so many biplanes this low-wing monoplane, the Hurricane, was something very different.

Foreman and rigger had been surprised by the sheer size of the great humped shape under the tarpaulin and on the November day Bulman took her up even Sopwith, Spriggs and Camm were struck by the contrast between the pale blue and silver monoplane and 'the dainty Fury standing by'.

When all was ready on the morning of 6 November 1935, the impression of size and strength given by the new fighter was accentuated by the small, slim, bald-headed figure of George Bulman, trotting over to the first Hurricane and slipping quickly into the cockpit.

Bulman taxied for take-off at the controls of the fastest fighter aircraft in the world, the first to offer its pilot more than 300 mph; indeed Bulman would soon record 318 mph at 15,500 feet. But this November morning he would feel his way at speeds with which he was familiar, condition himself to the claustrophobic canopy and the absence of the wind and unmuffled engine sounds which always told him so much.

Anxiety over the unproved Merlin heightened the tension of Sopwith and his party. Much work lay ahead before Rolls-Royce got it right and its performance

An inverted Audax, one of the Hurricane's biplane predecessors, over Brooklands in the period of K 5083's maiden flight there is a reminder that biplanes still defended Britain. *(British Aerospace)*

Hardly the expected outfit for a chief test pilot but George Bulman sometimes flew the prototype in a trilby hat. *(RAF Museum)*

supported the company's international reputation for reliability. This morning, however, all was well. The Merlin and the two-blade Watts fixed pitch wooden propeller gave Bulman an easy exit from the soup plate grass airfield within the concrete Brooklands motor-racing circuit.

Now the Hawker party could only wait. Camm was to admit that he worried. Not that there might be a disaster: he was confident of his design and the results of extensive wind tunnel tests on scale models. Camm's thoughts as Bulman and K5083 disappeared were on his disappointment that the aeroplane was not as good as it could have been. Strength had been the company's keynote for construction. He pondered the performance that had been surrendered in pursuit of this quality: 'if only the wing had been thinner . . . '.

After half an hour Bulman returned and as he made his approach Camm noticed that the undercarriage was fully extended. In fact Bulman, knowing that its hand-pumped hydraulic jacks were uncertain, had not retracted it. He taxied to the narrow strip of tarmac by the Hawker sheds and opened the 'conservatory'. Camm climbed on to a wing and the chief test pilot said quietly: 'Another winner, I think'. Camm respected Bulman's qualification. He would not have wished it otherwise. He knew George Bulman as a disciple of Roderic Hill whom he had joined in 1919 as a Farnborough test pilot. Hill, at that time a Squadron Leader and already gaining a reputation as an artist and a philosopher, had taught Bulman to reject temptation to show off; to fly without flamboyance, report without fuss. Hill had also taught Bulman that a test pilot should accept that he is complementary to his designer.

Bulman's apprenticeship under Hill had brought another and very practical asset to Hawkers. At Farnborough he had flown in the engine flight. In the course of Bulman's

The prototype at Brooklands. *(British Aerospace)*

Bulman's maiden flight was on 6 November, 1935. This shot was taken shortly afterwards. *(Flight)*

long partnership with Camm, the performance of Hawker machines had benefited from Bulman's dedication to the flight development of engines. Both designer and chief test pilot knew that, if eventually the new fighter was to become a real winner in squadron operational service, it could be only as good as its engine.

Camm and Bulman were aware that the Merlin C engine powering the prototype Hurricane had failed to obtain the civil 50-hour certificate of airworthiness. But Hawkers were in a hurry. The threat posed by German rearmament under Adolf Hitler and domestic competition represented by a monoplane fighter designed by Reginald Mitchell to a similar specification and on the way from Supermarine, now a Vickers Aviation subsidiary, dictated the earliest possible maiden flight. By 18 December, when certification was received, K5083 had completed seven fights totalling about six hours. After that the Merlin gave trouble and the prototype was grounded between its eighth flight on 26 December and ninth flight on 5 February 1936, with a new engine.

For all the great regard in which the Rolls-Royce Merlin that powered the Hurricane, Spitfire, Mosquito and Lancaster — among other Second World War aircraft — was to be held, the PV 12 engine of the prototype Hurricane encountered serious early difficulties.

Three years before Bulman's maiden flight work had started on the engine at Derby, where it was the last to be nursed into life by Sir Henry Royce who did not live to see it through its teething troubles. After these had been overcome it was evident that 'Pa' Royce, as his men knew him, had produced an engine capable of rapid development. At the centre of its excellence was the capability of increasing supercharger boost and strengthening crankshaft and bearings in accord; a design legacy which after Royce's death in April 1933 was to enable his successors led by E. W. Hives, first as head of the Experimental Department, later as general manager and chairman, to raise the Merlin's horsepower from the 790 hp of the PV 12 to more than 2,000 hp.

In the New Year of 1936 the RAF was

Prototype pictured in 1937 after its acceptance by the RAF at Martlesham Heath. *(RAF Museum)*

agitating to test the prototype Hurricane for itself, but Bulman was loath to part with her. Philip Lucas, who had joined Hawkers at Brooklands in 1931, was sharing experimental flights with the chief test pilot. He has recalled that after the maiden flight K5083 'soon ran into the inevitable teething troubles one expects with a prototype'. Nothing dissuaded Bulman from his first belief that the fighter could be a winner, but as pressure mounted for delivery to the Aircraft and Armament Establishment at Martlesham Heath in Suffolk, engine installation, sliding hood and retractable undercarriage were giving trouble. In the wintry conditions of a New Year such flying as was possible was restricted to evaluating control and stability and trying out remedies for the most prominent faults. Bulman, never truly at home in an enclosed cockpit, discovered that the canopy could not be opened at speeds exceeding a slow climb. After the third flight the hood fell off. Cautiously, it will be recalled, he had not retracted the undercarriage on the maiden flight. Subsequently he discovered that it was difficult to retract and lock using the hand-operated hydraulic pump. At this stage the undercarriage was not powered.

Such problems were trivial compared with the scares the Merlin was providing. Bulman and Lucas realised that if Hawkers were to meet Martlesham's demands for delivery they would have to treat the Merlin gently. Yet however much they nursed it, mechanical trouble persisted, denying them the opportunity to compile performance measurements beyond, as Lucas described them, 'scratch readings in level flight to get

Not yet in the hunt, but the new monoplane fighters provide an incongruous background for the Puckeridge meeting at RAF Debden. *(Flight)*

Dick Reynell helped test and demonstrate the prototype. During the Battle of Britain as a Flight Lieutenant on the Reserve he reported to Hawkers on the fighter's performance in combat. In September, 1940, he was killed while flying with No. 43 Squadron. *(Flight)*

some idea of the suitability of the wooden propeller'. Diving K5083 to check stability and control when flying faster than in level flight was precluded. Cossetting the engine also forbade spinning and aerobatics.

It was not until after K5083 had been flown with a new engine on 5 February that, on 7 February, Bulman agreed to pass the prototype on to the RAF for its assessment. But there were considerable misgivings about the hand-over. Lucas described them: 'Although initial difficulties were converted at least to a usable standard we were far from happy at letting Service pilots fly our precious prototype before we had time to find out much more about it ourselves'. When Bulman delivered K5083 to the RAF's experimental team at Martlesham Heath it had flown eight hours in ten flights.

The prototype did not remain long as a guest of the RAF, with whom it behaved rather better than Bulman and Lucas had expected. Squadron Leader D. F. Anderson, responsible for trials which took place between 18 and 24 February, reported favourably. Martlesham pilots were accustomed to the unknown by virtue of their role, but they were impressed by how different this monoplane was. They complimented the comfort of the conservatory cockpit and, contrary to Bulman's reservations about the weaving required to see ahead, noted that the view was acceptable. They relished the novelty of the retractable undercarriage and reported that the aircraft handled easily, although controls became heavy at high speeds. Maximum speed attained was 315 mph at more than 16,000 feet, handsomely topping the Air Staff's 275 mph requirement. However, the engine — it was changed several times during the trials — continued to give trouble. It was apparent to Hawkers, Rolls-Royce and the RAF that the Merlin would have to undergo intensive development.

In March, notwithstanding the Merlin's unreliability, Hawkers plunged into production preparations for a run of as many as 1,000 aircraft. Sopwith and Spriggs took the view that if orders were not forthcoming from the Air Ministry then the export market would mop them up. On 3 June 1936, the company's risk and perseverance were rewarded with a contract for 600 — the largest such order in peacetime — and on 27 June, Camm's monoplane design to Specification

Pilot's-eye view of cockpit of an early Hurricane I, emphasising gun button on the control column spade grip and basic nature of instruments. *(RAF Museum)*

No. 111 Squadron was put through its paces before hostilities began by its commander, 'Downwind' Gillan. *(RAF Musem)*

F36/34 received Air Ministry approval for the company's choice of name. Henceforth K5083 would be known as the Hawker Hurricane.

Although there existed but one Hurricane, one single-seat monoplane fighter, faster by 100 mph than the biplanes defending the United Kingdom, no attempt was made to conceal it. Within weeks of the production order the prototype was presented — to the British public, representatives of friendly nations and any potential enemy — at the 1936 Hendon Air Display. Squadron Leader Anderson, who had assessed it for the Service at Martlesham Heath, put on a dazzling performance. The aircraft was to reappear regularly in domestic and international air shows until the Brussels exhibition on the very eve of war in the summer of 1939.

But Hawkers' purposeful presentation of the new fighter has to be viewed against the company's initial private venture risk and production scheme for 1,000 aircraft before receiving an order for 600. In 1936 it still seemed almost inconceivable that Europe would again resort to war to settle its differences. The company was pursuing its highly developed commercial instincts. The lack of orders after the First World War had hastened Sopwith Aviation's liquidation. It seemed prudent to Sopwith and Spriggs to seek export business.

The air displays served an equally useful purpose for the rising Luftwaffe, whose senior officers used them as a happy hunting ground in which to gather intelligence and establish a somewhat fretful fraternisation with senior RAF officers. Their persistence was rewarded with an exchange of visits in which Hermann Göring's airmen sought to stimulate a boisterous bonhomie as between former open-cockpit opponents of the Western Front. the Luftwaffe officers had a tendency to show off and the RAF gained from it. But Göring's leaders were not without style, Generals Udet, Junck and Schoenebeck, a technical triumvirate, landing a smart Me108 'Taifun' at Hendon for the 1937 display which featured the Hurricane. In the event buyers from Hawkers' customary export market were more impressed by the Hurricane than the window shoppers from Germany who were well content with the Me 109, already proven in the Spanish civil war. Despite the insistence of Inskip, Swinton and Sir Kingsley Wood, his successor as Air Minister, on the

No. 111 Squadron photographed by Charles E. Brown while based at Northolt before the outbreak of war. *(RAF Museum)*

urgency of production of monoplane fighters for the RAF, orders were to be accepted from Yugoslavia, South Africa, Belgium and Romania. In retrospect this may appear foolhardy in the extreme, but they should be judged in the context of Prime Minister Neville Chamberlain's 'peace in our time' return in September 1938 from his historic meeting with the German Chancellor, Adolf Hitler, at Munich. Moreover, Yugoslavia was a regular customer and had provided a steady market in the 1930s for Hawker Hinds and Furies.

The first of 24 Hurricanes for the Royal Yugoslav Air Force was flown from Brooklands on 15 December 1938, refuelling in France and Italy en route to Belgrade. In addition Yugoslavia was licensed to build Hurricanes and ordered 100 from factories in Belgrade and Zemon. Only 20 of these machines had been delivered by 6 April 1941, when Yugoslavia was invaded. The Royal Yugoslav Air Force's Hurricanes were engined with exported Merlins, excepting one aircraft which was fitted experimentally with a Daimler Benz.

South Africa, another previous purchaser of the Hawker Fury, was also eager to move up to the Hurricane and in November 1938 shipment began of seven aircraft released by the Air Ministry from storage. These aircraft were delivered before the provision of tropical air filters and succumbed to climatic conditions.

In the same period, King Carol of Romania, visiting Britain, was much taken by the Hurricane at an RAF presentation of the aircraft and the Air Ministry agreed to the sale of 12 machines. Delivery started a few days before the outbreak of the Second World War.

Belgium received 20 Hurricanes in 1939 and was licensed to build 80, of which only two were completed before the German invasion. Turkey took 15. Persia ordered 18. Two were delivered, the remainder of the contract being honoured after the war. The hapless Poland received just one.

Chamberlain's return from Munich was also followed by the shipment to Canada of 22

Delivery of Hurricanes, ordered for the Royal Yugoslav Air Force before the outbreak of the Second World War, began on 15 December 1939. *(British Aerospace)*

aircraft ordered by the Department of National Defence to re-equip No. 1 Squadron of the Royal Canadian Air Force. Hawkers supported the delivery with two sets of production drawings on microfilm, thus assuring production in Canada should war come. Among the many decisions made along the way by Sopwith, Spriggs and Camm, this must rank as one of the more important. Subsequently, the Air Ministry contracted the Canadian Car and Foundry Company in Montreal to build Hurricanes, 40 of which arrived in time to take part in the Battle of Britain. In all 1,451 Hurricanes were built in Canada.

At the time of Munich, as former cavalry officer Winston Churchill was to note, five squadrons had been 'remounted on Hurricanes'. Of Fighter Command's 750 fighter aircraft 93 were eight-gun Hurricanes. The Spitfire was not in squadron operational service. 'Remounting' would have been more rapid had it not been for the Merlin's troubles, which delayed production for four months. Housing the Merlin II exercised Camm and his staff as they reshaped the nose fairing for the re-designed engine mounting. There were also modifications to the cockpit canopy and the tail. The strut bracing the tailplane in Camm's prototype had long since gone and now an extended rudder and small ventral fairing were introduced to counter problems experienced during spinning trials at Brooklands and Martlesham.

In the RAF, even before production aircraft had reached it, there had been stories, rumours, exaggerations about the new type. There always were. With the Hurricane, surmise attained an almost unhealthy extreme. A Hurricane pilot, it was put about, would have to be something very special. He would live on an Air Ministry diet of steak and carrots, sleep at least ten hours a night and be checked by a medical officer after each landing. Unfortunately, shortly after No. 111 Squadron, flying Gauntlet biplanes at Northolt, began to be equipped in December 1937, and No. 3 Squadron at Kenley exchanged its Gladiator biplanes for Hurricanes in March 1938, fatal accidents lent credence to this erroneous mystique. The main difficulties as the monoplane fighter was introduced were that, after being nursed towards squadron operational service by Bulman, Lucas and the Martlesham pilots, it was getting into the hands of comparatively inexperienced young pilots in a rapidly expanding air force; and also that Kenley was too small.

Squadron Leader J. W. Gillan, the 31-year-old son of an RAF padre, commanding No. 111 Squadron — the nucleus of the Air Fighting Development Establishment — mastered the new type so that he could give

Hurricane I of No. 3 Squadron based at Biggin Hill shortly before the outbreak of war.
(Aeroplane-Quadrant)

On a clear day — aircraft of No. 601 (County of London) Squadron patrol the patchwork quilt so characteristic of rural England before post-war destruction of hedgerows changed the countryside. *(Imperial War Museum)*

his pilots all the help they needed. Gillan trained himself to be at one with the Hurricane, much as a leading jockey acquaints himself with a thoroughbred Derby entry. On 10 February 1938, Gillan put man and machine to a test which he intended should dispel any doubts about the Hurricane among his pilots and those who would follow.

Almost without notice he flew a round trip to Scotland. After flying to Turnhouse (Edinburgh) against strong afternoon headwinds Gillan made a quick turnround. At 17,000 feet with an 80 mph tailwind he raced for home, averaging 408.75 mph over 327 miles. This feat was splashed in the Press, the reports mostly ignored the tailwind. It was a remarkable achievement for a Hurricane I with a two-bladed wooden propeller and fabric-covered wings. Most significant was the manner in which the aircraft's Merlin II, subjected to almost take-off boost from start to finish, had withstood the punishment. It would be 18 months before the introduction of the constant speed propeller to allay such stresses.

The Hurricane won international acclaim and, of more consequence to Gillan, the confidence of his young pilots. Gillan, henceforth known as 'Downwind', nannied them firmly, teaching them to come to terms with gravity and blackouts when recovering too sharply from a dive, and drumming in the lesson of lowering the undercarriage before landing. Air Commodore Roy Dutton, then a Pilot Officer and who was to fight in the Battle of Britain and end the war with at least 19 victories, remembers Gillan's painstaking leadership. New pilots were told to make three take-offs and landings without retracting the undercarriage and with the cockpit open before the CO allowed them more rein.

A metal covered wing Mark I of 1940. *(British Aerospace)*

Obviously opinions differed among pilots flying the Hurricane for the first time, but as its ease of handling became more and more apparent, the stories that it required a superman at the controls evaporated. Former biplane pilots did, however, find that they had to get used to engine vibration and noise, acceleration and speed, and their sometimes disconcerting effects. For instance, Dutton experienced the wing gun-bay panels partially falling out and the wing fabric 'distending like sausages between the ribs'. On the whole pilots agreed that the Hurricane was forgiving when things went wrong.

No squadron could have been more delighted to convert to the aircraft than No. 43 at Tangmere. While Chamberlain appeased Hitler, its pilots had wondered just how effective they could be as their gleaming silver Furies were camouflaged in 'sand and spinach' warpaint. They knew that they could neither outpace Do 17 and He 111 bombers, nor were their guns effective above 15,000 feet. Shortly after conversion they were badly shaken, however, by the death of a Sergeant Pilot who, gliding back to the airfield with a faulty engine, dived headlong into the ground. Although having plenty of height to land he turned too slowly and the Hurricane fell out of his hands.

The future Group Captain Peter Townsend, then a young pilot of No. 43 Squadron, had recently exchanged his Fury for a Hurricane when he found 'the occasional phenomenon known as surging accompanied by a sudden loss of power' particularly disconcerting at night when, with the sudden loss of power the blue exhaust flames 'faded to an unnerving yellow'.

But overall the pilots' verdict was a hearty thumbs-up, as expressed by Graham Leggett, a former Hawker company student who noted after his first flight at No. 5 Operational Training Unit, Aston Down 'There's much to learn, but already I know the Hurricane's secret — superb manoeuvrability, the quality above all others that is to make her a legend'.

Chapter 3
Going to War

'The Hurricane inspired solid affection . . . ' Air Marshal Sir Peter Wykeham.

Conditions as the Hurricane went to war in the autumn and winter of 1939 exercised more mundane qualities than its manoeuvrability in combat. French airfields available to the four squadrons of the Air Component covering arrival of the British Expeditionary Force required the aircraft to rough it. Camm's provision of a strong, broad-track undercarriage enabled Nos 85, 87, 1 and 73 Squadrons to operate from poorly drained fields. Subsequently Nos 1 and 73 Squadrons transferred to become the fighter element of the Advanced Air Striking Force of 12 Blenheim and Battle squadrons. The fighter strength in France was reinforced later by Nos 607, 615, 3, 79, 504 and finally, 501 Squadrons of Hurricanes. Considering that one year after Munich no more than 497 Hurricanes had been delivered, equipping 17½ squadrons with the remainder in reserve, and that there were only nine squadrons of Spitfires, the Hurricane squadrons of the Air Component and Advanced Air Striking Force represented a substantial commitment.

If at the outset the Hurricane's fighting qualities were little exercised, the aircraft's

The novelty of the monoplane fighter early in the Second World War is emphasised by the Gladiators' presence at this December, 1939, inspection of the Air Component in France by King George VI. Hurricanes in the foreground belong to No. 85 Squadron. *(Imperial War Museum)*

strong physique was hard tested. In the opening weeks of the Second World War its campaign serviceability established a reputation, squadron pilots recognising its ruggedness and stamina as its chief assets. Some pilots in France said the Hurricane had 'the strength of a battleship'. Pilots of No. 87 Squadron at Lille Vendeville, a muddy, round field with draughty wooden huts, found refuge from the winter by sitting in their cockpits with the canopies closed.

At home in these early weeks, in the absence of enemy custom, the weather posed more problems than the Luftwaffe. Accidents increased pilots' confidence in the aircraft's strength. On a pitch-black night in February 1940, John Simpson of No. 43 Squadron, which had been moved from Tangmere in the south to Acklington near Newcastle in the north-east, had engine trouble. Too low to bale out and unable to lower the flaps he kept the Hurricane straight and, as best he could judge, at 100 mph. He bounced off a haystack, losing half his propeller, sliced a telegraph pole and ploughed into a wood of larch trees. Although badly bruised, suffering a broken nose and cheekbone, Simpson was sufficiently mobile to inspect the wreckage in the morning. Only the cockpit remained intact amid 36 cut-down trees.

During the winter at home and in France many young pilots sensed that they were themselves maturing and hardening as they discovered how much of a weather-beating the Hurricane could take. This was particularly so of squadrons such as No. 43 which found the harsh north-east of England a discomforting contrast to Tangmere and the soft south. Covering coastal convoys, often from a snowbound airfield, No. 43 flattened and hardened the snow into a runway by tearing a door off the dispersal hut, sitting three men on it, and towing the improvised 'roller' behind a tractor! There was no snow plough.

By this time some squadrons had flown the Hurricane for almost two years and reasonably might have been expected to agitate for conversion to the Spitfire, now being slowly introduced. However, neither the Spitfire's speed nor its more aesthetic appearance could impair their loyalty. John Simpson of No. 43 Squadron confided in his friend, the author Hector Bolitho: 'We have had our Hurrybugs since December 1938, and we still think they're the tops'. A companion squadron, No. 152, operating with Gladiators since the outbreak of war, was being re-equipped with Spitfires when Flight Lieutenant Peter Townsend and Flight Lieutenant Caesar Hull were permitted to try them out, looping and rolling in close formation over the airfield. Simpson commented afterwards; 'Caesar and Peter still feel the same after their line-shooting in the Spitfires . . . It may well seem nonsense, but I wouldn't change over if they asked me'.

It was as well that the Hurricane was the object of so much esteem and affection. It would be many months before the Spitfire would be as readily available. Although the Spitfire's maiden flight had taken place at Eastleigh in the hands of 'Mutt' Summers, the Vickers chief test pilot, on 4 March 1936, its production had proved more troublesome than that of the Hurricane. Each type had been late in delivery, but construction similarities between the Hurricane and the Hawker biplanes had given the monoplane fighter the production edge over the Spitfire. Camm, recognising that availability would encourage orders, had taken the production factor into account in his design. Mitchell, breaking away from the aerodynamic practice of the 1930s, had designed a wafer-thin, metal wing of low thickness-chord ratio in contrast to Camm's thick, and at that stage, fabric-covered wing. He knew that to gain Air Ministry acceptance the Spitfire would have to offer a far better performance than its competitor. He had succeeded, but in the New Year of 1940 Hurricane pilots could still echo the comment of a Group Captain comparing the aircraft when they were at Martlesham Heath for acceptance trials. Looking at the Spitfire he said: 'There's a racehorse for you'. Then, approaching the hump-backed Hurricane, he added: 'That's more like an aeroplane'. Air Marshal Sir Peter Wykeham was to take another view, writing: 'The

Hurricanes of No. 3 Squadron 'cuckoo' a Gladiator out of the nest at Kenley.
(RAF Museum)

Hurricane inspired solid affection and respect, the Spitfire devotion'.

Over the next four years the Hurricane would not be short of heroes, but expeditionary conditions of the winter of the 'phoney war' of 1939-1940 were not conducive to producing them. Consequently it was an achievement for a young New Zealander, Flying Officer 'Cobber' Kain to earn recognition as the RAF's first Hurricane ace by shooting down five enemy aircraft, including three Me 109s, between November 1939 and March 1940. Such exploits against the 109 and other successes against the Me 110 heartened pilots and public alike, although the public were not aware of the problems being encountered by Hurricane pilots. One deficiency discovered in this period was the absence of armour to protect a pilot's back. No. 1 Squadron experimented with armour plate from a Fairey Battle with the eventual result that Hurricanes were fitted with it. Another snag was that Browning guns were jamming because ammunition, some of which had been stored for 30 years, had deteriorated. Beyond the need for modifications revealed by operational experience, peacetime formation practices were found to be far too rigid. Roland Beamont of No. 87 Squadron has recalled getting 'clobbered badly in the process of sailing into battle with the immaculate formations of before the war'.

On 9 April 1940, after occupying Denmark, Germany invaded Norway. Anglo-French and Polish forces went to the aid of Norway. Neville Chamberlain, who would not be replaced by Winston Churchill as Prime Minister until the invasion of the Low Countries on 10 May, hoped to avert German access to the North Atlantic and counter the threat of enemy naval and air bases in Scandinavia to Britain's east and north-east coastline. Moreover, the northern port of Narvik provided year-round facilities free of ice for exporting rail-freighted Swedish iron ore for the German armaments industry. But, if Allied efforts were to hold any credence then, in the absence of a long-range fighter, monoplane fighters must reach Norway fast. In practice, this meant Hurricanes.

From the start, the absence of Hurricanes

Hurricanes of No. 73 Squadron over France during the period of the 'phoney war'.
(Imperial War Museum)

was reflected in swift enemy success assured by air superiority. Courageous attempts to provide cover by biplanes from the carriers *Ark Royal* and *Glorious* were inadequate and the fate of 18 Gladiator biplanes of No. 263 Squadron flown ashore from *Glorious* on 24 April underlined the urgent need for Hurricanes. Not one Gladiator survived more than 72 hours at the RAF squadron's operational base, the ice of Lake Lesjaskog near Aandalsnes. They were destroyed on the 'ground'. Expeditionary troops in Central Norway were evacuated.

Although No. 263 Squadron had lost its aircraft, the pilots had returned home by sea. 21 May found them flying their replacement Gladiators ashore from the carrier *Furious*. It was abortive. Two aircraft followed a guiding Swordfish into a mountainside and the remainder returned to the carrier. The next day the squadron succeeded in establishing itself at Bardufoss.

The biplanes, for all their obsolescence, were to put up a magnificent performance, but the need remained for Hurricanes. As it happened, No. 46 Squadron had embarked its Hurricanes with No. 263's Gladiators in *Furious*, only to sail home with the carrier because their base at Skaanland was not ready to receive them. However, by 26 May they had returned to Norway, after being transferred from *Furious* to *Glorious*. Because three

Hurricanes of No. 306 Squadron demonstrate the difficulties of operating at Turnhouse in Scotland during the winter of 1940-1941.
(RAF Museum)

Hurricanes had nosed over in the soft conditions at Skaanland, No. 46 was despatched to join No. 263 at Bardufoss. Although the Hurricane would later establish itself as a carrier-borne fighter, the decision to ferry No. 46 Squadron in *Furious* and *Glorious* was an innovation. The RAF pilots had no experience of deck landing and take-off, nor were their aircraft fitted with arrester hooks for landing. When the aircraft were transferred from *Furious* to *Glorious* for the return passage to northern Norway they were hoisted laboriously in and out of lighters.

The Hurricanes put immediate heart into the troops landing on 27 May at Narvik. Morale lifted as No. 46 Squadron circled overhead and immediately the expedition seemed more feasible. Not that the 15 remaining Hurricanes were destined to cover a prolonged stay. Defeat in France ordained a second withdrawal, from Norway.

Between 3 June and 8 June most of the Hurricane and Gladiator squadrons' efforts were devoted to covering the evacuation. The fighters were given a hard time because by 2 June the Luftwaffe, much reinforced, was

Roughing it on farmland, Hurricanes withstood the rigours of unsatisfactory airfields in France, thanks to the sturdiness of Camm's construction.

concentrating bomber and dive-bomber attacks on shipping, covered by Me 110 fighters. But the Hurricanes had enabled completion of the vital demolition of port facilities at Narvik. It would be the New Year of 1941 before Germany could resume shipment of iron ore from that source.

After the evacuation there was the puzzle of what to do with the surviving ten Hurricanes. Their pilots could be embarked, but not their aircraft. The Gladiators, despite the absence of arrester hooks, with their low speed, could reasonably be expected to land on *Glorious*. Consequently No. 46 Squadron was ordered to fight on and then destroy its aircraft. But Squadron Leader Kenneth 'Bing' Cross could not bring himself to supervise their destruction. The only alternative was to attempt to land on *Glorious*. Any Hurricane that failed would probably be destroyed. Cross borrowed a Gladiator, flew out to the carrier and persuaded her reluctant Captain G. d'Oyly Hughes that he could devise a method of halting the Hurricanes on deck without arrester hooks. In the event sandbags were secured below the tail surface of each fuselage. The modification may not have had the finesse of a design detail in Camm's Kingston office, but it worked. Three Hurricanes, sent ahead under Flight Lieutenant P. Jameson, a New Zealander, to test the scheme on the evening of 7 June, landed safely. At Bardufoss Cross awaited confirmation. It did not arrive. Nevertheless he decided to lead his seven Hurricanes out to sea in the early hours of 8 June. Each landed without mishap. That afternoon *Glorious* fell in with the battle-cruisers *Scharnhorst* and *Gneisenau*. She was sunk with 1,100 men and the Hurricanes. Two pilots survived. They were Squadron Leader Cross and Flight Lieutenant Jameson, rescued by a Norwegian fishing boat after three days on a Carley float.

Loss of Hurricanes in support of the Norwegian expedition would have been serious at any time. In the wake of the lightning German advance on the Channel ports and Paris, it was disastrous. In France, since the 10 May invasion of Holland, Belgium and Luxembourg, and the consequent turning of the Maginot Line, ten Hurricane squadrons, falling back on improvised landing strips and reinforced on 13 May by 32 Hurricanes from home, had fought as best they could against great odds.

While the dwindling numbers of Hurricanes were dividing their presence between covering the retreat of the British Expeditionary Force to the Channel ports and the defence of Paris, a somewhat different conflict was developing between Fighter Command headquarters at Bentley Priory and 10 Downing Street. Dowding knew that if Hurricane losses continued to be sustained in France there would be too few left to defend Britain.

On 13 May, by which day the RAF had lost more than 200 Hurricanes in support of the BEF and the French army, he was obliged by the War Cabinet to send 32 more. Dowding, who already regarded France as a lost cause, now took the bold and unusual step of seeking to put his case to the Cabinet. He felt he could not rely on support from his Service and political colleagues at the Air Ministry for his determination to keep the Hurricanes at home. Dowding was to recall that on 15 May, before leaving headquarters for Whitehall, he had drawn a simple graph of the heavy fighter losses. In the Cabinet room he got up from his seat at the table, walked to Churchill's place and laid it before him. He said: 'If the present rate of wastage continues for another fortnight we shall not have a single Hurricane left in France or in this country'. Lord Beaverbrook, who was not present, also enjoyed repeating this account of the 15 May Cabinet meeting. Oddly, as John Terraine writes in *The Right of the Line,* no such intervention appears in the minutes.

There can be no doubt Dowding said something very effective on the case for keeping Hurricanes at home, but the story may have improved over the years. No matter, Dowding was rewarded with a Cabinet decision in his favour, but the very next day Churchill reversed it and he was ordered to send four more Hurricane squadrons to France. Dowding now wrote a formal letter, addressing it to Captain Harold

Balfour, the Under-Secretary of State at the Air Ministry.

He stated: 'I must point out that within the last few days the equivalent of ten squadrons have been sent to France, that the Hurricane squadrons in this country are seriously depleted, and that the more squadrons which are sent to France the higher will be the wastage and the more insistent the demands for reinforcements'.

After reminding the Air Council that 'the last estimate which they made as to the force necessary to defend this country was 52 squadrons, and my strength has now been reduced to the equivalent of 36 squadrons', he emphasised that the new circumstances had very much extended the line to be defended 'at the same time as our resources are reduced'.

He concluded: 'I believe that, if an adequate fighter force is kept in this country, if the fleet remains in being, and if Home Forces are suitably organised to resist invasion, we should be able to carry on the war single-handed for some time, in not indefinitely. But if the Home Defence Force is drained away in desperate attempts to remedy the situation in France, defeat in France will involve the final, complete and irremediable defeat of this country'. This document resulted in the conservation of enough Hurricanes to tide over Fighter Command and keep Britain in the war.

While Dowding, shamefully unsupported in the Cabinet room by Sir Cyril Newall, that very same Chief of the Air Staff who had put bombers before fighters in the crucial late 1930s, had battled to hoard his Hurricanes, numerous dramas beset the doomed squadrons. Of these, possibly the oddest concerned Louis Strange, the much decorated former Lieutenant-Colonel and Wing Commander of the First World War who, aged 49, had rejoined as Pilot Officer, the lowest commissioned rank in the RAF. Demanding to fly, he was ordered a test in a Tiger Moth. By a coincidence Strange had signed the instructor's father's flying certificate!

Towards the end of May, Strange was part of an operation to fly spares and mechanics to Merville to make Hurricanes sufficiently airworthy to fly home. He was to recall: 'We quickly got busy servicing the Hurricanes we had come to rescue. The first was soon away, a good many bullet holes in it, the variable pitch airscrew control tied into fine pitch with a bit of copper wire and a piece of telephone cable back to the cockpit to enable the pilot to change pitch by breaking the copper wire with a good tug, and other simple devises to make good broken controls and shot-away instruments'. In the event the pilot who made it home in this machine used it for his second attempt. He had already baled out of a blazing Hurricane over the airfield. 'Have another Hurricane', Strange offered, as the pilot landed. Strange, who had never flown a Hurricane, took the next one out. It was unarmed, but he ran the gauntlet of anti-aircraft fire and enemy fighters.

On 21 May the few remaining serviceable Hurricanes of the Air Component, less than three squadrons, were ordered home, but not all survived the evacuation and the cross-Channel flight. Meanwhile, the fighting in France was not over. That Hurricanes of the Advanced Air Striking Force should continue to be lost in support of a demoralised French army may now seem incomprehensible. But Churchill had replaced Neville Chamberlain

'Cobber' Kain. First Hurricane ace, he killed himself making a farewell beat-up in France. *(Imperial War Museum)*

A Hurricane of No. 46 Squadron being hoisted inboard from a lighter for transport to Norway. *(RAF Museum)*

as Prime Minister as recently as 10 May. France was Britain's Ally and, beyond that, the French were a people to whom Churchill felt emotionally attached. The Hurricanes, by now about 30, paid the price, fighting in defence of Paris between 16 May and 2 June from airfields south-east of the capital. Amid much remarkable air fighting, an action on 27 May by No. 501 Squadron stands out. Flying from a strip at Boos near Rouen, 13 Hurricanes encountered 24 He 111s and 20 Me 110s, destroying at least 11 bombers. But the Hurricanes' days in France were numbered. On 3 June the tattered Advanced Air Striking Force of Hurricanes, Blenheims, Gladiators and Lysanders — most of its Battles had been lost attempting to stem the German offensive at the outset or on the ground — withdrew to six strips south-west of Paris. By 15 June the remaining Hurricanes moved to cover the closing stages of the British evacuation. In all Fighter Command had lost 477 aircraft in the May and June Battle of France. Of them 386 were Hurricanes.

Among the casualties was Cobber Kain, the first Hurricane ace. Credited with 17 enemy aircraft destroyed, he killed himself in a farewell beat-up of his airfield.

Chapter 4
Most of the few

'The Hurricane was great and we proved it . . . ' Group Captain Peter Townsend.

On 18 June Winston Churchill, addressing the House of Commons and that evening broadcasting to the nation, said: 'What General Weygand called the Battle of France is over. I expect the Battle of Britain is about to begin'. History demands dates. When the time came to honour aircrew, those who served in operational fighter squadrons between 10 July and 31 October 1940 were privileged to wear a Battle of Britain rose gilt emblem on the ribbon of the 1939-1945 Star.

On the very first day of the Battle of Britain an action took place which typified the numerical disadvantage at which the Hurricane was to find itself throughout the summer and autumn of 1940. At 1.40 p.m. on 10 July six Hurricanes of No. 32 Squadron, approaching their patrol line 10,000 feet above a convoy off Dover, flew into a rain cloud. The flight split into two sections. Emerging, Green section, Flying Officer J. B. W. Humpherson, Sergeant L. Pearce and Sub-Lieutenant (A) G. G. R. Bulmer, on loan from the Fleet Air Arm, saw the enemy. 'Waves of enemy bombers coming from the direction of France in boxes of six', Bulmer reported. In fact the enemy comprised a mixed force of Me 109s, 110s and Do 17s. As the first three Hurricanes engaged, 20 more fighters from Nos 111 and 56 Hurricane squadrons and Nos 64 and 74 Spitfire squadrons were on the way to support them. When the Spitfires arrived over the convoy their pilots saw that enemy bombers and fighters had spiralled into three layers, creating a cylinder over the target, 109s atop, 110s in the middle and Do 17 bombers below. Among the reinforcements were eight Spitfires of No. 74 Squadron. Climbing to 13,000 feet, 1,000 feet above the guardian 109s, the Spitfires dived into the cylinder. The convoy sailed on after losing one small ship. The Luftwaffe lost four fighters to the RAF's three Hurricanes, one of which had rammed a bomber. Despite their losses the Hurricane squadrons derived some consolation in that the engagement confirmed the Hurricane's ability to deal with the Me 110, whose pilots had sought refuge in a defensive circle. This was, however, about the only solace on a day which produced further evidence of the difficulties that lay ahead for Hurricane squadrons and the air defences.

Air Vice-Marshal Keith Park, the New Zealand Scot who commanded No. 11 Group defending the vulnerable invasion corner of south-east England and who visited his sector stations in his personal Hurricane, could not know, as any plot built up, whether it was the beginning of the enemy's big throw; possibly the preliminary to invasion. On this July day, as on following days, he responded cautiously. A total of 200 Hurricanes and Spitfires, about one-third of Britain's first-line fighters, were under his command: 13 squadrons of Hurricanes and six squadrons of Spitfires. In the west of England, north of London, in the north of England and Scotland respectively, Nos 10, 12 and 13 Groups mustered 16 single-seater monoplane fighter squadrons of which four Hurricane squadrons were forming or re-equipping. For the rest, Fighter Command's Order of Battle comprised six Blenheim squadrons, two squadrons of the power-turreted Defiant and one flight of Gladiator biplanes — in all some 600 serviceable fighters of varying performance, of which the majority were Hurricanes. Of an authorised Fighter Command establishment of 1,450 pilots only

1,253 fighter pilots were available, more than 50 of whom were on loan from the Fleet Air Arm.

Park, as he visited the sector stations, flying his personal Hurricane, knew that a mistake on his part could lose the war, that No. 11 Group must stay in the fight until more Hurricanes, which in the foreseeable future would continue to outnumber the Spitfires, were available. Hence his caution in committing so few of his precious Hurricanes. Both Dowding at Fighter Command's Stanmore headquarters and Park at Uxbridge, conscious of the loss of 15 fighters in the past seven days, were guided by the paramount need to husband Spitfires. Hurricanes were no more expendable, but there were more of them and they could be the more readily replaced. By 1 September there would be 34½ Hurricane to 19 Spitfire squadrons; evidence that, even allowing for the heavy fighting in August, production, reserves and repair of the Hurricane allowed new squadrons to be formed. Spitfire production was stretched to meet losses and maintain 19 squadrons.

Determined to conserve their fighters, Dowding and Park recognised that radar stations, fighter airfields, aircraft factories building Hurricanes and Spitfires, and London itself, were now vulnerable to bombers based across the Channel. Moreover, enemy fighters were capable of escorting the bombers to their objectives and back although this would leave little margin for the Me 109s over London.

Just as he had prevented the nightmare possibility of sacrificing the defence of Britain, hoarding and cossetting the Spitfire at the expense of the Hurricane when France was falling, Dowding acted now to avoid losses over the Channel in defence of convoys. He warned the Navy that convoys might have to fend for themselves.

While the sun was still rising on the second day of the battle Fighter Command was faced with this problem. Six Hurricanes of No. 501 Squadron in Park's most westerly sector, Middle Wallop, were scrambled with six Spitfires of No. 609 Squadron. Ten Ju 87 Stuka dive-bombers and 20 Me 109s were heading in from the Cherbourg area. The Hurricanes engaged the 109s and one Hurricane was shot down. The Spitfires, arriving afterwards, lost two to the 109s, but the convoy sailed on without loss.

Only two days into the battle and Park's parsimony, blessed of course by Dowding, was already bewildering pilots whose knowledge of the situation was understandably limited to squadron and sector. Hurricanes and Spitfires, together with their pilots, were being lost against impossible odds. There were further engagements in the afternoon of this second day, but it is not the purpose here to tell the story of the Battle of Britain, day by day, phase by phase. Rather to follow the fortunes of the Hurricane and its pilots in relation to the development of the battle — and to its partner the Spitfire.

In the folklore of the Battle of Britain the Hurricane and Spitfire are indivisible. Even today in the Battle of Britain Memorial Flight Hurricane and Spitfire are tenderly maintained for annual exhibition duets in the summer and autumn season of air displays. Theirs is a partnership as inseparable in public remembrance as were their show business contemporaries Flanagan and Allen or, in a cricket context, Compton and Edrich. But that is as far as the analogy goes, because the basic roles of the Hurricane and Spitfire were disparate and dictated by their respective performance and availability.

Each was a star in its own right, where possible the Hurricane attacking the bombers, dive-bombers and Me 110 twin-engined fighters; the faster, better-performance-at-altitude Spitfire pitted preferably against the high-flying Me 109 escorts. Of course, amid the confusion of battle and as the pressures mounted in August and September, demarcation could never be as neat as that. Frequently the Hurricane had to be committed by ground controllers, regardless of such copybook considerations, or by pilots according to the circumstances in which they found themselves.

Somewhat perversely, the general

Cramped conditions on a 1940 production line, but a sight to rejoice Lord Beaverbrook. *(Flight)*

inferiority on paper of the Hurricane to the Spitfire as an opponent of the Me 109 enhanced its pilots' chances. Even before the opening of the Battle of Britain the Luftwaffe tended to under-estimate the Hawker fighter and suffered in consequence. As early as the Spring of 1940 Flight Lieutenant Peter Townsend of No. 43 Squadron, defending the naval base at Scapa Flow, identified this 'Spitfire snobbery' as he termed it. After shooting down a Heinkel 111 he returned to his airfield to find that another Heinkel, after being crippled by a fellow Hurricane pilot, had crash-landed there. On ditching, as they believed, the German crew took off their boots, threw out a dinghy and dived after it. Townsend whose Hurricane had been badly damaged, learned later that the Heinkel crew, who thought they were in the sea, insisted they had been attacked by a Spitfire.

German fighter pilots repeatedly claimed they had been in combat with Spitfires after falling victims to the Hurricane's manoeuvrability. The ultimate for a Luftwaffe fighter pilot was to claim a Spitfire shot down. Helmuth Wieck, a pupil of Major Wernher 'Daddy' Molders in the Spanish Civil War, and who by November 1940, was himself a 25-year-old Major, boasted: 'In the first great air battle over the Channel I shot down three Spitfires after bitter fighting'. Heinz Knoke, author of *I flew for the Führer*, confided in his diary: 'Achtung Spitfire! German pilots have learned to pay particular attention when they hear this warning shout in their aeroplanes'. 'Achtung — Hurricane'! — there is a faintly ridiculous ring about it, and yet there were many many more Hurricanes than Spitfires in the Battle of Britain. Major Adolf Galland, later General, touched the heights of adulation of the Spitfire at the expense of the Hurricane when in the summer of 1940 he urged Hermann Göering: 'Give me one wing of Spitfires and we'll finish this job'. Later Galland scoffed: 'The Hurricane was hopeless, a nice aeroplane to shoot down'.

But many Battle of Britain pilots were never in any doubt about the wrong-headedness of such contempt for the Hurricane, resulting as it so often did from the self-aggrandisement obtainable through Spitfire snobbery. Peter Townsend has recalled in *Duel of Eagles'*. We ourselves thought the Hurricane was great and we proved it'. He quotes the Air Ministry in support: 'The total number of enemy aircraft brought down by the single-seat fighters was in the proportion of three by Hurricanes to two by Spitfires. The average proportion . . . serviceable each morning was approximately 63 per cent Hurricanes and 37 per cent Spitfires. In proportion . . . Spitfires brought down six per cent more than the Hurricane'. As Townsend comments: 'This was no reason for the Hurricanes to blush, considering they were slower than the Me 109 and Spitfire'. Indisputably the Hurricane's record in the Battle of Britain rebuts the assertion of Field Marshal Kesselring, commander of Air Fleet 2 that 'only the Spitfires worried us'.

In all the discussion since the battle on the comparative merits of the two fighters, some of the more generous tributes to the Hurricanes's role have come from Spitfire pilots. Jeffrey Quill, the Vickers test pilot who had shared the early flying of the Spitfire with J. 'Mutt' Summers after Summers' maiden flight on 5 March 1936, is on record as saying: 'It took both of these great aeroplanes to win the battle'. Quill, who as a 34-year-old Reserve Regular Air Force officer took leave from Vickers 'to put in a spot of practical' in the battle with No. 65, a Spitfire squadron, is convinced that neither aircraft would have won the battle on its own.

Camm, sacrificing performance in the Hurricane for ease of handling, speed of production and simplicity of maintenance, had assured the Spitfire's greater fame in posterity, and yet in combat, Quill believed, the edge was marginal. Comparing the prototypes, his opinion is that Camm's Hurricane, with a very thick wing, fabric covering and a humped-back fuselage and the same power, performed remarkably in relation to R. J. Mitchell's Spitfire with its metal-skinned thin wing of an unusually low thickness/chord ratio in defiance of all contemporary aerodynamic design. Quill's verdict after fighting in the battle: 'The Hurricane and Spitfire ideally complemented each other'.

Extraordinarily, however, during the summer of 1940 there was one particular aircraft which looked like a Hurricane, was a Hurricane, but performed like a Spitfire. Elegantly monogrammed 'H. B.', the initials of its 'owner', Harry Broadhurst, it was powered ahead of its Mark 1 contemporaries by the very latest two-stage supercharged Merlin XX which the recently promoted Wing Commander had charmed out of Rolls-Royce. Even more unusual, the aircraft really was Broadhurst's very own private Hurricane for a while.

Air Chief Marshal Sir Harry Broadhurst tells the story: 'On 19 May 1940 when I was commanding 60 Wing in France I received orders to prepare to evacuate the wing back to the UK. That evening the wing moved to Merville where I was joined by the aircraft of another wing — both had been well decimated by then. I then received detailed instructions for the evacuation, which were that I should retain a minimum number of airmen to enable me to continue to operate whilst the remainder were to be sent off by road to one of the ports in NW France under the command of Wing Commander Finch who had been the commander of the other wing. The arrangements then, were that sufficient transport aircraft would arrive at 1800 hours on 20 May to pick up the remaining airmen as quickly as possible, whilst the Hurricanes would circle overhead to protect the airfield and then escort the transports back to England.

'All went to schedule except that I left my Hurricane ticking over in a corner of the airfield whilst I supervised the loading of the transports, intending to take off and join the party for the trip home. Unfortunately when I got back to my Hurricane I became involved in a slight argument with some Army officers who wanted a lift back to England. By the time I took off I was alone in the sky and a ripe target for four Me 110s who intercepted me en route. When I had shaken them off my Hurricane was very badly shot up, but I managed to struggle back to the UK. I landed at Northolt because I knew everybody there having been stationed there with 111 Squadron before my promotion to Wing Commander. The next day I had to report to the C-in-C Fighter Command (Dowding) to tell him all about the air fighting in France. I was then sent on a tour of all the squadrons in Fighter Command to lecture them on my

'Leader of the Few' Air Chief Marshal Sir Hugh Dowding was bowler-hatted after the Battle of Britain during which he was acutely conscious that the majority of his pilots flew the Hurricane. On 14 September 1941, he was reunited with some of them. Although Spitfire pilots are included in this company, readers will recognise the names of some pilots who figure in this account, among them Wing Commander Ian Gleed and Wing Commander Max Aitken.

Pictured from left to right are: S/Ldr. A. C. Bartley, D.F.C.; W/Cdr. D. F. B. Sheen, D.F.C.; W/Cdr. I. R. Gleed. D.S.O., D.F.C.; W/Cdr. Max Aitken, D.S.O., D.F.C.; W/Cdr. A. G. Malan, D.S.O., D.F.C.; S/Ldr. A. C. Deere, D.F.C.; Air Chief Marshal Sir Hugh Dowding (in civilian clothes) F/Officer E. C. Henderson, M.M., W.A.A.F.; F/Lt. R. H. Hillary; W/Cdr. J. A. Kent, D.F.C., A.F.C.; W/Cdr. C. B. F. Kingcombe, D.F.C.; S/Ldr. D. H. Watkins. D.F.C.; Warrant Officer R. H. Gretton. *(Imperial War Museum)*

experiences, which Dowding calculated would soon be happening over England when the Germans were established in Northern France.

'I reported back to him a week later and was told that I was posted to the fighter station at Wittering which was equipped with Spitfires, Hurricanes and Blenheim night-fighters. I had only been there a week when Northolt rang up to say they had repaired my Hurricane and asked what they were to do with it. It suddenly dawned on me that I had my own Hurricane! So I collected it and had it painted black with my initials on it, and used it at night. Meanwhile Rolls-Royce, whom I knew well, offered to re-engine it with the most up-to-date Merlin which revolutionised its performance.

'Later that year I was posted to Hornchurch which had a wing of Spitfires. However, I took the Hurricane with me and continued to use it at night whilst flying Spitfires by day. About the middle of 1941 a visiting senior engineering officer from Fighter Command spotted the lone Hurricane in a hangar at Hornchurch, and learning its history, reported the illegality and regretfully I lost my Hurricane! I never did find out what happened to it after it left Hornchurch'.

While the more advanced Merlin enabled the freak Spitfire-like performance of Broadhurst's Hurricane, as the battle progressed both the Hurricane and the Spitfire were to benefit from the rushed conversion from variable pitch to constant speed propellers. This improvement had been urged for some time by Captain Geoffrey de Havilland, the pioneer aircraft designer and manufacturer (later Sir Geoffrey de Havilland), who was convinced that the margin between variable pitch and constant speed propellers could lose the war. His company, with the personal blessing of Lord Beaverbrook, Minister for Aircraft Production, privately initiated the conversion programme and from 24 June 1940, it surged ahead. Speed was raised from an estimated 317 mph with the two-bladed wooden Watts propeller (Merlin II) to 320 mph with the de Havilland Hamilton two-speed metal propeller (Merlin III); 325 mph with the de Havilland constant speed metal propeller (Merlin III) and 328 mph with the three-bladed Rotol constant speed propeller (Merlin III).

Although Wing Commander Harry Broadhurst commanding a Spitfire wing sometimes flew his 'private' Hurricane in 1940 after the fall of France, by 1944 the Hawker fighter had been wholly superseded and Air Vice-Marshal Broadhurst returned to France in a Spitfire.
(RAF Museum)

In his official Despatch Dowding refers to obtaining an average speed of 305 mph after testing six representative Hurricanes, but Group Captain Tom Gleave, among other survivors of the battle, regards this as a conservative average obtained from some war-weary aircraft. Be that as it may, the Luftwaffe had latched on to the constant speed propeller far in advance of the RAF. Me 109 pilots, blooded as members of the Condor Legion in support of General Franco in the Spanish Civil War, had already familiarised themselves with the Hamilton two-blade variable pitch propeller. By 1939 the constant speed propeller was standard 109 equipment.

The Luftwaffe had also stolen a march on the Merlin-engined fighters by recognising the advantages of a fuel injection system in engines. Erhard Milch, promoted Field Marshal in July 1940, had picked up the potential of fuel injection in conversation on its theory with a member of the Bristol Aeroplane Company technical staff at a pre-war Hendon air display. While Britain neglected it, German prescience in adopting it bestowed a combat advantage on its fighter pilots. Too often Hurricane pilots, managing through skill and manoeuvrability to get on the tails of 109s, were frustrated by enemy pilots flopping from the horizontal into a vertical power dive; an aerobatic gift entirely due to the Daimler Benz engine's injection pump. Air Marshal Sir Peter Wykeham has emphasised in *Fighter Command* that Luftwaffe pilots, particularly the ace Adolf Galland, 'learned to use this quality in a number of disconcerting ways'. Galland himself was to credit it with preventing the engine from conking out in critical moments of combat. Repeatedly in combat in 1940 Hurricane pilots were disadvantaged by the Merlin's reliance on a carburettor. Wykeham again: 'Carburation caused little trouble in aircraft that stayed the right way up, but in a fighter there is no right way up, and in air combat every position is normal'. Hurricane pilots (as also with Spitfire pilots) had to turn on their backs and dive. That Rolls-Royce's remedial modifications were not available until after the Battle of Britain gave rise to much subsequent comment. Derek Wood and Derek Dempster note in *The Narrow Margin* that it seemed 'extraordinary that this problem was not tackled earlier or that Rolls-Royce did not fit an injection pump in place of a carburettor'. But they didn't, and as the battle built up towards its autumn crescendo this omission was to become increasingly tiresome.

Throughout July Hitler had brooded on his hopes that Britain would see reason; that a struggle for air superiority as the essential prerequisite of invasion could be avoided; that he could preserve the Luftwaffe for an eventual assault on the Soviet Union in which a defeated, compliant Britain might acquiesce, even assist.

The Luftwaffe's experiences since the fall of France had confirmed what some of its senior officers already accepted, namely that for all such technical advantages as the constant speed propeller and fuel injection system, it was not ideally equipped for air battles over Britain; for reducing ports, airfields and the airframe and engine plants capable of reinforcing the RAF.

The Luftwaffe had been conceived, planned and equipped for blitzkrieg, the new lightning war which had placed the German army and its tanks on the Channel coast. Its Ju 87 Stukas were the 'artillery', its Me 109 and 110 fighters assuring cover for the advancing tanks and infantry. Yet, because of the very nature of their roles its aircraft were limited in range; sufficient to move forward with and cover an advancing army on the continent, but hard stretched to sustain a short, sharp campaign over southern England and between the sea and London. Nor were there any four-engined bombers with which to attack Britain's aircraft and other armaments industries. A strategic bomber was designed, but production had been vetoed.

Flight Lieutenant J. B. Nicolson of No. 249 Squadron was recovering from Battle of Britain wounds when this picture was taken shortly before the announcement of his VC. *(Flight)*

At the end of July Hitler's patience, sorely tested by Fighter Command — in essence by Dowding's most available fighter, the Hurricane — ran out. He ordered Göering to put the Luftwaffe into immediate readiness for the 'Attack of the Eagles'. Hitler directed

Airfleets 2, 3 and 5 to prepare 'to destroy the flying units and ground installations of the RAF and the British air armaments industry'.

In early August the weather, Britain's changeable ally, delayed execution of the directive until on 8 August improvement enabled the Luftwaffe to step-up its efforts to reduce Dowding's fighter resources by again enticing Hurricanes over the Channel in defence of shipping. In the run-up to the *Eagle* offensive Göering had convinced himself that, given four days of good weather, Airfleets 2 and 3 could establish air superiority over south-east England. In the early hours of 8 August the better weather and the Royal Navy offered the Luftwaffe the opportunity it had awaited. The Navy sent a convoy of 25 merchant ships into the Straits of Dover. By 9 a.m., following attacks by E-boats which sank three ships and damaged two others, the convoy was in the vicinity of the Isle of Wight when the first wave of some 80 Stukas arrived, accompanied by up to three times their number in fighters. It was an outright challenge to Fighter Command, the opening of the first of the 9 a.m.—5 p.m. August days during which Hurricane and Spitfire pilots made as many as four or five operational take-offs in what they came to call their regular office hours.

Five squadrons of Hurricanes and two of Spitfires were scrambled from Nos 11 and 10 Groups. Squadron Leader J. R. A. Peel, leading No. 145 Squadron's Hurricanes from Westhampnett in the Tangmere sector had climbed his squadron to 16,000 feet when he saw a swarm of little black dots off the Isle of Wight. As the Hurricanes dived the dots enlarged until the pilots could pick out their targets among the Ju 87 dive-bombers. 'Look out! 109s!' The hunting Hurricanes in the act of savaging the Stukas were themselves the hunted.

Stepped-up in the sun to 20,000 feet the 109 pilots had seen the peril of the Stukas. In moments they were on the tails of the Hurricanes forcing the pilots to break off and defend themselves. Peel, jumped by two 109s, reported: 'The enemy fighters were half-rolling and diving and zooming in climbing turns. I fired two five-second bursts at one and saw it dive into the sea. Then I followed another up in a zoom and got him as he stalled'. The 109s revenged themselves on Peel who came down in the sea close to the French coast. Rescue boats reported they might have to turn back, but some of the squadron leader's fellow Hurricane pilots passed the message: 'Tell the boats they'll be shot up by us if they do'. Peel was rescued. The convoy sailed on, after losing a total of six ships, the Stukas adding three to the E-boats' earlier score of three.

Despite these shipping losses the RAF was well pleased. The Air Ministry announced that in one action 12 Hurricane pilots had engaged 50 Ju 87 and 50 Ju 88 bombers and declared: 'The German Air Force today suffered their heaviest losses since the air war round our coasts began'. It claimed 24 bombers and 36 fighters. The claim was revised after a post-war scrutiny of the Luftwaffe's books to 31 enemy aircraft destroyed for the loss of 19 RAF fighters. Even so the result was highly satisfactory considering the vastly superior numbers of the enemy had been met by Nos 145, 43, 238, 257 and 601 Hurricane Squadrons and Nos 41 and 609 Spitfire squadrons operating in dribs and drabs and never banded together. It should be added that the Luftwaffe claimed 46 fighters, including 36 Spitfires — under the customary influence of Spitfire snobbery.

On 12 August the grouse-shooting season opened. The significance of the date in the British sporting calendar was not lost on Berlin which broadcast spuriously that on the previous day the 'Nazi cads unsportingly had bagged' 90 RAF warplanes. (The tally was 38 German aircraft for the loss of 32 British.) Quaintly, news items about the production of Hurricanes to shoot down the Luftwaffe and grouse shooting on the moors were linked in a BBC broadcast as 'work of national importance' because King George VI was presenting game from royal estates to military hospitals.

As the battle continued raids concentrated on the coastal radar stations and No. 11 Group airfields, each so essential to the

Squadron Leader Peter Townsend (with stick) and members of No. 85 Squadron in 1940.
(Imperial War Museum)

Hurricane squadrons defending the invasion corner of England. Deployment of fighter squadrons by ground controllers, depending largely on radar, would be a key factor in Fighter Command's survival of the next phase of the battle. Dowding had geared the defence system to his expectation of radar and now Kesselring and Sperrle, commanding Airfleets 2 and 3, came to recognise the full significance of the tall radar masts featured in reconnaissance photographs. It was plain to them that if the *Eagle* offensive was to win air superiority in the south of England then the radar chain and the forward airfields whose squadrons, predominantly Hurricanes, were guided by it, must be eliminated.

Eagle Day, when finally the code name was signalled on 13 August, was something of an anti-climax and in the beginning almost a farce. Shortly after the launch it was cancelled; an about-turn which was not received by all Luftwaffe units involved. Changeable weather, not expected after the improving conditions of the previous day, was the cause. A mix-up over the cancellation resulted in a formation of 70 unescorted Dornier 17 bombers attacking the Coastal Command airfield at Eastchurch in Kent at 7 a.m. As it happened No. 11 Group was little better organised that morning because of cloudy weather and an unusually weak radar plot. All that could be managed was to attack the enemy bombers on their way home. Fortunately, Hurricanes of No. 111 Squadron, led by Squadron Leader John Thompson and patrolling over Folkestone, were nicely placed for the task. Without an escort of 109s the Dorniers presented a tempting target. The Hurricanes tore into them, shooting down five in as many minutes. Hurricanes of No. 151 Squadron and No. 74 Squadron's Spitfires assisted. Two squadrons of Hurricanes to one of Spitfires typified the ratio which was to place the burden of countering the *Eagle* offensive so squarely on the Hawker Hurricane.

To the west a force of Ju 88 bombers also encountered cloudy conditions in their search for the fighter station at Odiham and the RAF's research and development establishment at Farnborough. They failed to locate the targets and were engaged by aircraft of Nos 43 and 601 Hurricane squadrons and Spitfires of No. 64 Squadron — another example of the two-to-one ratio as between Hurricane and Spitfire squadrons.

Among the first pilots to scramble with No. 601 Squadron at 6.45 a.m. on *Eagle Day* was Pilot Officer W. M. L. 'Billy' Fiske, a volunteer from the United States which was not to ally itself to Britain until the Pearl Harbour attack by Japan on 7 December 1941. Son of a wealthy American banker, he need not have been looking for trouble before breakfast in a Hurricane. Fiske was credited with a Ju 88 probably destroyed and another bomber damaged.

Later that morning the Luftwaffe compounded the error which had left the Dorniers unescorted, a fighter escort of some 30 Me 110s failing to rendezvous with their bomber charges for a raid on Portland. Five Me 110s were destroyed in six minutes, Hurricane pilot Flight Lieutenant Sir Archibald Hope, a baronet in No. 601 Squadron, reporting: 'I fired a short burst at one enemy aircraft head-on and as I passed I took another the same way. He tightened his turn and pulled straight up across me so that I could see his pale blue underneath. I finished my bullets into his bottom . . . ' With good radar notice two Hurricane squadrons and one Spitfire squadron had operated as a wing in this action. The pilots were greatly encouraged by what they regarded as the enemy's headlong flight from superior numbers. Despite continued bad weather the Luftwaffe intensified operations in the afternoon. In the post-war count it was learned that it had lost 45 aircraft to the RAF's 13, of which 12 were Hurricanes.

After a comparatively quiet 14 August, during which the defences were tested by the diversity of enemy raids, the offensive took on a new dimension. For the first and only time in the battle Göering hurled three air fleets at Britain. To the Germans 15 August, now the weather was better and the unco-ordinated start was behind them, represented the true beginning of the *Eagle* offensive in which they expected Fighter Command would be destroyed. Non-stop raiding along a broad front from the east to the west coast. Total destruction of the radar stations and airfields. Force the remaining fighters up to defend the radar sites and their own bases and shoot them down. This was the programme.

Hitler intended doomed Britain to be in no doubt about its approaching fate. On *Eagle Day*, Berlin broadcast in English: 'England lies on a silver salver awaiting the German Air Force's attack. She cannot escape. John Bull will be smoked out. Either he will surrender or England will be annihilated'. Cartoons depicted an encircled England, the German eagle at her throat.

From dawn the Luftwaffe kept No. 11 Group squadrons on their toes. The wear and tear on men and machines was beginning to tell, although the strong construction, wide-track undercarriage and comparative ease of repair of the Hurricane, were already paying off. The main peril of repeated take-offs and landings was the increasing likelihood of being caught rearming and refuelling on the ground. In the pre-war planning of the Air Defence of Great Britain it had been assumed that enemy bomber bases would be behind the River Meuse. But the blitzkrieg advance to the Channel coast had exposed the most forward airfields to attack with little or no warning. Hurricane pilots flying from them were required frequently to climb inland to reach an altitude from which to return and fight.

The front-line airfields of Lympne and Hawkinge in Kent were selected as the main targets for the morning of 5 August. Forty Ju 87s, escorted by some 60 Me 109s, attacked Lympne. Although Hawkinge also suffered, it was spared Lympne's degree of devastation by the courageous efforts of No. 501 Squadron which lost two Hurricanes — their pilots baled out — in destroying two Stukas.

Spitfires of No. 54 Squadron were also involved in the defence of the airfields, Mitchell's machine complementing Camm's monoplane by tackling enemy fighters whenever possible while the Hurricane attacked bombers. But the combination of talents had not been sufficient to prevent serious damage to the airfields and, worse, radar breakdowns at the ancient Cinque Port towns of Rye and at Dover because power cables were severed in the raids. Damaging though they had been there was at least an increasingly familiar pattern about the morning attacks and cross-Channel feints in south-east England and this helped Fighter Command headquarters and No. 11 Group to measure their response.

However, after mid-day a novel situation began to develop. In the north, hitherto quiet enough to enable Dowding to rest and reserve fighter squadrons, particularly his minority of Spitfire squadrons, the radar plot picked up abnormal and unexpected activity on the part of Airfleet 5 operating from bases in occupied Norway and Denmark.

General Stumpff's airmen, impatient while their comrades in Airfleets 2 and 3 were 'winning the war', were about to receive their opportunity to share the honours for the defeat of the RAF, which they believed to be imminent. Airfleet 5 was under orders to destroy airfields in north-east England and in Yorkshire. Believing that the air defence of the north and the Midlands had been weakened to reinforce the invasion front, Stumpff's bomber and fighter crews surmised they were in for a joyride.

But Luftwaffe intelligence had got it wrong. Dowding had maintained the defence of the north and the Midlands, though some of No. 13 Group's squadrons were resting after exchanging with fresh units. In contrast to the south-east the majority of the fighters scrambled by Air Vice-Marshal R. E. Saul's No. 13 Group to intercept 65 He 111 bombers and 34 Me 110 fighters were Spitfires; Dowding had saved them for 'a rainy day'.

Saul sent up three squadrons of Spitfires, two of Hurricanes and even one of Blenheims.

Rare occasion when the rivalry between the Hurricane and Spitfire ended in tears. This Mark I Hurricane of No. 17 Squadron was in collision with a Spitfire I A of No. 266 Squadron at Martlesham Heath. *(RAF Museum)*

Given the advantage of time, usually denied Hurricanes in the south because of the short Channel crossing, the Spitfires outclimbed the North Sea raiders on their way to intercept. Eight Heinkels and seven Me 110s were destroyed to No. 13 Group's nil. It proved a costly excursion for the bombers and fighters of Airfleet 5 which had set off so confidently from Stavanger in Norway. The Hurricanes, including No. 605's which had flown 80 miles from Scotland to engage enemy bombers over Tyneside, accounted for nine.

Some 100 miles to the south, 50 of Airfleet 5's faster Ju 88s swept across the North Sea from Aalborg in northern Denmark. Approaching Flamborough Head they encountered 12 Spitfires of No. 616 Squadron and six Hurricanes from No. 73 Squadron, both from No. 12 Group. Air Vice-Marshal Trafford Leigh-Mallory, the No. 12 Group commander, and his pilots welcomed the opportunity, eager as they were to play a more prominent part in the battle. Heavily engaged, the bomber force split up, but about 30 attacked the bomber airfield at Great Driffield in Yorkshire, destroying ten Whitleys on the ground. A raid on a fighter base such as No. 73 Squadron's at Church Fenton would have paid a better dividend for Airfleet 5's losses. No. 73 Squadron's Hurricanes shot down seven of the eight Ju 88s destroyed. Losing a total of 23 aircraft out of 123 serviceable bombers and 34 fighters Airfleet 5 was not to reappear in any strength in daylight for the remainder of the battle.

In the south the Luftwaffe continued to play the hand Dowding and Park feared: raids to rub out the front-line fighter airfields. In addition to the midday attacks on Lympne and Hawkinge, the Kent cliff-top airfield of Manston was raked by cannon and machine-gun fire, two Spitfires being destroyed on the ground. By 3 p.m. Martlesham Heath, where the RAF had put the prototype Hurricane through its paces, was dive-bombed by unintercepted Stukas escorted by 109s. As the raiders approached, Hurricanes of No. 17 Squadron were scrambled but did not locate the enemy in time. Simultaneously, a mixed force of 100 bombers and fighters were detected approaching the Kent coast, followed 30 minutes later by 150 enemy aircraft. Four fighter squadrons on patrol as the raids came in were supplemented by another three — just one squadron of Spitfires, No. 64, and six squadrons of Hurricanes, Nos 1, 17, 32, 111, 151 and 501. If ever there was an example of the preponderance of Hurricanes over Spitfires in the Battle of Britain this was it. The Hurricanes fought valiantly to break up the large Luftwaffe formations but they were outnumbered and roughly handled by the 109s.

In the later afternoon the fighting moved to the west, some 250 Airfleet 3 raiders fanning out along the south coast from Sussex to Dorset. As at Lympne, Hawkinge and Martlesham Heath, airfields were the principal targets. Hurricanes scrambled to protect their bases in the face of far superior numbers of enemy fighters. Of the eleven Nos 10 and 11 Group squadrons involved, Nos 32, 43, 111, 601, 87, 213 were of Hurricanes, the remainder being one Blenheim squadron and four of Spitfires. No. 601's Hurricane pilots excelled themselves, destroying five Ju 88s for the loss of two whose pilots baled out.

By early evening the battle had swung back to the 'invasion' skies of south-east England, radar plotting more than 70 bandits approaching from the direction of Calais. They were briefed to bomb Park's key sector stations at Kenley and Biggin Hill. Hurricanes of No. 501 Squadron, almost out of fuel, helped to intercept the force as it crossed the coast. Under attack the raiders split up and, unloading on the nearest possible target, the less vital West Malling, failed to press on to Kenley and Biggin Hill. Shortly afterwards the last daylight raid developed, 15 Me 110s and eight Me 109s heading for Croydon, a course so familiar to peacetime Lufthansa airline crews.

This comparatively small force wrecked Hurricane repair facilities at the Rollason and Redwing works, demonstrating again the implications of the Luftwaffe's eventual failure to persevere with the destruction of

Refuelling in July, 1940, B Flight of No. 85 Squadron at Castle Camps refreshes itself while the bowser stands by to fill up one of their aircraft. *(RAF Museum)*

radar, airfield and aircraft industry targets. Between them, No. 111 Squadron, officially not yet operational at Croydon, and No. 32 from Biggin Hill, exacted some retribution, shooting down four of the raiders as they raced for the sea. The RAF tally for the day was 182, amended after the war to 75 enemy aircraft shot down for the loss of 34 fighters.

While the Luftwaffe named 15 August 1940 as 'Black Thursday', Hawkers and the RAF were entitled to take a more optimistic view of its events and results. More Hurricanes had been in action than on any day since the outbreak of war, their pilots justifying beyond measure the company's faith in Camm's concept of a monoplane fighter and Sorley's insistence on eight guns.

Cannon would have been more effective than the .303 Brownings. Hawkers had favoured installation of this heavier armament for almost five years. As it happened it was at this stage of the battle that No. 151 Squadron at North Weald received a Hurricane armed with cannon. The squadron already had a limited experience of cannon. In *Hurricane* Adrian Stewart reveals that a trials cannon-armed Hurricane, hitherto thought to have lain unblooded in a Martlesham hangar in 1940 and then scrapped, had been collected in July by a Flight Lieutenant of the squadron, who had so damaged a 109 on 14 July that it had crash-landed at base. On *Eagle Day* the cannon-firing Hurricane pilot had destroyed a Do 17. Experimental cannon-firing Hurricanes took little further part in the battle, although in early September Flight Lieutenant Rabagliati of No. 46 Squadron succeeded in blowing up a 109. The cannon were unreliable, not because of the guns themselves, but mainly because of installation and feed problems. Hurricane IICs were not to come into their own until the New Year. If Camm had been listened to, the Hurricane could have been armed with cannon very much earlier and no doubt its teething troubles would have been overcome in time for the battle. A prime factor in pre-war official opposition to Hawkers' wish to experiment with cannon had been concern about speed. Certainly the weight of the Swiss Oerlikon or French Hispano, then under consideration, would have reduced the performance of K5083. However, the advent of the Merlin XX mitigated loss of speed and on 6 February 1941 a prototype IIC, capable of up to 336 mph, made its first flight.

Meanwhile, Lord Beaverbrook, the Minister of Aircraft Production, had become a forceful advocate of cannon. Hawkers, authorised at last, got to work on 30 pairs of wings in for repair.

Hurricane repair was as vital to making up squadron losses as production. The Canadian-born proprietor of the *Daily Express, Sunday Express* and London *Evening Standard,* had not long been in office when he stimulated the development of an emergency repair organisation. Since his appointment by Churchill as 'Aircraft Minister', as he preferred to call himself, on 14 May 1940, the Beaver's drive and nervous energy had capitalised on Camm's design bonus — ease of production and repair — to get badly 'winged' Hurricanes back into the battle. He remembered that Trevor Westbrook, a brilliant if contentious aircraft production engineer, was unemployed. He traced Westbrook to a golf course and summoned him to London. 'Have a drink?' Beaverbrook offered when Westbrook arrived. Westbrook declined. 'I'm not drinking until I get work'. — 'You've got it, and now have a drink'. Westbrook headed the repair organisation of 25 companies which returned damaged Hurricanes to operational squadrons. It was quicker to refer a damaged fighter to one of Westbrook's Hurricane 'hospitals' than send it back to Hawkers.

In August 107 Hurricanes were repaired, rising to 179 in September. Respective figures for new production Hurricanes were 251 and 252. It was estimated that, of the Hurricanes that crashed on land in Britain during the battle, 61 per cent were mended and returned to squadrons. Those beyond recovery were stripped of spares. Dowding and Park were highly appreciative of Beaverbrook's determination to keep them in business. Park was particularly reassured by the Beaver's nightly telephone call to ask how many Hurricanes and Spitfires were required the next day. Shortly after the battle, David Farrer in *The Sky's The Limit,* wrote: 'In no single branch of MAP's activities did Beaverbrook see his innovation and inspiration bring about such remarkable results as in repairs'.

Dowding credited Beaverbrook with such 'magical' production and repair improvement that the supply of trained pilots to fly fighters became 'the primary danger'. That Beaverbrook's son, Squadron Leader the Hon Max Aitken of No. 601 Squadron, flew Hurricanes in the Battle of Britain, enabled the Minister to learn at first hand about the aircraft and its performance. Late on summer evenings in 1940 Max Aitken's pilot friends would gather for a drink at Stornoway House, Beaverbrook's St. James's home. On at least one occasion the Beaver took them down the road to No. 10 Downing Street because the Aircraft Minister thought there were things the Prime Minister ought to know.

Resumption on 16 August of widespread raiding in which the emphasis remained on airfields and radar sites brought further pressure on the repair organisation. At Tangmere, No. 11 Group's most westerly sector station and home of two Hurricane squadrons, Nos 43 and 601, with a third, No. 145, at its satellite Westhampnett, pilots underwent the nightmare experience of landing to refuel while the airfield was being bombed. Hangars, workshops, stores, sick-quarters, a Salvation Army hut, all were written off. Seven Hurricanes were destroyed on the ground. Bombs falling among them, pilots landed into a smoking scene of devastation. In No. 601 Squadron, Pilot Officer Billy Fiske, the United States volunteer who need not have been there, his Hurricane on fire, undercarriage retracted and jammed, attempted a belly landing. Momentarily it seemed that the American was safe and then his aircraft was enveloped in flames. Billy Fiske died from his injuries and is commemorated in St. Paul's Cathedral by a tablet: 'An American citizen who died that England might live'; a Hurricane pilot from the United States remembered in the Cathedral with Nelson and other British heroes. During the attack Fiske's fellow squadron, No. 43 had taken its toll of the Ju 87s, shooting down seven, but losing the squadron hangar to them. It had been built in 1914-18 by German prisoners of war.

Losing Hurricanes in combat was acceptable, if regrettable, but destruction or damage on the ground was wasteful and squadrons from Nos 10, 11 and 12 Groups fought valiantly to protect the airfields. They could not be everywhere and on the evening of 16 August two Ju 88s, breaking inland, scored a success of the kind that Fighter Command could least afford. With direct hits on hangars at No. 8 Maintenance Unit and No. 2 Service Flying Training School at Brize Norton in Oxfordshire they destroyed more than 40 aircraft of which 28 were Hurricanes.

On this same summer's day a fighter pilot, surviving a blazing Hurricane, won Fighter Command's only Victoria Cross. Flight Lieutenant J. B. Nicolson, formerly a Spitfire pilot of No. 72 Squadron and now with No. 249 Squadron, was patrolling Southampton in a cloudless sky and wondering if the baby which his wife was expecting in Yorkshire had arrived. He was hoping for a 'squirt' at the enemy — and then there they were, three Ju 88 bombers just ahead. In company with the other two Hurricanes of his section Nicolson was closing when he saw the 88s 'fly straight past into a squadron of Spitfires'. He said later: 'I used to fly a Spitfire myself and I guessed it was curtains for the three Junkers. I was right and they were all shot down in quick time, with no pickings for us. I must confess I was very disappointed for I had never fired at a German in my life and was longing to have a crack at them'.

Nicolson began to climb his section to rejoin the remainder of the squadron at 18,000 feet over Southampton, but he was not to reach them. An Me 110 had slipped onto his tail and was pumping cannon shells into the Hurricane. In seconds it was ablaze. Nicolson was blinded in one eye by blood and wounded in a leg. He said: 'The first shell tore through the hood over my cockpit and sent splinters into my left eye . . . the second cannon shell struck my spare petrol tank and set it on fire . . . the third shell crashed into the cockpit and tore off my right trouser leg . . . the fourth shell struck the back of my left shoe and made quite a mess of my left foot . . . the effect of these four shells was to make me dive away to the right to avoid further shells . . . I was just thinking of jumping out when suddenly a Messerschmitt 110 whizzed under me and got right in my gunsights . . . I plugged him the first time and I could see my tracer bullets entering the German machine. He was going like mad, twisting and turning as he tried to get away from my fire. So I pushed the throttle wide open. Both of us must have been doing about 400 mph as we went down together in a dive'.

Nicolson kept the burning Hurricane on the tail of the 110, giving him a 'parting burst'. Then he started thinking about saving himself. He had trouble getting out. His thumb on the firing button and hand on the throttle were badly burned and it was a struggle to free himself from the cockpit straps. Once out he was closely inspected by an enemy fighter. 'I don't know if he fired at me. The main thing is that I wasn't hit'.

As he began to drift towards the sea, Nicolson realised how badly injured he was. He could see the bones of his left hand showing through the knuckles and blood was seeping through the lace holes of his left boot. 'My right hand was pretty badly burned too'. The oxygen mask was still over his face, but his hands were in such a poor state that he could not remove it. Getting lower, he realised that he might fall into the sea which would have been fatal because he was in no condition to swim. Wriggling about he managed to float inland. He dodged a high-tension cable only to be fired at by an over-enthusiastic member of the Local Defence Volunteer force, predeccessor of the Home Guard, 'Dad's Army', receiving a bullet in a buttock. Thus did a fighter pilot who had exchanged his Spitfire for a Hurricane win Fighter Command's only VC. In May 1945 Nicolson took time off from commanding No. 27 Squadron of Mosquitoes and Beaufighters in the Far East to observe a Liberator raid on Japanese targets. He was killed.

Chapter 5
Saving the nation

'Best of all it was a marvellous gun platform . . .' Group Captain Sir Douglas Bader.

Despite reasonable weather 17 August was a comparatively quiet day for the defenders. Next day, a Sunday, the Luftwaffe renewed its onslaught against the fighter airfields. The raids were not so heavy as on the 15th but were pressed home with great determination. Biggin Hill, Kenley, Croydon and West Malling were attacked. More aware of the effectiveness of Fighter Command's radar-aided interception tactics the Airfleet 2 and 3 commanders resorted to the ruse of following high-level, escorted bomber waves with a low-level attack by unescorted bombers flying below the radar scan. That this did not work out as intended owed more to the Luftwaffe's own muddle that to the defence. The high altitude Ju 88s which were supposed to have indicated a smoking Biggin Hill for nine hedge-hopping Dornier 17s were involved in a rendezvous mix-up over France, exposing the Dorniers to the full blast of ground and air defences. Between them Nos. 32 and 610 Hurricane and Spitfire squardons, hastily scrambled on the initiative of the station commander, together with the ground guns, saved the airfield from serious damage. The tally after the Ju 88s eventually arrived was four Ju 88s and six Dornier 17s.

Kenley did not escape so lightly. Experiencing a raid based on a similar ruse,

Mark II machine — one of a batch of 1,000 Hurricanes built at Kingston, Brooklands and Langley, 1940-41. *(British Aerospace)*

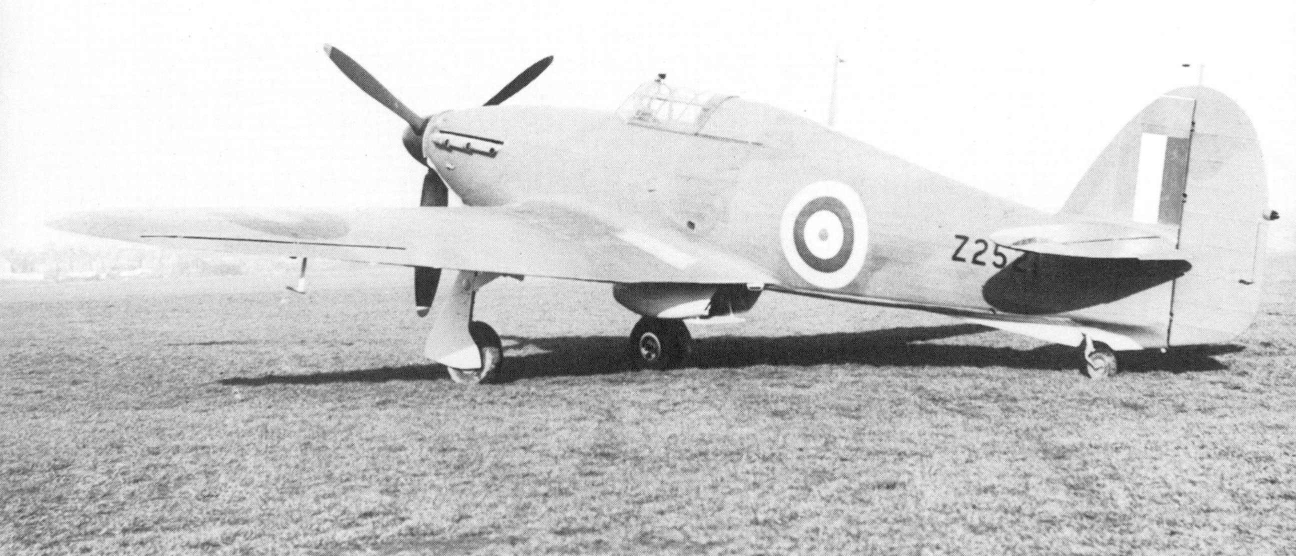

except that Do 17s comprised both high- and low-level forces, it lost ten hangars and many other buildings. With No. 615 Squadron of Hurricanes confronting a raid over Hawkinge, Kenley's two remaining squadrons, No. 111 Hurricane, and No. 64, Spitfire, tackled some nine low-level Dorniers and 50 Me 109-escorted high-level bombers respectively. Unfortunately their efforts did not prevent the loss of six Hurricanes destroyed on the ground.

In all it was a hard day for the Hurricanes, 29 being lost although 20 pilots survived, but placed to their credit were some 35 of the 65 enemy aircraft destroyed. Serious though such losses were when set against the mounting toll of August and reinforcement possibilities, they would have been far worse but for the capability of Camm's rugged design to withstand punishment. A No. 85 Squadron pilot landed his aircraft minus a wing tip and Flight Lieutenant F. R. Carey of No. 43 Squadron was astonished to climb out and inspect what remained of his machine. There was an enormous hole in one wing and an elevator and the rudder had gone. Carey, wounded in combat, suffered the additional inconvenience of anti-aircraft fire as he returned to his airfield. His aircraft was so battered that the gunners had failed to recognise it as a Hurricane. More will be heard of Frank Carey, a pre-war aircraft apprentice and Sergeant Pilot, especially of his exploits in the Far East.

If there was a message to Fighter Command from this hectic Sunday it was — though neither Park nor Dowding needed such a reminder — that the Hurricane in its greater numbers was saving the nation. To underline it No. 56 Squadron at Rochford in the North Weald sector destroyed six Me 110s without loss.

As the sun went down there ended the four days in which Göering had pledged the Luftwaffe to achieve air superiority over the south of England. The Hurricane had made the main contribution towards frustrating this intention, keeping Airfleet 5 at home in daylight, deterring further Stuka dive-bombing attacks and with all the perils they held for the radar sites, sector and satellite airfields. After the four days of intensive fighting on August 13, 15, 16 and 18 Winston Churchill, addressing the House of Commons on 20 August, immortalised the Few: 'Never in the field of human conflict was so much owed by so many to so few. All hearts go out to the fighter pilots whose brilliant actions we see with our own eyes every day . . .'.

Now Göring, as with the gambler who plays to recoup on the next 'investment', convinced himself that, given another four days of fine weather, he could claim air superiority. He ordered Kesselring and Sperrle to subject the defences to round-the-clock raiding. But poor weather conditions intervened and bought a crucial respite for Hurricane (and Spitfire) squadrons. The battle was not to resume in all its full fury until 24 August, a fine and cloudless day over the south of England. In No. 11 Group, where the lull had assisted the reinforcement of depleted Hurricane squadrons with aircraft and pilots, this beautiful Saturday morning was greeted with apprehension. From 8 to 18 August 121 Hurricanes (against 54 Spitfires) had been lost, with 25 Hurricanes badly damaged.

There was no repetition this day of Luftwaffe fighters missing their rendezvous with bombers. In they came. As the fighting swayed across the southern counties, Hurricane airfields — Kenley, Croydon, Biggin Hill, West Malling, Hornchurch, Rochford, North Weald, Debden, Hawkinge, Lympne, Manston, guardians of the invasion coast and the way to London — were imperilled. After four raids in not many more hours, Manston in the Biggin Hill sector was abandoned. Should withdrawal be enforced elsewhere, closing down the Hurricane squadrons' No. 11 Group refuelling grounds, then the situation would be indeed be critical.

As August faded into September these airfields remained under extreme pressure. The general courage and individual acts of bravery of groundcrew and members of the Women's Auxiliary Air Force, particularly at Biggin Hill on 31 August and 1 September, are recorded in more specific accounts of the Battle of Britain, yet merit credit here for their contribution to keeping Hurricane squadrons refuelled, airborne and in contact with the enemy.

Daily, the bombed airmen and airwomen kept Dowding's 'few' in the battle. Of the 'few' the 'most' flew the Hawker Hurricane against formations which, beginning as waves of 200 to 300 bombers and fighters, fanned out over the Channel and broke up into small groups to attack their target airfields. The partnership of controllers, WAAF plotters, fitters and riggers, pilots and, for the most part, Hurricanes, wrecked Göering's rhetoric about removing the RAF from the skies of southern England. But this is not to deny that the Luftwaffe was exacting a high price from Fighter Command for its resistance, especially in Hurricanes and the more experienced pilots whom it could least afford to lose.

One of these was Squadron Leader Tom Gleave of No. 253 Squadron who had shot down four 109s in swift succession on 30 August. Leading his section of three Hurricanes this 32-year-old regular was 17,000 feet over Maidstone in Kent when 'stretching as far as the eye could see were rows of Me 109s riding above the haze'. They were silver with yellow bellies, 75 to 80 of them. Gleave and his companions, Flight Lieutenant George Brown and Pilot Officer Colin Francis, attacked. Tom said the 109s tended to fly at not much more than 270 mph to economise on fuel. They were, therefore, often 'sitting ducks'. Tom always thought he had got four, although they were not to be confirmed until after the war. Nothing was known of the fate of 19-year-old Colin Francis until August 1981, when his remains were found in the wreckage of a Hurricane near Wrotham in the Sevenoaks area of Kent. Brown was shot down shortly afterwards.

The next afternoon at about 5 pm Tom Gleave climbed nine Hurricanes from Kenley and into 'a wheeling mix of Me 109s and Hurricanes, each firing at the chap in front'. He recalls: 'Then I saw a Me 109 blasting bits off the tail of a Hurricane'. Gleave shot it down — confirmed as in the sea off Dungeness.

After landing he was amazed by the punishment his Hurricane had taken. He stepped out of 'just a few tubes and thin air'. Within hours Tom Gleave had been shot down in flames. Fire was a particular hazard in the Mark Is of 1940. In front of the pilot, forward of the instrument panel, there was a small gravity-fed fuel tank, offering the risk of groundcrew forgetting to replace the screw cap. More petrol from the filling trap ran down just behind the red hot exhaust manifolds. A pilot, reacting by closing the throttle quickly, could set off a spark and ignite himself and the Hurricane. In time Hawkers fitted a spring-loaded cap.

Tom Gleave fell to a Ju 88 gunner. His right wing fuel tank was hit by a cannon shell. The fire engulfed him rapidly and he felt for his revolver which he wore in the cockpit for just such an emergency. His clothes on fire, the skin of his hands and wrists blistering in white bubbles and the flames licking at his legs, he rejected the option and struggled to get out, only to be thwarted by his radio lead and oxygen tube which refused to disconnect. Clawing off the helmet to which they were attached he opened the canopy and then an explosion ejected him more suddenly and forcefully than he would have wished.

Tom Gleave's extensive burns to face, hands, arms and legs — 'standard Hurricane burns' — were to require many months of surgery and treatment at the Queen Victoria Hospital, East Grinstead, as a patient of Sir Archibald McIndoe, the New Zealand-born consultant in plastic surgery to the RAF. From the wooden army hut, Ward 3, accommodating the RAF's most badly burned aircrew, Tom Gleave helped to found the Guinea Pig Club, at that time exclusively for aircrew treated there. To this day he is the Chief Guinea Pig, presiding over the annual Lost Weekend reunion, fostering the club's fund-raising and welfare activities, more than ever needed as surviving members face old age.

It might be supposed that death or grievous injury suffered in flaming Hurricanes would have soured pilots' opinions of the aircraft. To the contrary; far from being diminished

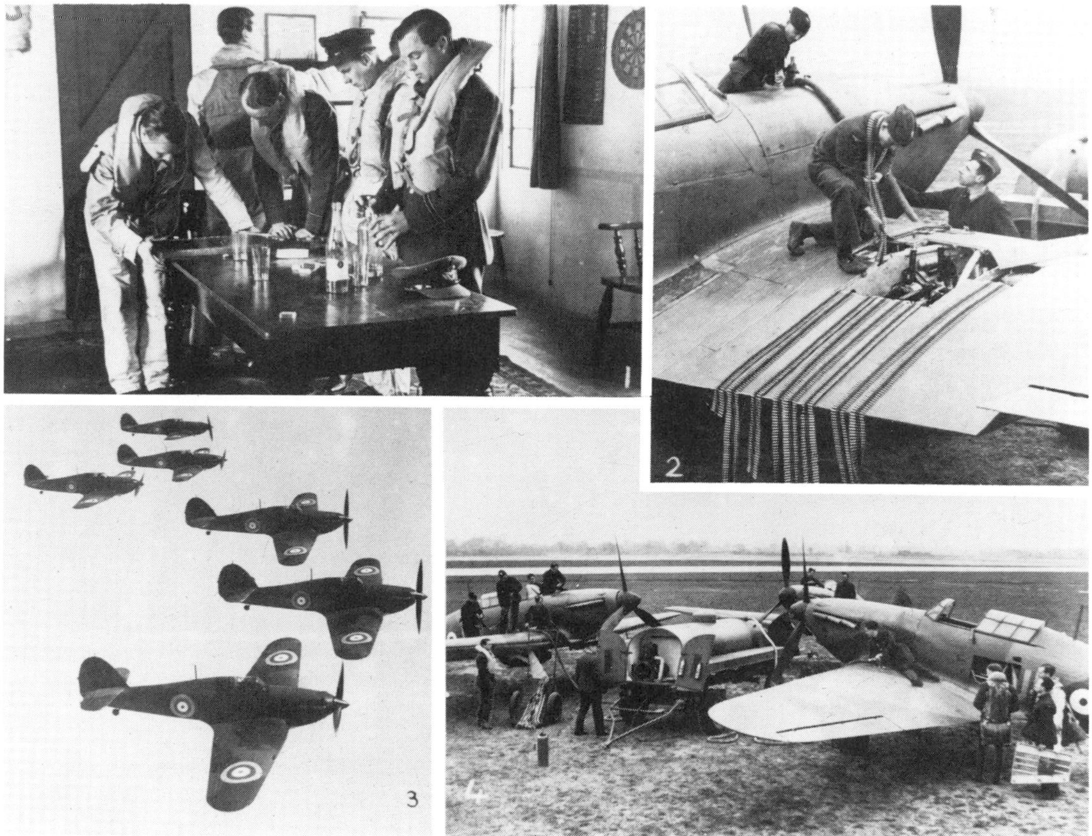

Composite picture: (1) Pilots of No. 601 Squadron, Tangmere. Standing with syphon is Max Aitken, son of Lord Beaverbrook. (2) Rearming. (3) No. 601 airborne. (4) Refuelling. Max Aitken is to the left wearing Mae West.
(RAF Museum)

during the Battle of Britain, the Hawker fighter's reputation was enhanced by the daily evidence of its strength and absorption of punishment. Despite his experience, Tom Gleave can still say: 'She was a true fighting lady if ever there was one'.

The odds faced by Gleave, Francis and Brown were symptomatic of the background to the Big Wing controversary developing over Park's sparing commital of fighters; an enduring argument in historical debate on the conduct of the Battle of Britain. From the outset Park's usual tactic had been to meet the enemy as early as possible — which of itself generally implied small numbers. The No. 12 Group commander, Air Vice-Marshal Trafford Leigh-Mallory favoured assembly of a Big Wing of up to 60 fighters, of necessity mostly Hurricanes, to savage enemy aircraft on the way home, even though they may have first reached and bombed their targets.

In July, August and early September the proximity to the Luftwaffe's bases of Park's crescent-shaped defence lines of airfields defending south-east England and London, did not normally permit the assembly of a Big Wing in No. 11 Group. The defence system had not been prepared in the expectation of fighter and bomber units of two Airfleets operating from little more than 20 miles away. Dowding always took the view that fighters should be used in the greatest strength circumstances would permit, but the best Park could manage from the frontline

The Hurricane of Squadron Leader Douglas Bader's No. 242 Squadron bore the symbolic emblem of Hitler getting a kick in the pants.
(RAF Museum)

airfields of No. 11 Group was to pair squadrons. Throughout the battle Fighter Command's dependence upon the slower climbing Hurricanes militated against Park — hard-pressed to defend coastal radar stations and airfields — putting together a formation of more than two squadrons. The alternative — and this would not have conformed with Dowding's orders at this stage — might have been to assemble large formations to harass raiders returning from their targets. Since, however, these targets were principally No. 11 Group's own airfields during August, and also Hurricane and other aircraft factories, such a tactic held little appeal for Dowding and Park.

Towards the end of August, however, Park desperately needed reinforcements because his airfields, notably Biggin Hill, faced the possibility of abandonment. So he introduced the 'Tally Ho' procedure aimed at enabling fighters in contact with the enemy to call up assistance. Very soon there were too many tally-ho's seeking reinforcement by too few fighters — 'Thirty bombers 40 fighters, Angels 20, proceeding North Guildford' was to become a cliché of the Battle of Britain.

Thus the vulnerability of No. 11 Group's airfields and the handicap of the slower climbing Hurricane bolstered the Big Wing theory, which Leigh-Mallory, No. 12 Group commander, had mulled over since June.

It was at this stage that a legless pilot in No. 12 Group, Squadron Leader Douglas Bader, commanding No. 242 Squadron at Coltishall, sought to vary the conduct of the battle, presuming authority far beyond that normally vested in his rank and experience. That almost a year afterwards he was flying a Spitfire when he collided with a Me 109 near Bethune in France, has encouraged a public misconception that Bader led a Spitfire squadron at the height of the Battle of Britain. Bader's parachute descent after falling several thousand feet attached to the Spitfire's cockpit by a duralumin leg until a belt gave way, was to strengthen that belief. Moreover, earlier as a member of No. 222, a Spitfire squadron, he had shot down a 109 and a 110 over Dunkirk as the evacuation ended and had been stationed subsequently at Duxford in No. 19, another Spitfire squadron.

Bader, therefore, came to the Hurricane from the Spitfire and when he returned to the Spitfire after the Battle of Britain he left part of his heart with the Hurricane. He was to acknowledge: 'Like all pilots who flew and fought in the Hurricane I grew to love it. It was strong, highly manoeuvrable, could turn inside the Spitfire and of course the 109. Best of all it was a marvellous gun platform . . . The Spitfire was less steady when the guns were firing'.

When the guns were firing . . . Bader, as with so many of his peacetime Cranwell contemporaries, had progressed from a boyhood appetite for adventure story exploits of First World War aces to a professional study of their careers and tactics. Steeped in McCudden, Mannock, Bishop and Ball he was dogmatic about the virtues of assembling wing formations before engaging the enemy, then breaking off into individual attacks and dogfights. 'The boys in the last war knew' was a favourite assertion. The trouble was that Bader's training of his Hurricane squadron pilots, his style of fighting, conflicted with Fighter Command's opinion that the Hurricane — and more so the Spitfire — was too fast for the dogfight tactics of the First World War. Given this background, Bader's frustration during the heavy fighting at the end of August intensified as he sat in the dispersal hut at Coltishall while No. 11 Group's Hurricane squadrons were losing aircraft and pilots in what he regarded as wasteful piecemeal attempts to intercept mass raids.

After 1940 the Hurricane appeared in new roles, particularly as a fighter-bomber. The ubiquitous Mark II B featured in Europe, the Middle East and the Far East. *(Aeroplane)*

Bader's representations were welcomed by Leigh-Mallory who, as group commander, was impatient of No. 12's comparatively passive role. Finally, on 9 September Bader deliberately disobeyed orders leaving No. 11 Group's North Weald, base of two Hurricane squadrons, and Hornchurch airfields unprotected.

Much of this battle within the battle might have merged with the mass of incident of the fighting over south-east England but for the colourful mix of men which war had brought into the Hurricane squadrons. It so happened that No. 242 Squadron's adjutant was a Member of Parliament named Peter Macdonald.

The MP, subject daily to Bader's forceful suggestions took them up with Harold Balfour, the Under-Secretary of State for Air, an RFC pilot of the First World War, and who after sampling the Hurricane, found it 'a nice aeroplane for an old gentleman to fly'. Balfour arranged for Macdonald to see the Prime Minister. The results of this irregular lobbying behind Dowding's back will become apparent as the Hurricane's role in defending London in the climactic week of 7-15 September are to follow. But first there occurred the mistakc or 'miracle', as Dowding sincerely believed it, which would lift the burden of repeated attacks on the airfields of Hurricane and other fighter squadrons.

On the night of 24/25 August some 10 of the 170 bombers over Britain, briefed to attack Thameshaven oil targets but losing their way, unloaded on the City of London, the narrow streets of the commercial centre of what was still the British Empire. The very next night Wellingtons, Hampdens and Whitleys of Bomber Command retaliated against Berlin. As a consequence, just as the hammering of No. 11 Group necessitated consideration of withdrawal of fighter squadrons from its reeling sector stations, an infuriated Hitler stormed: 'I haved waited three months without responding, with the thought that they might stop this mischief. Herr Churchill saw in this a sign of weakness . . . When they declare that they will attack our cities in great strength, then we will eradicate their cities'. One city was at the top of Hitler's mind.

Events between the Berlin raid and the launch of the blitz on London underlined thc importance of the 'miracle'. At the beginning of September the Luftwaffe had scheduled some 30 aircraft industry plants for attack. Since Spitfire snobbery did not restrict attempts to disrupt fighter production to the Supermarine Works at Woolston, targets included Hurricane production lines at Brooklands, Kingston and Langley. Brooklands was attacked on 4 September and, appropriately, two Hurricane squadrons, Nos. 249 and 253, already on patrol, were ordered to the defence of the works and airfield where Bulman had so cautiously nursed the Hurricane prototype over the rim of the motor-racing circuit. Fortunately for Hurricane production the Wellington shops were hit, largely because a force of 20 Me 110 fighter-bombers, losing six of their numbers to No. 253 Squadron, failed to press home their intended attack on the Hawker area and sought refuge in a defensive circle. A hold-up of Hurricanes would have been a grievous blow. Wellingtons, the legacy of the 1930s priority for building a bomber force at the expense of fighters, could wait. On 6 September Me 110s of the same unit, aiming to make the most of their speed of up to 340 mph at a best altitude of 22,000 feet, made a dash for Brooklands. Some damage was caused to the Hurricane shops, but production was not affected. Had not Hurricanes of No. 1 Squadron intervened, scoring two victories, it might have been much more serious. In 1940 Brooklands accounted for half the total output of Hurricanes.

Chapter 6
Hurricane's victory

'Spitfire snobbery still persisted . . .'

Among the Hurricane pilots defending London on 7 September, as Göering rolled up in his personal train in the Pas de Calais to cheer on the 300 bombers and 600 fighters massing overhead, was Flight Lieutenant R. C. 'Dick' Reynell, who had joined No. 43 Squadron from test flying for Hawkers at Brooklands. Reynell knew rather more about the Hurricane than the majority of his fellow pilots, some of whom were now joining operational squadrons with ten hours or less Hurricane solo experience. Dick Reynell, an officer on the regular reserve, had rejoined temporarily, not so much because of the shortage of pilots, but because of the need for feedback to the company. At least that is how it was said he had convinced the RAF and Hawkers that his place in this critical period was in combat. He had succeeded Hawker test pilot John Hindmarsh, after Hindmarsh had been killed on 6 September 1938 in a Hurricane accident, and was supremely qualified for this task. It was also said that he had refreshed his pre-war service experience and display aerobatics in K5083 in mock dogfights over Brooklands, particularly when his friend Stanford Tuck happened to be in the vicinity.

Reynell, who had destroyed a 109, was himself shot down during the heavy fighting in the defence of London in early September. Separated from the squadron, not even his experience could save him from the 109s which set his Hurricane on fire. Squadron Leader Caesar Hull, who had only just succeeded Squadron Leader J. V. 'Tubby' Badger — shot down and killed on 30 August — in command of No. 43 Squadron, dived to assist, only to become another victim of the swarming 109s.

With the deaths of Tubby Badger, Dick Reynell and Caesar Hull, No. 43 Squadron had lost every one of its key pilots within eight days. Squadron Leader John Simpson, Badger's predecessor as CO, recovering from wounds in Cornwall wrote: '. . . when the news came I cried for the first time since I was little. . . Poor 43. But we can take it. We will have to begin all over again. New CO. New pilots. But the squadron spirit is safe. Dear old Caesar, he commanded the squadron he began in as a Pilot Officer'.

As the daylight blitz on London wore on the breed in Hurricane cockpits was changing. Regulars such as Badger, Reynell, Hull and Simpson were replaced by fresh-faced teenagers, hardly more than schoolboys; surely those most in Dowding's mind when he referred affectionately to his 'chicks'. There were also pilots borrowed from the Fleet Air Arm; Fairey Battle pilots, pilots from Army Co-operation Command — and there too were the Poles, the Czechs and the Canadians.

To the Poles the Hurricane was a God-given weapon of revenge, enabling their No. 303 Squadron to claim 69 Me 109s in the battle. Recognising the 109's superiority over the Hurricane apart from manoeuvrability — the Poles tended to use a tactic enforced during the invasion of Poland by their inferior aircraft. This was to fly low and in a tight circle when sighting a 109. When the 109 sought combat the Pole in his Hurricane would eventually be on the enemy's tail — and open fire. But they also gained a great reputation for their aggressive handling of the Hurricane and it was this which earned them such plaudits on 7 September and thereafter.

The huge force which Göering had cheered

on from a Cap Gris Nez cliff-top met little opposition on its way to London. Insufficent credence had been given to Hitler's threat and it was not thought the Luftwaffe would relax its effective attacks on fighter airfields and aircraft factories. Consequently, Park's No. 11 Group of 13 Hurricane and seven Spitfire squadrons were not positioned to meet a mass attack on London. Dockland in the East End of the capital was set ablaze and pounded by 300 tons of high-explosive bombs. German bomber crews had been astonished by the ease of it all, but it was not to be the same on the way home. For by now, newcomers to the battle, the Poles of No. 303 Squadron, and Canadians of No. 1 (RCAF) Squadron, had paired-up in their Hurricanes from Northolt, and Bader's wing of one Spitfire and two Hurricane squadrons, Nos 19, 242 and 310 Squadrons, had climbed from Duxford in No. 12 Group to come forward and protect Park's airfields.

The keenness of the Poles to employ their Hurricane skills in battle had been evident on 30 August before No. 303 Squadron became operational. Although still training, Flying Officer Paszkiewicz had broken away to dive on an enemy formation and shot down a Do 17. On 7 September the Poles were officially in action. Led by their British commanding officer, Squadron Leader R. G. Kellett, they shot down or badly damaged 10 of 40 Dorniers heading for the Channel. The Poles were well pleased with the performance of their Hurricanes; confidence which had been boosted by news of the punishment Kellett's aircraft had withstood the previous day. Exploding ammunition boxes had holed the wings, the tailplane was in tatters and part of one aileron was shot away.

On 7 September, however, Bader's Wing had not justified its creation. No. 242 Squadron — mostly Canadians under Bader's leadership — did well enough, scoring a number of victories, but No. 310 and the Spitfires of No. 19 had not climbed in time to participate. That night the attack on London was renewed. The bombers were virtually unopposed in the air and the glow from the day's fires lit the way. Hurricanes were not yet employed as night fighters and after dark the defences depended on two Blenheim squadrons and a small unit experimenting with airborne radar.

The combination of day and night raiding and reconnaissance evidence of invasion preparations implied that an invasion attempt was imminent. But 8 September was a quiet day, an opportunity for Fighter Command to plan not to be caught off-balance again. Thus on 9 September successive waves heading late in the afternoon for London received a warm reception. Yet, however well nine of Park's No. 11 Group squadrons were positioned after the lessons of 7 September, there was much anxiety about their ability to block the way to London and protect airfields and Hurricane production at Brooklands and Kingston.

Help was sought from No. 12 Group, specifically for watching over the airfields and aircraft factories. But Douglas Bader ignored the order to patrol between North Weald and Hornchurch at Angels 20 — 20,000 feet. He climbed his Wing of three squadrons to 22,000 feet over the fringe of London until he saw the raid he was expecting — two great swarms of bombers. Bader sent No. 19's Spitfires even higher to provide cover and then, instructing his pilots 'line astern, we're going through the middle', he dived the Hurricanes of Nos 242 and 310 Squadrons, causing the enemy bombers to jettison their loads and enabling his pilots to claim a bag of 20 for the loss of four Hurricanes. Bader, who had disobeyed orders, received an immediate offer from Leigh-Mallory of a Wing of 60 fighters, mostly Hurricanes.

Park, for his part, was now finding it practicable to operate Hurricane squadrons in pairs because, London being the Luftwaffe's main objective, there was longer warning. A pair of squadrons, a Wing, either might appear more impressive than a flight of six aircraft or a single squadron, but many a Hurricane pilot reflecting on this over the years has wondered how much it mattered. 'Ginger' Lacey, who on 13 September as Sergeant J. H. Lacey in No. 501 Squadron, his Hurricane on fire, shot down a Heinkel 111

The ebullient Caesar Hull (centre) with pilots of No. 43 Squadron. L-R Sgt J. A. Buck, F/O C. A. Woods-Scawen, F/O Wilkinson, Sgt G. W. Garton. Squadron Leader Hull was killed in September, 1940, within days of receiving command of the squadron he had joined as a Pilot Officer.

after it had bombed Buckingham Palace and then baled out, has commented: 'The basic fighting unit was, and is, a section. Whether this was of two or three aircraft made no difference'. Lacey firmly believed the Hurricane pilots' task was to get to the enemy bombers before they bombed the fighter airfields or other targets.

If the Battle of Britain has its 'Trafalgar Day' then that day is Sunday, 15 September 1940 . . . 'One of those days of autumn when the countryside is at its loveliest', as Park was to recall.

Shortly after half past ten, Women's Auxiliary Air Force 'croupiers' shuffling counters on the plot table, were astonished to see Mr. and Mrs. Churchill walk into No. 11 Group's operations room at Uxbridge. 'I don't know whether anything will happen today. At present all is quiet', Park told them. By half past eleven, when the first German aircraft crossed the coast, Park's squadrons were airborne, ten squadrons in five pairs. From No. 10 Group in the west No. 609 Squadron's Spitfires were called in to cover the Hurricane works at Brooklands and also Windsor Castle where Beaverbrook was concealing in the grounds new Hurricanes awaiting delivery to squadrons. Behind London a wing of 60 fighters from five of Leigh-Mallory's No. 12 Group squadrons was assembling under Squadron Leader Douglas Bader.

A force of 100 Do17 bombers escorted by 300 fighters was crossing the south coast. The lessons of 7 September had been learned. Churchill watched and listened as the controllers applied Park's remedial instruction of 11 September, pairing like with like — Hurricane squadron with Hurricane squadron, Spitfire with Spitfire. The Hurricanes were to engage the bombers and their close-escort fighters while the Spitfires tackled the fighter screen. Churchill could not fail to appreciate the contribution of the Hurricane squadrons on a day which had started with the destruction by Hurricanes of No. 87 Squadron over Start Point in south Devon of a 'met' Heinkel.

At much the same time as the Prime Minister arrived at No. 11 Group headquarters Squadron Leader J. Sample, a Northumberland estate agent and pre-war weekend flier, had been introducing No. 504 Squadron's Hurricane pilots to two visiting US Army Air Corps Generals and a US Navy Rear-Admiral at Northolt when, as if on cue, the squadron was scrambled.

The first wave of Airfleet 2 bombers and fighters was in trouble from the moment it crossed the coast over east Kent. Stepped up from 15,000-25,000 feet the force was harried all the way to London, its crews persevering in the belief that they only had to appear over the capital often enough and in strength to hasten the end of the war. Over the Medway on their way in they encountered particularly determined head-on attacks from the Poles in Hurricanes of No. 303 Squadron. Over London the Hurricanes of Nos 17, 73, 504 and 257 Squadrons engaged so effectively that the bombers unloaded indiscriminately, mostly in the south-eastern suburbs and wheeled for home. It was now that Bader's wing of Britons, Canadians, Poles and Czechs in three Hurricane and two Spitfire squadrons, the most formidable fighter opposition the Luftwaffe had yet encountered, swept the enemy into retreat, harrying them from Hammersmith to Dungeness, the Hurricanes attacking the bombers while the Spitfires occupied the fighters.

Many were the exploits of Hurricane pilots on this September Sunday. The most representative description of the first mass raid of the day was provided shortly afterwards by Squadron Leader Sample, the leader of No. 504 Squadron whose public relations exercise with the American VIPs had ended so abruptly. He said: 'At lunchtime on Sunday, my squadron was somewhere south of the Thames estuary behind several other squadrons of Hurricanes and Spitfires. The German bombers were three or four miles away when we first spotted them. We were at 17,000 feet and they were at about 19,000 feet. Their fighter escort was scattered around. The bombers were coming in towards London from the south-east and at first we could not tell how many there were.

'We opened our throttles and began to climb towards them, aiming for a point well ahead where we expected to contact them at their own height. As we converged on them I saw there were about 20 of them and it looked as though it was going to be a nice party, for the other squadrons of Hurricanes and Spitfires also turned to join in. By the time we reached the bombers we were over London — central London I should say. We had gained a little height on them too, so when I gave the order to attack we were able to dive on them from their right.

'Each of us selected his own target. Our first attack broke them up pretty nicely. The Dornier I attacked with a burst lasting several seconds began to turn left away from his friends. I gave him five seconds and he went away with white smoke streaming behind him. As I broke away and started to make a steep climbing turn I looked over the side. I recognised the river immediately below me through a hole in the clouds. I saw the bends in the river, and the bridges, and idly wondered where I was. I didn't recognise it immediately and then I saw Kennington Oval. I saw the covered stands round the Oval and I thought to myself: "That is where they play cricket". It's queer how in the middle of a battle one can see something on the ground and think of something entirely different from the immediate job in hand. I remember I had a flashing thought — a sort of mental picture — of a big man with a beard, but at that moment I did not think of the name of W. G. Grace. It was just a swift, passing thought, as I climbed back to the fight.

'I found myself very soon below another Dornier which had white smoke coming from it. It was being attacked by two Hurricanes and a Spitfire, and it was travelling north and turning slightly to the right.

'As I could not see anything else to attack at that moment I went to join in. I climbed up above him and did a diving attack on him. Coming into attack I noticed what appeared to be a red light in the rear gunner's cockpit, but when I got closer I realised I was looking right through the gunner's cockpit into the pilot's and observer's cockpit beyond. The red light was fire. I gave it a quick burst and as I passed him on the right I looked in through the big glass nose of the Dornier. It was like a furnace inside. He began to go down and we watched. In a few seconds the tail came off and the bomber did a forward somersault then went into a spin. After he had done two turns in his spin his wings broke off outboard of the engines, so that all that was left as the blazing aircraft fell was half a fuselage and the wingroots with the engines on the end of them. This dived straight down just past the edge of a cloud, and then the cloud got in the way and I could see no more of him. The battle was over by then. I couldn't see anything else to shoot at, so I flew home. Our squadron's score was five certainties — including one by a Sergeant Pilot who landed by parachute in a Chelsea garden. (R. T. Holmes who shot down a Do 17 which fell at the front entrance of Victoria station) An hour later we were in the air again, meeting more bombers and fighters coming in . . . '

The enemy returned after lunch, crossing the Kent coast in waves totalling 150 bombers — Do 17s, Heinkel 111s and Junkers 88s — escorted by more than 300 fighters. For the second time within three hours paired squadrons of Hurricanes and Spitfires, in all some 200 fighters, intercepted the aerial armada and Bader's wing rose up behind London.

The bomber crews, accepting their losses stoically, pressed on to the capital. Bombs were dropped blindly through cloud, some damaging railways and other essential services. German pilots were astonished at the numbers of 'Spitfires' they encountered. Spitfire snobbery still persisted. Germany had been assured that more than 2,000 RAF fighters had been destroyed since the fighting over England began.

One Hurricane still very much in evidence was the personal aircraft of Group Captain Stanley Vincent, station commander at Northolt. It was not really his business, as a station commander aged 43 and a veteran of the Royal Flying Corps, to be in the battle. However, the Group Captain excused his habitual presence as being necessary to keep

Fighter ace Squadron Leader Bob Stanford Tuck. *(RAF Museum)*

an eye on his squadrons. Possibly the most elderly pilot to fight in the battle, Vincent was near Biggin Hill at 19,000 feet when he saw a formation of 18 Do 215s escorted by 20 Me 109s some 3,000 feet above. He reported: 'There were no other British fighters in sight so I made a head-on attack on the first section of bombers, opening at 600 yards and closing to 200 yards'. After further attacks Vincent noted that most of the bombers had turned south, deciding apparently that discretion was the better part of valour.

The Luftwaffe coupled the afternoon raid on London with a sharp attempt by 30 bombers of Airfleet 3 to damage the naval dockyard at Portland. Shortly before 6 p.m. an Airfleet 3 formation of some 20 Me 110 fighter-bombers made a quick lunge at Supermarine's Spitfire works at Woolston near Southampton. Five Squadrons which were scrambled to intercept arrived too late, but fortunately the raiders failed to hit the target. After dark London was bombed again, with Bristol, Cardiff, Liverpool and Manchester sharing the attentions of almost 200 raiders.

Next day when Churchill walked into his map room he read the score: Destroyed 183, Probables 42, Damaged 75, Lost 28. After the war the tally was amended to 58 enemy aircraft destroyed for the loss of 26 fighters, of which 20 were Hurricanes from 19 Hurricane Squadrons taking part in the day's actions. Twelve squadrons of Spitfires were engaged but most of the victories, possibly as many as 40, went to Hurricane pilots. Among the kills were the Hurricane pilots of No.303 Polish Squadron who accounted for at least eight.

It had been the Battle of Britain's' Trafalgar Day' and on it the Hurricane had assured its place in the history books as the fighter in the battle that destroyed more of the enemy than the sum total credited to other fighters and ground defences.

Towards the end of September, in the late autumn of the battle, Hurricane squadrons had to contend with Me 109s converted into fighter-bombers. As if to emphasise the peril which an absence of Spitfires would present in the face of this new tactic, 15-20 bomb-carrying 109s raced unchallenged up the Solent and attacked Supermarine at Woolston near Southampton, killing nearly 100 workers in an air raid shelter. Next morning the Bristol Aeroplane Company was badly damaged and there were more than 250 casualties. Reduced raiding of London and renewed attacks on the aircraft industry suggested that the Luftwaffe was returning to some of the professionalism of its earlier raids on radar sites and fighter airfields. Hurricane squadrons that had been reasonably capable of taking on bombers and their close-escort fighters — especially when Spitfires were taking on 109s above — were hard put to deal with the ruse of interlarding fighter formations with bombed-up fighters. Hurricane pilots became painfully aware that the enemy was recovering some of the initiative. A number of successful attacks on fighter factories could still give the Luftwaffe a measure of air superiority before winter; dispersal of Hurricane and Spitfire manufacture was not yet fully effective. Moreover, after the summer's losses too many unpolished pilots were expected to meet the new menace; boys whom pre-war professionals such as 'Downwind' Gillan, would not regard as operationally fit for combat in a Hurricane. In *Dowding and the Battle of Britain*, Robert Wright quotes Francis Wilkinson, his predecessor as Dowding's personal assistant during the battle and subsequently a Central Flying School instructor: 'I used to wonder how some of them had managed to survive. I had youngsters with DFCs who really couldn't fly, in the strict sense, the aircraft they had been fighting with . . . '

Unblooded Hurricane pilots, however limited their combat experience, were not short of confidence in their aircraft. Aware of their seniors' respect for the Hawker fighter's sturdiness, some were tempted in the heat of action to push their luck almost too far. On 7 October Pilot Officer Kenneth Mackenzie a 24 year-old volunteer reserve officer from Northern Ireland, serving in No. 501 Squadron, had shot down his first 109 and damaged another which he then chased out to

Two leaders who relied heavily on the Hurricane. Sholto Douglas (left), leaning into Europe, raised the morale of post-Battle of Britain Hurricane pilots, while the Hawker aircraft was indispensable to Tedder in the desert war. *(Imperial War Museum)*

sea. Finding himself out of ammunition he manoeuvred his starboard wing to knock off the 109's tail, losing part of his wingtip in the process. The 109 fell into the sea. Mackenzie's machine was now a 'winged' bird, but two 109s on his tail failed to get him and he crash-landed in a field after just clearing the cliffs at Folkestone.

If the resort to using fighters as bombers was challenging the Hurricane's effectiveness in daylight over Britain, its earlier prey, the Dornier and Heinkel bombers joined the Stuka as being too vulnerable to operate in day raids. The Hurricane, itself already heading for obsolescence in defence of Britain, had obliged bombers that were to have spearheaded a German victory to take refuge in the night.

Meanwhile, the 109 and 110 raiders increased the difficulties of Hurricane squadrons by operating at 30,000 feet and Park revised his tactics. Because it took a Hurricane up to 30 minutes to reach 30,000 feet he ordered readiness patrols. Park reminded his controllers: 'Bitter experience has proved time and again that it is better to intercept the enemy with one squadron above him than by a whole wing crawling up below, probably after the enemy has dropped his bombs'. A reproof if ever there was one for the Big Wing advocacy of No. 12 Group.

Park's message was issued against a background of high-flying fighter-bombers raiding London in daylight. On 15 October, a typical day, 30 of them bombed the capital at 9 a.m., hitting Waterloo station. Before 10 a.m. 50 more bombed the City of London. Within an hour and a half another formation had swept in across the Thames estuary and that night the real bombers were back, bombing throughout the hours of darkness. There was no respite for Park's Hurricane and Spitfire squadrons. In August and in the first half of September Hurricane pilots had indulged the luxury of resting on their airfields between scrambles, affording opportunities for some maintenance of their aircraft. But now the necessity of readiness patrols at 30,000 feet or more was physically exacting on tired pilots, some of whom were flying operationally for five hours a day. Life expectancy of a Battle of Britain pilot was later put at 87 flying hours or little more than a fortnight at worst. For some Hurricane pilots 'who really couldn't fly' life expectancy was lessened by a readiness to 'take one with them'. Polish and Czech Hurricane pilots exemplified this spirit, but the experience of Pilot Officer Mackenzie who got away with ramming a 109 shows that such desperation was not exclusive to pilots from occupied Eastern Europe.

Daylight raiding tailed off as winter closed in, although on 11 November the Italians, who had entered the war on 10 June in search of easy pickings, provided Hurricane pilots with a bonus. Wearing tin hats and bayonets, aircrew of the Regia Aeronautica crossed the east coast in ten Fiat BR 20 bombers escorted by 40 Fiat CR 42 biplane fighters. It might have been fairer to match them with Gladiators but Hurricane squadrons prevented the formation from hitting its target, Harwich harbour, and shot down seven bombers and four fighters without loss. Several probables were also claimed. At first the Italian aircraft posed a recognition problem, but soon the Hurricane pilots realised that here was a different enemy.

The action became, in the words of Flight Lieutenant H. P. Blatchford from Martlesham Heath, 'the best party I ever had'. Blatchford, running out of ammunition, drove his Hurricane's propeller into the upper wing of a CR 42. Possibly the Italians thought they were also on the way to a party, or at least a picnic, for a crashed bomber yielded a bottle of champagne, some chianti and a five-pound cheese. One Italian biplane looped the loop, his Hurricane opponent looking in astonishment at this aerobatic display until he realised the pilot had pulled the stick back as he was shot dead. It was appropriate that Martlesham Heath, where the RAF had accepted the Hurricane prototype K5083, should accommodate some of the Hawker fighter's more renowned pilots. Stanford Tuck was CO of No. 257 Squadron when the Italians appeared, Douglas Bader's No. 242 Squadron was posted there shortly afterwards, and there was also Flying Officer Count Manfred Czernin who had joined the RAF before the war. Shot down while flying from Martlesham on 17 November with No. 17 Squadron — 13 enemy aircraft to his credit — the Austrian-born aristocraft fell to the guns of the Luftwaffe ace, Major Adolf Galland. Czernin survived and served later with Special Operations Executive. After Czernin's death in the 1960s the engine of his Hurricane was disinterred from the depths of a Suffolk field and restored as a memorial to him.

Chapter 7
New roles

'We seem to be forgotten . . . nobody loves us . . .' Hurricane squadron commander.

In late November, the day battle done, Dowding was replaced and after an interlude in the United States, and writing his Despatch on the Battle of Britain, was retired, resuming briefly at Churchill's request, only to be retired finally at his own wish. The rights and wrongs of what was tantamount to the dismissal of the 'Leader of the Few' have been argued elsewhere. Suffice it here that Hurricanes enabled Dowding to deny the Luftwaffe the prerequisite of invasion — air superiority over Britain — and that but for his Cabinet intervention in May there might not have been enough of them. His plea to conserve their dwindling numbers after wasteful losses during the fall of France was as unwelcome as is any home truth. Churchill had pledged reinforcement. Possibly Dowding's fate and that of the Luftwaffe were sealed in the same moment. Thereafter the Hurricane, more available, more robust, more readily repaired and quickly manufactured than the Spitfire, influenced Dowding's tactical decisions and thus the conduct and outcome of the battle.

This is not to suggest that Dowding

Night fighter-intruders of No. 87 Squadron in 1941. *(RAF Museum)*

harboured any illusions about the fighter's performance. Indeed he was candid in his Despatch: 'As regards the fighter types in the Command, the bulk of the force consisted of Hurricanes and Spitfires; the former were beginning to be outmoded by their German counterparts. They were comparatively slow and their performance and their manoeuvrability were somewhat inadequate at altitudes above 20,000 feet'.

By December, Air Marshal Sir William Sholto Douglas, covert supporter of Leigh-Mallory's Big Wing advocacy from the Deputy Chief of the Air Staff's chair at the Air Ministry, was in Dowding's room at the Bentley Priory headquarters of Fighter Command and Leigh-Mallory was in Park's place at Uxbridge. New men for a new period now that the Hurricane had had its day over Britain; and the Spitfire, more available than hitherto and more suitable for the Big Wing, was in the ascendant at home.

Ironically, Fighter Command's musical chairs was accompanied by the reluctance of daylight raiders to reappear in any numbers, frustrating pilots and their leaders, particularly Dowding's successor, Sholto Douglas. Gainful employment was required for Hurricane squadron and wing commanders such as Douglas Bader and Stanford Tuck who had established their reputations during the summer battle. Product of a similar tradition in the First World War, in which he led Nos 43 and 84 Squadrons, Sholto Douglas understood only too well the eagerness for action which, understandably was keenest in the quieter sectors. Air Marshal Sir Peter Wykeham, then a young fighter pilot, has recorded the commander-in-chief's reaction to the complaint of a Hurricane squadron commander: 'We seem to be forgotten, sir. It seems that nobody loves us'. Of pugnacious appearance and speech Sholto Douglas's front masked an inner kindliness. He snapped at the squadron leader: 'What the hell do you mean, nobody loves you? I love you. Get that into your thick head', I love you!'

Of course it would have been imprudent in the winter of late 1940 and early 1941 to bank on the Luftwaffe's unwillingness to return to the offensive in the following spring and summer. Therefore, Sholto Douglas decided that he could best occupy his fighter pilots and aircraft, while keeping them on top line for a renewed onslaught, by experimenting with some as night fighters and launching aggressive sweeps and small raids against Channel shipping and over occupied France.

First, though the introduction of the Hurricane at night, a role in which it was disadvantaged.

It was a day fighter committed in some desperation to a task for which the twin-engined longer duration Blenheim and Beaufighter, carrying a second man and being equipped with air interception radar — and later the Mosquito — would be more suitable. As night raids replaced daylight attacks on London, provincial cities and towns, Hurricanes were used as night fighters, but knowledge of their presence among the probing fingers of the searchlights inspired the public with more confidence than was warranted. With no airborne radar and scanty help from ground radar, which was inefficient once raiders had crossed the coast, Hurricane night fighter pilots were seriously handicapped. Their best hope was to seek a bomber silhouetted against an incendiary blaze or to follow searchlight beams and anti-aircraft fire as indications of a raider's presence. Under pressure of the damage and casualties suffered from night bombing, and fears for civilian morale, ground and air radar systems advanced rapidly, but in the early stages a Hurricane pilot's night-flying experience, eyesight and personal resolution had to compensate as best they could for the absence of science.

Before the beginning of the Battle of Britain Squadron Leader the Hon Max. Aitken, Lord Beaverbrook's son, leading No. 601 Squadron on the night of 26/27 June 1940, had demonstrated the potential of a sharp pair of eyes and opportunism by shooting a Heinkel bomber into the sea. It had been illuminated by searchlights. By Christmas 1940 five Hurricane squadrons, Nos 73, 85, 87, 151 and 96, were flying night operations.

IIC of No. 1 Squadron based at Hawkinge on the Kent coast in early 1941. *(Aeroplane-Quadrant)*

On exceptionally heavy nights day squadrons adopted the night role; thus Squadron Leader Douglas Bader and two more Hurricane pilots of No. 242 Squadron were over Coventry on the night of 14/15 November when the cathedral was destroyed.

Such efforts went largely unrewarded, weather and conditions taking their toll of the hunters as they groped blindly around the night skies. No. 85, the most active Hurricane night fighter squadron of the 1940-1941 winter did not score until 25 February 1941, when its commander, Squadron Leader Peter Townsend, destroyed a Dornier 17. Success was more likely to come to the mature pilot, mature that is in flying hours and Hurricane operational experience. It also required patience and nerve to stalk the enemy in a fighter of short duration, at risk from indiscriminate anti-aircraft batteries and the hazard of being blinded by their powerful, searching beams of light.

In his mid-thirties and a former London-Paris airline pilot with 400 hours of night flying in his logbook, Pilot Officer Richard Stevens of No. 151 Squadron embodied the appropriate qualities. But there was something else. A German bomber crew had killed his wife and children in a night raid on Manchester.

On the night of 15/16 January Stevens shot down a Dornier 17, landed, refuelled and destroyed a Heinkel 111, being awarded the DFC. He pressed home his attacks at such close range that after one victory it was said there was enemy blood on the Hurricane's wing. On the night of 8/9 April Stevens bagged two Heinkels, scoring two further doubles in April and May, bringing his total to ten. Before transferring as a flight lieutenant in November 1941 to No. 253, which had fought in the Battle of Britain and which by this time was employed on night intruder missions over enemy airfields, four more bombers had fallen to his guns. In December, shortly after adding the DSO to the DFC, he failed to return home from a sortie across the Channel. In kills, Stevens alone in a Hurricane had beaten all the odds at night and had far out-performed the improving teams of pilot and radar operator in the twin-engined fighters.

To appreciate fully the fortitude of Hurricane night fighter pilots it has to be remembered that the aircraft was performing in a role and an element for which in the 1930s

IIC Head-on. *(Aeroplane-Quadrant)*

it had not been designed. For instance, neither Hawkers nor Rolls-Royce had foreseen that pilots might be attempting to close on an enemy bomber at maximum speed at night and thus be robbed of a clear view by flames from the Merlin exhausts.

Sholto Douglas believed that his predecessor, Dowding, had neglected 'the more simple hit or miss trial and error use of the single-engined fighters' at night. It is unlikely that Stevens would have been operating after dark had Dowding not been instructed by the Chief of the Air Staff to make more use of the Hurricane at night. Sholto Douglas was not too optimistic about the Hurricane's chances, but felt it had to be tried, encouraging the use of guile until radar became available. Hence, night Hurricanes were painted black with the occasional splash of colour to reflect a pilot's personality. The black-as-soot machine of Squadron Leader Ian 'Widge' Gleed, leading No. 87 Squadron, could be distinguished by its pale blue nose. As for guile, it started on the ground as Townsend, Gleed, Stevens and their fellow pilots sat patiently in dark goggle-like glasses to improve their night vision which, with the black aircraft and their experience, were their only resources.

With experience they improved and scored spasmodically. But the unguided one-man-in-a-Hurricane effort, despite the occasional Stevens, was insufficiently scientific to sustain a successful night campaign, so Fighter Command resorted to the ruse of pairing Hurricanes with a companion Havoc, equipped with an airborne searchlight, known as the Turbinlite. Each Havoc, the night fighter version of the Douglas Boston twin-engined bomber, carried a powerful searchlight in the nose and Air Interception radar. The idea was for the Havoc to locate and illuminate an enemy aircraft for its satellite Hurricanes, which would then go in for the kill. The difficulty was that it was a toss-up whether the Hurricanes would be correctly stationed at the critical moment of the beam lighting-up the target. Then, even if the combination of radar and light had offered this opportunity, an enemy bomber could quickly evade it, leaving the stalking Hurricane pilot in the dark. Hurricane squadrons which had established big reputations were assigned as available from normal day duties to provide the satellite aircraft, among them Nos 1, 43, 3, 32, 87, 151, 247, 253 and 257, but results did not repay the trouble. Nor did the provision of full-time Hurricane night flying satellites for the Havocs produce any better results.

Trials and development together with crew training were carried out by No 1422 (Air Target Illumination Unit) Flight at Heston under Wing Commander A. E. Clouston, renowned for his pre-war record-breaking flights to the Cape and New Zealand. Ten special flights were formed between May and December 1941. Bryan Winslett, who as a squadron leader commanded No. 1454 Flight, recalled each flight being attached to a Hurricane squadron, in his case No. 87 under Squadron Leader Ian Gleed, and also working with Peter Townsend's No. 85 Squadron. Winslett remembered ruefully: 'There were many problems. On one occasion the Havoc cockpit filled with smoke and its searchlight never lit up. Havocs were so heavily loaded with equipment, especially the batteries, that they were not manoeuvrable enough'.

With the advent of Spring and early Summer of 1941, the night intruder operations such as that in which Flight Lieutenant Stevens was lost, useful though they were in harassing German bomber airfields, were overshadowed by daylight

Night fighter-intruder of No. 87 Squadron, 1941-42. Mark IIC. Inscription on side of cockpit reads: United Provinces, Cawnpore.
(RAF Museum)

operations. The escort of Blenheim light-bombers, which had sustained attacks on the 'invasion' harbours in the Autumn and Winter of 1940 and the 'Channel Stop' harassment of shipping, provided the base for the development of a daylight, predominantly fighter offensive. However, it was recognised at Fighter Command that neither the Hurricane nor the Spitfire had been designed for such — for them — long-range activities. Flying up to 40 miles out from the English coast, by agreement with the Navy, in attempts to clear the Channel of enemy shipping, had underlined duration difficulties. Attacking targets in occupied territory and tempting Luftwaffe fighters to challenge them worsened the problems. Consequently, long-range fuel tanks were introduced, giving impetus to Sholto Douglas's determination to carry the war to the enemy; 'leaning forward into France', as he described the policy for which he won Air Ministry approval. The two fuel tanks contained 45 gallons apiece and could be jettisoned from under the wings.

Such aggressive operations appealed to squadrons which felt they had been kicking their heels since the hectic summer. They fell into two categories, 'Rhubarbs' and 'Circuses'. A Rhubarb usually involved a small number of Hurricanes, some armed with 250 lb bombs, attacking targets near enemy airfields with the aim of enticing fighters into combat with covering Spitfires. A Circus, as the name implies, was an offensive projection of the Big Wing evolved towards the end of the Battle of Britain. Battle of Britain Hurricane squadron aces, among them Stanford Tuck and Douglas Bader, were soon prominent in the large formations of up to five squadrons that assembled over airfields which the Luftwaffe had attacked during the summer, and usually accompanied by a small force of bombers, swept the skies of coastal France.

How the tide had turned. In May 1941, one year after the fall of France the Hurricane equipped 29 of the 56 squadrons and, committed to Rhubarb and Circus operations, was carrying the war back over the Channel. Sholto Douglas had at his disposal a formidable force for 'leaning forward into France' of which the Hurricane component consisted mostly of Mark IIAs and bomb-armed IIB aircraft with 12 Brownings in the wings. Nevertheless, the fact that the Hurricane now equipped only half the squadrons in Fighter Command indicated that Camm's monoplane fighter was losing its advantage of quick and simple production to Mitchell's endowment of the Spitfire with scope for improvement. Rhubarb and Circus squadrons, which had made early war reputations as Hurricane units, began to re-equip with Spitfires. But pilots who still flew the Hurricane remained steadfastly loyal — and not through any false sentiment. Repeatedly, its tight turning circle and readiness to be shot to pieces and return home kept a much-needed pilot in the war. Squadron Leader Tuck, at that time commanding No. 257 Squadron, has recalled: 'My God, the punishment those Hurricanes could take. The airframe could stand almost anything'. On 21 June 1941, after shooting down two Me 109s over the sea, Tuck, his Hurricane IIC badly shot up, was attacked head-on by a third 109. With no throttle and a faltering engine Tuck managed to drive off the enemy pilot, the 109 itself in serious trouble from the Hurricane's cannon-fire. Tuck nursed the Hurricane, 100 miles out from Southend, to the coast. Then the starboard aileron dropped away and flames appeared in the cockpit. Tuck baled out, inflated his rubber dinghy and was rescued after two hours.

If the value of Rhubarbs and Circuses was debatable in terms of results set against losses of pilots killed or taken prisoner, they served

Built as a Mark IIB in 1942 this aircraft was modified as a Mark IV armed with eight three-inch rocket projectiles.

other less tangible purposes. They lifted Fighter Command and Home Front morale and enforced a presence in the West on the Luftwaffe, which, by mid-summer, would have somewhat more pressing duties in the Mediterranean, the Balkans, the Middle East and in Russia.

In June 1941, Fighter, Bomber and Coastal Command leaders met at Bentley Priory, Fighter Command headquarters, and agreed fighter priorities for the remainder of the year. They were: Day and night air defence, 'Circus' operations; offensive fighter sweeps; escorting anti-shipping sweeps; night intruder operations, 'Rhubarb' sorties. In the context of these calls on Fighter Command the Hurricane was subjected to a critical reappraisal. It could continue to contribute to home defence, but it was no longer up to the demands for *fighting* over German-occupied territory. True it was more powerfully engined and armed, but it could not produce the performance to challenge the speed, rate of climb and dive characteristics of enemy fighters. It will be remembered that in putting the Hurricane into early and rapid production Hawkers had always recognised that prospects of subsequent development were being sacrificed. Camm had stolen a long march on Mitchell, but now the Spitfire was demonstrating how supremely capable it was of development. Even the Hurricane's manoeuvrability was to become a wasted asset in the face of such superior fighters as the Me 109 F and FW 190, while the Spitfire continued to develop to meet new criteria. In any event Camm had moved on. The Typhoon, the Hurricane's successor which had been on the drawing board since 1938, aimed at accommodating a 2,000 hp engine, eventually the Napier Sabre. In a sense the beginning of the Hurricane's superannuation as a first-line fighter at home and in the RAF's aggressive sweeps over occupied France and the Low Countries was advantageous. It freed the Hawker fighter in ever-increasing numbers to reinforce hard-pressed squadrons overseas, fill gaps, undertake special roles and take on a new career as a fighter-bomber. Shortly it would feature in the Battle of the Atlantic, fight for the Russians, from carriers and in the Middle, Near and Far East.

Chapter 8
Seatime

'If an old boy like me can do it, it won't mean a thing to lads like you . . .'
Squadron Leader Louis Strange.

Camm had not designed the Hurricane as anything other than the straightforward land-based fighter which the Air Ministry specification had called for. But in the lean years following the Sopwith liquidation Hawkers had learned to be adaptable and respond to the market. If the country needed it and there was an order in it then the Mark I could be adapted to go to sea. Norwegian operations had brought home the vulnerability of ships to air attack. After the Battle of Britain, the reconnaissance and bombing activities of the long-range Focke-Wulf Condor sharpened the lesson.

In the Battle of the Atlantic U-Boats and Condors — sometimes collaborating — were exacting an increasing toll. Since there were not enough aircraft carriers, and since new carriers were so long in building, a simple if temporary counter-measure was required. It was provided by the combination of Hurricane, catapult and merchant ship. The idea was kicked around in the winter of 1940-1941, the much-needed decision being held up by disagreements between the Admiralty and Air Ministry. At length, under the spur of increasing losses attributed to the Condor and a directive from the Prime Minister, action was taken to introduce the Hurricat or Catafighter . . . On 6 March 1941, Churchill directed: '. . . We must assume the Battle of the Atlantic has begun . . . Extreme priority will be given to fitting-out ships to catapult or otherwise launch fighter aircraft against bombers attacking our shipping. Proposals should be made within a week'. By the end of March, 60 Mark I Hurricanes with Merlin III engines had been set aside. Hawkers, anticipating the order, had already delivered a modified Hurricane to the Royal Aircraft Establishment at Farnborough and conversion was rushed forward. Chiefly, this involved fitting an arrester hook and catapult spools. The Sea Hurricane Mark I A was evolving. The strength inherent in Camm's design was about to pay another dividend.

While the aircraft were prepared, 35 Catapult Merchantmen were made ready, a considerable reduction from the 200 ships at first suggested. The cutback owed more to conservatism about the scheme than to concern over the supply of aircraft. Numbers of former Battle of Britain machines were available, and since they were to be expendable in the empty wastes of the Atlantic such worn aircraft commended themselves. That they were not necessarily fit or fast enough — modifications reduced the Hurricat's speed to 245 mph — was discovered later.

Provision of ships to carry aircraft and catapult apparatus was made in two ways. Predominantly they were to be cargo-carrying merchant vessels of some 9,000 tons. However, the Royal Navy, long experienced in catapult operations for reconnaissance at sea, insisted on contributing five of its own auxiliaries. These, typified by *Maplin*, the adapted banana boat *Erin,* were known as Fighter Catapult Ships. Excepting *Maplin*, which at first carried two Hurricanes — later three — the naval vessels proved largely ineffective other than as ocean-going scarecrows. This was because they were equipped with the under-performing Fairey Fulmar.

More demanding than providing the aircraft and ships for the Catapult Aircraft Merchantmen was the recruitment and training of pilots and supporting crews. For

Deck-landing practice for a Mark IA pilot — a piece of cake compared with taking a chance in the sea. *(Imperial War Museum)*

the Navy and its Fighter Catapult Ships it was routine. Fleet Air Arm pilots were appointed as to any warship. But the RAF, recognising that the sea was not the natural environment of aircrew, and also the suicide pilot undertone of the task, sought volunteers.

Preponderance of the Hurricane in fighter operations throughout the preceding summer and the flow of the new pilots from Operational Training Units assured the availability of pilots, but mere competence in a Hurricane cockpit was insufficient. Selectors of the newly formed Merchant Ship Fighter Unit, part of Fighter Command's, also new, No. 9 Group at Speke, Liverpool, established their own criteria. Only commissioned officers would be eligible in order to assure their status with Merchant Navy officers and Fighter Direction Officers, mostly naval. Pilots also had to be capable of adjusting to periods of inactivity at sea.

Many of the volunteers were former Battle of Britain pilots disenchanted with the routine of Circus and Rhubarb sorties; pilots dazzled by the prospect of a short leave among the bright lights of North America; misfits eager to leave their units and those who were adventurous and game for anything. When they joined ship they found that the Hurricane and its catapult were the least of their problems.

But first the pilots had to acquaint themselves with the catapult apparatus. At the start of the scheme this introduction was made by a Mr. Charles Crowfoot of the Royal Aircraft Establishment who emphasised his civilian status by wearing a bowler hat at each launch. In July 1941 training was transferred to Speke, where Mr. Crowfoot explained the mysteries to Squadron Leader Strange, that very same veteran of the First World War who had led the Hurricane rescue team as France fell. At Speke, Strange characteristically insisted on flying the first Hurricat launch before taking over Crowfoot's responsibilities. While warning pilots that handling a Hurricane on the rocket catapult was an altogether different proposition to take-off from a runway, Strange helped their confidence with his favourite dictum: 'If an old boy like me can do it, it won't mean a thing to lads like your'.

Yet there were daunting handling problems. To begin with there were the

Sea practice for a one-way ticket. Rocket launch of a Merchant Ship Fighter Unit Sea Hurricane Mark I A. *(Imperial War Museum)*

awsome roar and the blinding flash of light as the launch party took cover and the pilot realised he was alone. Then, although the Hurricane's fuselage had been strengthened, there was the shock as pilot and aircraft hurtled down a 70 foot steel ramp, the launcher's 13 rockets producing a speed of 75 mph. Together with something like 3.5 G, the effect of all this reduced pilot aptitude. But, if this is how it was at Strange's school on dry land, how would it be in Atlantic seas with a 40 foot drop at the end of the ramp? There would be only one chance and Strange rehearsed his pilots painstakingly. He taught them that for all its robust reputation, the Hurricane — as with its pilot — was under severe and unforeseen stress as a Catafighter. He counselled pilots to counter the Hurricane's congenital swing to the left and longitudinal instability. Once clear of the catapult ship's rail the drop towards the sea would be so noticeable that a pilot would want instinctively to pull the stick back. Strange sent his pilots to sea fully aware that they must accept the sinking feeling or face the likelihood of stalling into the Atlantic. Each RAF pilot had volunteered for a possible one-way ticket, so survival was an important part of thc training. The Hurricane had never been expected to float, but unfortunately it had a record of sinking more rapidly than other fighters. The trouble was that the distinctive air scoop ploughed into the sea, hurling the aircraft onto its back so that it went straight down. Rather than ditch, pilots were advised to bale out and use the dinghy attached to their parachutes.

The desperate need for air cover of convoys was painfully demonstrated by the experiences of CAM-ships themselves. Eleven were lost in action of which, the first, the *Michael E,* was torpedoed before its Hurricane could be launched. Although *Michael E* was sunk by a U-boat, a Condor could have been instrumental. German sea and air arms were co-operating closely in the search for victims.

When *Michael E* sailed from Belfast on 28 May 1941 she carried a Fleet Air Arm pilot, Sub-Lieutenant M. A. Birrell, aged 21, because no RAF pilot was yet available. Birrell had flown a Hurricane as a midshipman during the Battle of Britain. After transferring to a naval Fighter Catapult Ship, *Ariguani,* he was torpedoed off Lisbon. He survived. Naval and merchant catapult ships were priority targets.

From the Merchant Ship Fighter Unit's inception until its disbandment in July 1943, its Hurricanes operated in the North Atlantic, with Russian convoys and on the Gibraltar run. Almost every passage produced a drama.

Inevitably such a desperate occupation produced its characters. One such was Lieutenant R. W. H. 'Bob' Everett, senior pilot in HMS *Maplin,* the former banana boat. He had served as a midshipman in the First World War and as a National Hunt rider had come home a 100-1 winner on Gregalach in the 1929 Grand National.

On 18 July 1941, after being launched against a Condor making a low-level attack on a convoy, Everett was robbed of this opportunity for a kill by the accuracy of gunfire from one of the ships, the *Norman Prince.* Since he was within range of Northern Ireland, 300 miles away, Everett elected to make for land rather than bale out or ditch.

On 2 August 1941 *Maplin,* in company with three destroyers, was detached from a Gibraltar-bound convoy to meet a homeward-bound convoy from Sierra Leone. On a Sunday afternoon Everett was completing his watch — two hours on, four hours off — in the Hurricane's cockpit 80 feet above the deck when a Condor was seen 10 miles astern. He was launched and shot down the Condor but could not manage to bale out. Twice he flew upside down, intending to fall out as the forward trim lifted the nose. Perversely, the nose dipped and Everett found himself still in the cockpit. He decided to ditch. In the sea the Hurricane turned turtle and dropped like a stone. The pilot was probably 30 feet down before escaping. In the New Year of 1942 Everett's luck ran out. Delivering a Hurricane from Belfast to Abingdon he suffered engine trouble and the aircraft plunged into the sea only 150 yards short of a beach. Bob Everett's naval friends claimed that he had been the victim of a worn-out, RAF cast-off Hurricane.

For all the suspicion about the maintenance records of some of the Hurricanes supplied to them, only one pilot of the more numerous CAM-ships was lost after a launching. Nor was the condition of the aircraft responsible for this death.

Convoy QP 12 was homeward-bound from Russia on the morning of 25 May 1942, when Flying Officer J. B. Kendall was launched from the CAM-ship, *Empire Morn.* After scaring away a vulnerable BV 138 flying-boat, Kendall shot down a Ju 88. After patrolling for a further hour while fuel permitted he baled out, but his parachute opened only partially. John Kendall died shortly after being picked up by a destroyer and was buried at sea.

Dry run for a Catafighter pilot before going to sea. *(Imperial War Museum)*

The attacks on Convoy QP 12 exemplified the pressures on the Hurricats and their crews. No convoy was accompanied by more than four CAM-ships, and this was an unusual maximum. In two years 35 CAM-ships, of which 12 were lost, undertook 175 voyages. Consequently, the responsibility resting on a CAM-ship's master, pilot and Fighter Direction Officer was heavy. At times on the Russian convoy route, other than ships' gunfire, the Hurricane, high up on its catapult perch in a cargo boat's bows, was all that protected a large convoy from Norway-based Condors, Ju 88s and He 111 torpedo-bombers — as on the day John Kendall died. Merchant Navy masters, in whom, subject to a pilot's approval of conditions, was vested the authority to launch, had mixed feelings about the Hurricane. It was their protector and yet it invited attack. Its presence was reassuring and yet it blocked the for'ard outlook from the bridge. At the same time, as a pet can unite a warring family, the Hurricane helped to bond such disparate individuals as a crusty ship's captain, a cocky young fighter pilot and a conservatively naval Fighter Direction Officer. That at least one ship's master insisted upon signing pilot and FDO as deckhands, indicates the difficulties.

Before the introduction of merchantmen converted into naval-manned escort carriers could end such human problems the last Hurricat launch, on 18 September 1942, in protection of a convoy to Russia, took place in circumstances typical of the odds heaped against one pilot, one Hurricane.

After the losses in the controversial and much described Convoy PQ of 17 July 1942, there were raised eyebrows among veterans of the Russian run when PQ18's escort commander, Rear Admiral R. L. Burnett, told them: 'Well gentleman I have not had the pleasure of doing this highly amusing little trip before, but I can tell you we're going to succeed'.

Totalling 40 merchant ships, Burnett's was

Out of fuel, a Hurricat pilot could only bale out or take his chance in the sea. *(Flight)*

The following photographs were taken aboard the escort carrier *HMS Striker* in 1943, whilst escorting a Russian convoy in the North Sea. *(Paddy Porter Collection)*

A Sea Hurricane IIc of No. 824 Squadron Fleet Air Arm comes in to land.

The port undercarriage leg collapses as it lands.

Sea Hurricane IIc NF.694 makes a crash landing.

Sea Hurricane Ibs of No. 801 Squadron Fleet Air Arm on the deck of *HMS Victorious*, August 1942.
(Paddy Porter Collection)

the largest Arctic-bound convoy yet attempted, joined as it was by United States ships off Iceland. As the escorts, including for the first time a US-built 'Woolworth' Merchant Aircraft Carrier, *Avenger* with 12 Sea Hurricanes, shepherded the convoy towards Archangel, the single Hurricane, on its ramp in the CAM-ship *Empire Morn*, seemed supernumerary. Prime responsibility for air cover lay with *Avenger's* Sea Hurricanes and three anti-submarine Swordfish for two days of air attacks until, some 300 miles east of Bear Island and nearing its destination, *Avenger* and most of the escort turned and joined QP 14, a homeward-bound convoy. *Empire Morn's* Hurricane was now the convoy's sole fighter protection.

In this circumstance there was an understandable desire to hoard the Hurricane. Consequently, the presence of an inquisitive Condor in company with a Ju 88 early on 18 September failed to entice the Hurricane. It was just as well, because a strong raid by Ju 88 bombers and torpedo-carrying He 111s was approaching. As ever when a convoy was dependent upon just one expendable Hurricat, the timing of the launch presented an agonising decision. In came a group of Ju 88s making a dive-bombing attack. No hits were scored and, as the raiders sought refuge in cloud, the Hurricat team, sensing that the Ju 88s had raised the curtains for the Heinkel torpedo-bombers, congratulated themselves on holding back a second time. And then they appeared, 12 He 111s wave-hopping from astern. but when the Fighter Direction Officer, on this occasion a Flying Officer John Carrique of the Royal Canadian Air Force, told the ship's master this was the moment to launch, permission was refused. The Merchant Navy captain was not prepared to hazard the Hurricane, which would have to clear the cables of the barrage balloons flown by the ships ahead. So the aircraft stayed put and, fortunately, anti-aircraft fire drove off the raiders, though not before one of 24 torpedoes found its mark.

Almost an hour later Carrique had cause to count his lucky stars for the master's veto. In came a second wave of some 15 Heinkels. This time there was no holding 23-year-old Flying Officer A. H. 'Jackie' Burr. But now the ships' gunners who had been so effective earlier mistook the Hurricane for a dive-bomber. Burr survived the fire and the balloons. And then he saw them, 15 Heinkels in what was known as 'Golden Comb' formation. Bellies almost touching the wavetops, the torpedo-bombers implied the menace of a sharp-toothed comb sweeping towards the convoy. Burr dived his Hurricane at the Heinkels with such desperation that one aircraft, seeking escape from collision, plunged into the sea. A second Heinkel was shot down and Burr was out of ammunition when the CAM-ship, *Empire Morn*, reported 10 aircraft in another raid. Feigning attack, Burr so worried the German pilots that they unloaded their

Flight Lieutenant J. K. Ross of No. 134 Squadron in Russia was chiefly responsible for instructing Soviet pilots. *(Imperial War Museum)*

Camm's sturdy construction paid off in Arctic conditions near Murmansk. *(Imperial War Museum)*

torpedoes and hurried away. There was time to drive off another force of Ju 88s before fuel considerations dictated a decision to bale out or chance reaching Archangel, 230 miles distant. Burr landed at Keg Ostrov airfield with four gallons in the tank. Of the 12 ships sunk in Convoy PQ 18, Admiral Burnett's 'highly amusing little trip', all but one had been lost to the Luftwaffe and U-boats before the Hurricat assumed responsibility.

An irony of the Arctic convoys was that invariably their cargoes included crated Hurricane IICs — faster and, with four cannon, more heavily armed fighters than the Hurricat defending them. The Russians could not get enough Hurricanes, a need which Marshal Stalin underlined in correspondence with Mr Churchill. The Red Air Force and the Soviet Navy had admired the Hurricane from the moment of its introduction in northern Russia in September 1941. Under constant pressure from Stalin's impossible demands for a Second Front in the West, Churchill responded with equipment, arms and munitions — and two Hurricane squadrons complete with RAF air and groundcrew. The Prime Minister emphasised the extent of this sacrifice and pledged 200 more Hurricanes if Stalin's pilots 'could use them effectively'. Stalin replied that he did not doubt that 'the Soviet aviators will succeed in mastering them and putting them into use'. Eventually this would be so, but not before the RAF and its Hurricanes had endured a most testing experience in the region of Murmansk.

The RAF had every confidence in the Hurricane's ability to operate on the Arctic front because it had proved itself in northern Norway and Iceland. More problematical were the logistics of moving a Wing and its aircraft to Russia. In August 1941, Fighter Command assembled No. 151 Wing of two new Hurricane squadrons, Nos 81 and 134, at Leconfield in Yorkshire. Their dual role, as Wing Commander H. N. G. Ramsbottom-Isherwood explained to his pilots, was to protect the Arctic convoy ports of Murmansk and Archangel and teach the Russians how to

Immediate readiness for Hurricanes of No. 151 wing at Vaenga near Murmansk.
(Imperial War Museum)

The Red Star replaced the roundel of the RAF as the Russians took over the Hurricanes.
(British Aerospace)

fly and maintain the Hurricane. The pilots were launched into the spirit of the enterprise by Czech pilots of other Leconfield units wearing shirts back to front like Russian peasant blouses and singing at a farewell party to the accompaniment of a violin played by a Czech squadron leader. Another memorable incident of that party was the placing of Flight Lieutenant J. K. Ross on a very high mantelpiece. About four foot in height, Ross was almost certainly the smallest pilot to fly a Hurricane, and he paid the price of his return to earth with a magnificent speech delivered from the mantelpiece. In time Ross, who was to do most of the instructing in northern Russia, won a very special place in the hearts of the Soviet pilots and especially with Captain Koharenk, a jovial extrovert seat-of-the-pants pilot. 'They are great friends', noted Captain Safanov, an ace of the Red Naval Air Fleet, 'because they are both practically dwarfs and have the same problems in being able to see out of a cockpit'.

But first the Wing had to reach Russia. Twenty-four of the aircraft were embarked, ready to fly, in the small and elderly carrier *Argus,* and 15 were crated as deck cargo in the convoy which sailed from Liverpool on 21 August, 1941. Arriving at Murmansk on 25 August, the aircraft were flown off *Argus* to the nearby airfield of Vaenga, but the liner *Llanstephan Castle,* accommodating some 500 of the Wing's personnel and the ships bearing the crated Hurricanes, being at risk to local air attack, sailed on to Archangel, 400 miles to the east.

From the start the Russians exhibited a strong affection for the Hurricane. The erection party under Flight Lieutenant Gittins, left at Archangel to assemble the crated aircraft, was astonished to see Russian technicians stroking the wings. Within nine days the Hurricanes had been assembled and flown to Vaenga, and Soviet pilots were soon given a glimpse of the fighter's operational possibilities.

Both Nos 81 and 134 Squadrons were involved in operational flying to begin with, although No. 134 was to concentrate on training Soviet pilots. There were some nasty moments for Flight Lieutenant Ross and Pilot Officer Cameron (later Marshal of the RAF Lord Cameron of Balhousie) when on 11 September four aircraft of No. 134 Squadron ventured for the first time over enemy territory. Their Merlins, resenting the lower octane rating of Russian petrol, experienced scaring engine cuts. On patrol the next day No. 134, scoring four victories, lost Sergeant N. I. Smith to Me 109s. The Wing's only pilot to be killed in Russia, he lies in the Cemetery of Soviet Heroes on high ground overlooking Murmansk Sound. Thereafter, operations were devoted mostly to escorting Soviet bombers raiding German positions threatening Murmansk. Cameraderie was at times almost ecstatic. On one occasion No. 134, returning from a raid and unimpressed by the bombers' formation flying, closed in wingtip to wingtip on two of them. Whereupon the Soviet pilots all closed up until, as one Hurricane pilot described it, 'there were the whole lot of us locked in tight together in the sort of wizard formation flying you used to get in the old Hendon Pageant days — with their rear-gunners leaning out of their turrets and holding up their thumbs at us and grinning'. On 30 September the Wing Commander was congratulated by Sir Archibald Sinclair, the Air Minister, who signalled: 'The destruction by your squadrons of 12 German aircraft for the loss of only one of your own is a brilliant achievement; it is a source of particular pleasure to us here that you are working so closely and so successfully with the Russian Air Force. Good luck to you, 151 Wing'.

Not exactly a Scramble by sledge, but unusual transport for pilots of No. 151 Wing in north Russia. *(Imperial War Musuem)*

In all the Wing accounted for 15 enemy aircraft in combat and successful pilots were astonished to learn that, in accordance with Russian custom, they had been awarded 100 roubles (about £20) for each victory. Determined to maintain their 'amateur' status they donated the money to the Royal Air Force Benevolent Fund.

When the Arctic winter denied operations the Wing completed its principal purpose of training Soviet pilots to take over the Hurricanes and provide instructors and maintenance crews for future deliveries. From the moment the base commander, Major-General Kuznetsov, a former instructor, had been presented with his own Hurricane with a Red Star painted on it, his pilots had trained hard, at times almost dementedly; one pilot insisted on flying his first solo in a snowstorm. On 20 October, by which day a Russian fighter pilot had scored his nation's first Hurricane victory by shooting down a Me 110, Ramsbottom-Isherwood signalled the Air Ministry: 'All aircraft handed over to Soviet pilots'. Moscow, or rather Kubishev, 500 miles east, to which the Government had moved, complimented the Wing's 550 airmen and some 50 pilots, with awards of the Order of Lenin to its commanding officer, two squadron commanders, Squadron Leaders Rook and Miller and Flight Sergeant Haw who, with three confirmed victories, held the highest individual score. As the Wing sailed

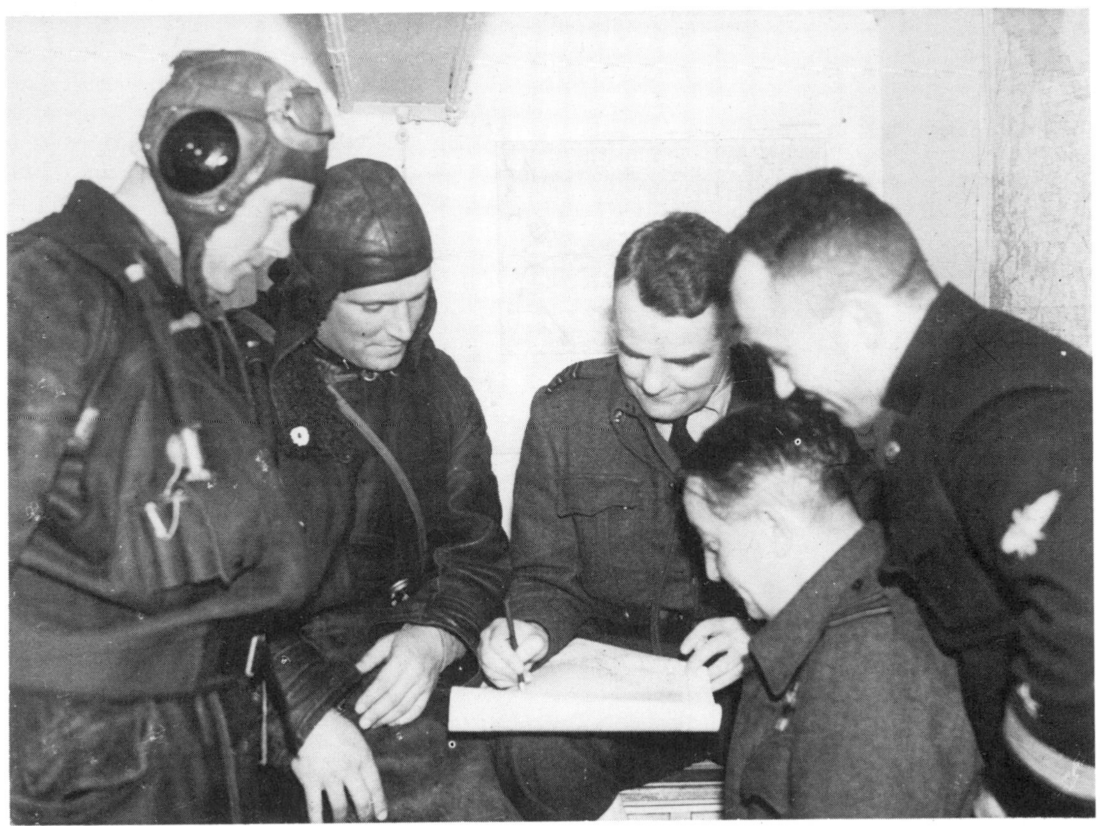

Wing Commander H. N. G. Ramsbottom-Isherwood, commander of No 151 Wing, briefs Soviet pilots before a Hurricane operation. *(Imperial War Museum)*

for home in late November two Hurricanes saluted the warships in which it was embarked. They were piloted by Kuznetsov and Safanov.

* * *

Channel Lessons

While the Hurricane would, as will be seen, remain a fighter at the start of its career in the Middle East it was becoming accepted at home in its developing role as a Hurribomber. With 57 squadrons in the United Kingdom in 1941 there was ample provision for conversion. Experience gained in Rhubarb and Circus operations over France and the Low Countries, and in the Channel Stop low-level attack on E-boats and merchant shipping, was excellent preparation for two events in 1942 — the surprise Channel dash by the battle-cruisers *Scharnhorst* and *Gneisenau* and the cruiser, *Prinz Eugen,* and *Operation Jubilee,* the Dieppe raid. Damaged by and at risk from repeated raids on their berths at Brest, passage of the three warships through the Channel and into the North Sea was ordered by Hitler. The Führer overruled naval objections and, assisted by massed fighter cover, British reconnaissance failures, low cloud and rain, the warships' survival of the Channel passage justified his decision.

Leaving Brest on the night of 11/12 February they reached the North Sea, though not without damage. It was lunchtime on 12 February before the escaping warships,

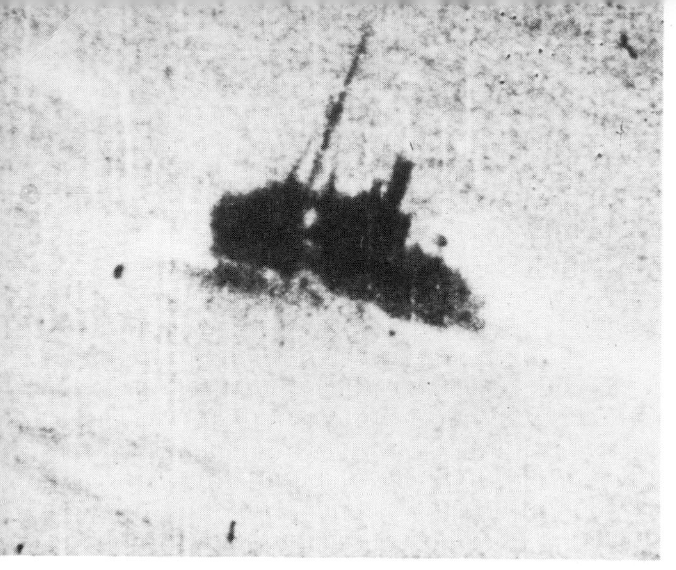

1. Hurricane 'shoots' the target as pilot opens fire.

2. A second Hurricane moves in to attack.

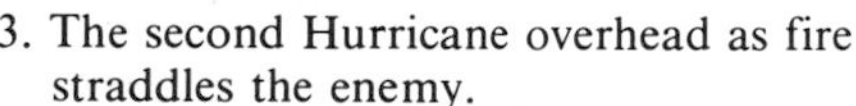

3. The second Hurricane overhead as fire straddles the enemy.

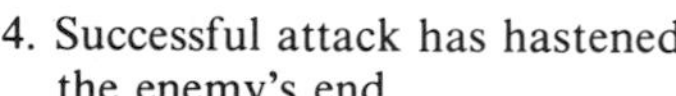

4. Successful attack has hastened the enemy's end.

In late 1941 and early 1942 anti-shipping strikes called for new skills from fighter-trained pilots.

(Imperial War Museum)

already through the Straits of Dover, were attacked by six Swordfish torpedo biplanes of the Fleet Air Arm's shore-based No. 825 Squadron whose leader, Lieutenant-Commander Eugene Esmonde, was awarded a posthumous VC. Not one Swordfish returned and subsequent RAF attacks were almost fruitless, pilots of Nos, 1, 3 and 607 Hurricane squadrons being the only British airmen to obtain some small satisfaction for the losses incurred. Between them these squadrons landed a 250 lb bomb on a flak ship and shot-up escorting E-boats and destroyers. Six Hurricanes failed to return. In the event Hitler gained little. The *Scharnhorst* and *Gneisenau* were damaged, not by direct air attack but by mines laid in the North Sea.

The *Prinz Eugen* reached Norway — as part of Hitler's plan to strengthen defences there — only to be neutralised by a submarine's torpedo. Subsequently, *Gneisenau* was bombed out of the war at Kiel on the night of 27/28 February 1942 and *Scharnhorst* was sunk on 26 December 1943, while trying to attack a convoy to Russia.

That Leigh-Mallory's No. 11 Group should lose 60 Spitfires on the day in *Operation Jubilee,* the Dieppe raid of 19 August 1942, is in itself evidence of changes that had taken place since the Battle of Britain and since Leigh-Mallory had moved from No. 12 Group to replace Park. In September 1940, 60 fighters represented the sum total of Bader's Big Wing of five squadrons, of which two flew Hurricanes. For all the Spitfire's success as it climbed the ladder of its Mark numbers, there was still a role for the Hurricane in the West even though it was surrendering numerical seniority as a fighter to its partner. The Hurricane was not done, and nor were some of its more illustrious squadrons. In the early hours of *Jubilee,* No. 43, the Fighting Cocks, one of 24 Hurricane squadrons involved, provided the first fighter aircraft over Dieppe. 'Poor 43 . . .' John Simpson had written after the deaths of Caesar Hull and succeeding commanding officers in early September 1940. Now led by Squadron Leader du Vivier, a Belgian, No. 43 was still equipped with Hurricanes and in the forefront of the disastrous test which contributed to the delay, until *Overlord* in June 1944, of Stalin's oft-requested second front in the West, and the November 1942, *Torch* invasion of Morocco and Algeria in French North Africa.

Although the Dieppe raid was master-minded by Vice-Admiral Lord Louis Mountbatten, Chief of Combined Operations, its army component was mostly Canadian. Coincidentally, some of the Hurricanes were Mark X products of the Canadian Car and Foundry Corporation, demonstrating yet again how inspired had been Sprigg's early decision to rush drawings to Canada. While some Canadian machines mounted four cannon, Nos 3, 32, 43, 87, 245 and 253 among the participating squadrons were generally equipped with two-cannon Hurricane IICs and IIBs. Aircraft of the IIB fighter-bomber squadrons, Nos 174 and 175, carried two 500 lb bombs apiece — until the heavier bombs ran out and only 50 lb bombs could be supplied.

The 'Light Brigade' nature of the Hurricane's part in the raid — 20 were lost as against 60 Spitfires — shines through J. Beedle's description in his *History of The Fighting Cocks* of No. 43 Squadron's 12 aircraft 'in line abreast against gun positions on the beaches and in buildings to the west of the harbour entrance'. The pilots encountered a hail of anti-aircraft fire and seven aircraft were hit, Pilot Officer Trenchard-Smith, an Australian, landing safely at Tangmere despite loss of much of the Hurricane's tail. At least one Hurricane pilot stepped out of a write-off only to obtain a replacement and fly three more sorties on the day.

Hurricane low-level attacks earned tributes from the Canadian troops and British Commandos but their determination was not repaid by results. The meagre armament of the IICs and IIBs made little impression on the gun emplacements. The combined operations lessons of Dieppe were costly — more than 4,000 casualties — but they were important in the context of the future Operations *Torch* and *Overlord.*

Dieppe also emphasised that the Hurricane's transition from fighter to fighter-bomber was incomplete. Within a year a 1,000 lb bomb load of two 500 lb bombs would be routine for Camm's monoplane fighter and possible firepower would increase, adding two 40 mm anti-tank guns and rocket projectiles.

Chapter 9
Desert Days

'Hurricanes doing magnificently loyal work . . .' Marshal of the Royal Air Force Lord Tedder

Everywhere the call was for Hurricanes and from mid-1941 when Spitfire production was sufficient to enable the re-equipment of Fighter Command, the Hawker fighter was more readily available to meet the overseas clamour — providing, of course, that it could get there.

From 1940, as Britain faced the likelihood of invasion, a first-line monoplane fighter had been as much needed in the Middle East as at home. If Dowding's Hurricane and Spitfire squadrons were all that stood between Hitler and London, then the obsolescent biplane fighters were all that provided the air cover for troops defending the Suez Canal and the land route to British oil supplies in Iraq and Iran.

Even more vulnerable was the Mediterranean naval base island of Malta, itself at one point defended for three weeks by three Sea Gladiator biplanes, enshrined in the story of the defence of Malta as Faith, Hope and Charity. Little wonder, therefore, that in a moment of exasperation, Admiral Sir Andrew Cunningham, the Mediterranean commander-in-chief, being told that he had been created Knight Grand Cross of the Order of the Bath, exclaimed: 'I would sooner have had three squadrons of Hurricanes!'

The problems eliciting Cunningham's crisis plea arose from events following Italy's expectation of easy pickings by entering the war as France fell.

Gladiators of No. 252 Wing, responsible for the defence of Cairo, more than held their own so long as the Italians were the adversary. An example of Italian ineptitude was the 'own goal' scored (28 June 1940) by anti-aircraft guns at Tobruk which shot down and killed Marshal Balbo, the Italian commander-in-chief. Air Commodore R. Collishaw, commanding the RAF's No. 202 Group in the desert sent a wreath and it was dropped by air for the funeral.

At about this time British troops were encouraged by the appearance overhead of a Hurricane. Neither they nor Italian intelligence officers were to know that it was one of only two Hurricanes in the command. Ceaselessly, Collishaw switched it from landing ground to landing ground to give the impression that Hurricanes had reinforced the desert squadrons. Its guns rendered unusuable by climatic conditions, it represented a ruse which may have paid off because the Regia Aeronautica was remarkably subdued considering that its Fiat biplane CR 42 outnumbered and outperformed the Gladiator.

Known as 'Collie's Battleship', this Hurricane had been sent by sea to the Sudan shortly after the outbreak of war in Europe. Unintended for combat, it had been despatched to test a tropical filter to protect the Merlin's carburettor air intake from the dust of the region's landing grounds. Subsequently, desert Hurricanes were fitted with the Vokes Multi-Vee filter, an indispensable ancillary even though it reduced speed and rate of climb.

The other Hurricane — it had been the only one in Egypt as Italy entered the war — was not often in evidence. In reasonable combat condition it was too precious for everyday use and Collishaw, a Canadian fighter ace of the First World War, was obliged by the commander-in-chief, Air Marshal Sir Arthur Longmore, to rein back his aggressive instincts and restrict its employment and also that of the Group's Blenheim light-bombers.

On the occasions this Hurricane was operational, it was effective, as on 19 June 1940, when piloted by Flying Officer Peter Wykeham-Barnes, later Air Marshal Sir Peter Wykeham, it accounted for two CR 42s.

Well before Hawker production became more plentiful, both at home and under licence in Canada, efforts were made to reinforce Egypt, however sparingly. Even as France fell, some 50 aircraft were flown, at much hazard from enemy action and empty fuel tanks, via France, Tunisia and Malta. They did not all arrive and of those that did four were sent back to Malta. The remainder were allotted to No. 80 Squadron, covering the Mediterranean Fleet at Alexandria; a godsend for Admiral Cunningham. A few more in crates survived a sea passage through the Mediterranean and joined No. 33 Squadron.

No situation better demonstrated the need for more Hurricanes between Gibraltar and Alexandria and the difficulties of reinforcing than the plight of Malta; a situation which would deteriorate in the early Spring of 1941 as Hitler acted to retrieve the Italian leader Mussolini's military failure in Greece.

After the Munich crisis in 1938 a conscious decision had been taken not to defend Malta, it being considered that in the event of hostilities the large Italian air force on the doorstep could not be countered. Hence the removal of Cunningham's fleet to Alexandria.

As war began in September 1939, there had been no fighter aircraft on the island, just four Sea Gladiators in crates; Fleet Air Arm spares. After assembly one of these aircraft crashed, leaving three.

It was unfortunate that ten crated Hurricanes, bound for Poland in 1939 and re-addressed to Aden, had vanished after leaving Gibraltar. They were now much needed. In the circumstances the best that could be done for Air Commordore F. Maynard, Malta's air commander, was to return four of the few

Hurricane reinforcements for Malta off Gibraltar on *Ark Royal's* flight deck.
(RAF Museum)

Mothered by a Hudson, badly needed Hurricanes head for Malta. *(RAF Museum)*

Hurricanes which had passed through Malta to Egypt.

On 28 June 1940, led by Flight Lieutenant Barber, a South African, they joined the three Gladiators. Even though they were under-armed by Sorley's eight-gun standards — mounting only six Brownings to save ammunition and facilitate take-off on the island's short runways — their arrival was a welcome tonic.

On paper the odds were impossible. In July these seven aircraft defended Malta against up to 200 Italian fighters and bombers based only 60 miles away in Sicily. Despite raids almost every day only one Gladiator and one Hurricane were lost and this was on a day when the RAF accounted for ten Italian aircraft damaged or destroyed.

It says much for this minuscule force and little for the spirit of the Italian airmen that it obliged the enemy to escort bombers by day until, wearying of losses, the Regia Aeronautica resorted to night raiding. In itself this was a magnificent achievement and a contribution to the essential need to develop Malta as a naval and air base astride the Italian supply route to North Africa and the British passage to Egypt. Yet if Malta and Egypt were to be reinforced for offensive operations, then the prerequisite was many more monoplane fighters on the island.

The only means by which Hurricanes could reach Malta reasonably quickly and ready for operations was by aircraft carrier. On 20 July 1940, 12 aircraft of *Operation Hurry,* as it was known, were embarked in the training carrier, *Argus*, reaching Gibraltar on 30 July. Astonished groundcrew were transferred to submarines for the rest of the journey. *Argus*, escorted by *Ark Royal,* two battleships and two cruisers, flew off the aircraft some 200 miles from Malta.

Guided by two naval Blackburn Skuas, the Hurricanes landed safely on 12 August to form the nucleus of No. 261 Squadron led by Squadron Leader D. Balden; a form of delivery which was to be repeated, though not always without loss. Meanwhile, this reinforcement sufficed for Malta, despite the desperate odds, until a similar delivery was attempted in November.

As with Malta, Egypt was vulnerable to

Knighted while in Malta, Air Chief Marshal Sir Keith Park resumed his Battle of Britain No. 11 Group practice of flying a personal Hurricane — OK 2. *(RAF Museum)*

vastly superior air strength in numbers, while on the ground, Marshal Graziani, Balbo's successor, outnumbered the Commander-in-Chief General Sir Archibald Wavell's forces by nearly seven to one.

Hurricanes headed the RAF's shopping list, but how were they were to be obtained, short of the long voyage round the Cape in crates on the ships of the military supply and reinforcement convoys?

The solution was to ferry them in aircraft carriers to a West African port and stage them nearly 4,000 miles across Africa to Egypt.

At much the same time as *Argus* was on passage to Gibraltar an RAF working party under Group Captain H. Thorold had begun to prepare the port of Takoradi on the Gold Coast — then a Crown colony, now Ghana — to receive Hurricane reinforcements and other aircraft.

Such an ambitious project required a prodigious effort. Toiling in the torrid conditions, unrelieved in the 1940s by air-conditioning and other aids to ease tropical service, susceptible to malaria, Thorold's men had within a month provided sufficient facilities for receiving the Hurricanes.

On 5 September, six Hurricanes together with six Blenheims were unloaded in crates. Next day 30 more Hurricanes flew ashore from *Argus.* Three weeks later the assembled aircraft were ready for take-off. In the 1940s it was a courageous decision to contemplate flying single-seat fighters across the heart of Africa, but the strength of Camm's design was repaid again, as it had been in the frozen Norwegian campaign, as it was doing in the concurrent Battle of Britain and as it would within the Arctic Circle in defence of northern Russia. Long-range 44-gallon tanks (90-gallon when Hurricane IIs were available) extended the range, but only the airframe itself and the wide undercarriage could contend with the rigours of the route. Even so, after as many as ten stages, from the humidity and squally downpours of the West African coast to the red dust of Kano, each Hurricane, as with the groundcrew malarial casualties in Takoradi, was in no shape for immediate action.

The 'stepping stones' across Africa from Takoradi to Sudan and the western Desert were perilous. *(RAF Museum)*

At home Winston Churchill was anxiously aware of the difficulties as reports were received of Hurricanes awaiting spares along the routes. After the war he admitted: 'The heavy wear on engines in their flight over vast barren sandy spaces reduced their fighting life'. Deeply concerned at the time that Hurricanes from this source could not be effective in 1940, he was to console himself in retrospect that without them 'the Army of the Nile and all its ventures could not have lived through the tragic events of 1941'.

In the desert, where the Hurricanes were so needed, a reluctant Graziani, urged on by Mussolini, moved against Egypt. Vastly outnumbered, British troops fought a four-day, 65-mile withdrawal across the Egyptian frontier to Sidi Barrani. There the Italians halted while Major-General Richard O'Connor retired his Western Desert force to a defence line at Mersa Matruh, 120 miles east of Egypt's frontier with Libya. There they remained. Six weeks later Mussolini had a new priority. On 28 October the Italian army in Yugoslavia invaded Greece, a campaign which was to fragment Middle East Air Command.

In an immediate gesture, pre-empting any request from Whitehall, Longmore offered aircraft from his meagre resources, albeit at the start only a squadron of Blenheims. It could only be a matter of time before the ace in his air pack, the Hawker Hurricane, would be committed.

On 31 October Longmore signalled the Prime Minister: 'It seems that it has become politically absolutely essential to send a token force to Greece, even at the expense of my Forces here. I have therefore arranged to despatch to Athens without any delay a Blenheim squadron'. Gladiators followed. For the time being, Blenheim bombers and fighters and Gladiators comprised the token force.

The widespread demand for Hurricanes delayed further reinforcement of Malta until 17 November 1940, when *Argus* sought to repeat Operation *Hurry* under the code-name Operation *White*. Unhappily it went wrong. Twelve aircraft were flown off, attended by two Blackburn Skuas to lead the way. On this occasion take-off was from more than twice Hurry's 200 mile distance from the island, requiring very careful consideration of range. The combination of this fuel factor, pilots not being briefed on the fuel economy settings for the constant speed propellers of the Hurricanes, their being instructed to fly far below the 10,000-foot most helpful altitude, reduction of speed and range by tropical radiators and an unexpected headwind, resulted in disaster. Two aircraft of the first six ran dry and fell into the sea, the remainder landing at Luqa in Malta on the last few drops in their tanks. The Skua guiding the second flight of six Hurricanes got lost and was shot down over Sicily. The Hurricanes, failing to reach Malta, disappeared. Aircraft and pilots were lost. This setback was all the more disappointing in the wake of the great naval aviation success at Taranto on 11 November when 21 Swordfish from the carrier *Illustrious* put three Italian battleships out of action for the loss of two of the torpedo-bombers.

Although Taranto was much celebrated it helped to stimulate Hitler into supporting Mussolini in Sicily, a move in the light of which the loss of eight of Operation *White's*

'Tin-opener' IID of No. 6 Squadron whose desert operations struck hard at enemy tank morale. *(RAF Museum and Imperial War Museum)*

IID 'tin-opener' of the type which excelled in the desert. *(Aeroplane-Quadrant)*

Hurricanes was even more serious. General Geissler's Fliegerkorps X would be in action from Sicily in the New Year.

Meanwhile, in the Western Desert Wavell's troops were on the brink of a venture which, in the New Year would result in the appearance of General Rommel and his Afrika Korps on the scene, with all that the Desert Fox's brilliance was to imply for Longmore's sorely stretched squadrons. Even as O'Connor's small force fell back to the Mersa Matruh line in mid-September, Wavell was contemplating Operation *Compass,* a surprise drive to push the Italians back, possibly as far as Derna. He considered this the speediest and most effective assistance he could render the Greeks. By 9 February 1941 he had reached beyond Derna, retaking Benghazi on that day and entering El Agheila. Thereafter pressures from London to reinforce Greece resulted in a much weakened desert army and air force just at the time when Italian failures in the Mediterranean and North Africa brought the Luftwaffe into Sicily and Rommel to Tripoli in Libya.

In all of this the Hurricane as the region's sole British monoplane fighter bore a crucial responsibility. Operation *Compass,* launched on the night of 8/9 December 1940, was only feasible in the first place because of deep and comprehensive reconnaissance. In the absence of more suitable reconnaisance aircraft the slow, vulnerable Army Co-operation Lysander was employed. But it could not have operated over Italian-held territory without a Hurricane escort. This essential was emphasised on 20 November 1940, when 60 CR 42s sought to disrupt one such photo-recce. The eight escorting Hurricanes and six Gladiators accounted for seven of the enemy biplane fighters.

The aggressive use of his fighter aircraft was much more in accordance with Collishaw's experience and nature. Off the leash now that more Hurricanes were becoming available, he relished Longmore's order for them to be sent in at low level against Italian fighter airfields and lines of communication. The intensity of Nos 274 and 233 Squadrons' operations required as many as four sorties a day from each pilot, an exhausting workload under desert conditions. Individual pilots seized their opportunities. On 11 December 1940, Flying Officer Charles Dyson of No. 33 Squadron chanced upon six CR 42s, escorting a SM 79. It seemed to him that he had hit all six, but any search for confirmation of shot down or damaged enemy aircraft was ruled out by the need to fight off more CR 42s, What Dyson did not know until he returned to his squadron after crash-landing in the desert was that troops in the vicinity had reported six fighters destroyed plus the bonus of the Italian bomber brought down by one of the falling Fiat fighters.

At about this time a certain Air Marshal A. W. Tedder arrived in Egypt to ease Longmore's burdens in the new appointment of deputy to the commander-in-chief. It was quickly agreed that Tedder assume responsibility for the Desert Air Force. After Sollum had been taken on 17 December and Egypt cleared of Italians, Tedder, eager to experience the desert environment of the squadrons, stood in at No. 202 Group headquarters while Collishaw took a week's sick leave in Cairo after flu'. The success of the Hurricanes in the wake of Collie's 'battleship' was a source of particular satisfaction to Tedder. Hurricane armament had been one of his responsibilities in the newly created post of Director-General of Research and Development in the Munich crisis autumn of 1938.

The desert took its toll of men and machines and neither stood on ceremony. None less so than No. 73 Squadron.

During the Battle of Britain Hurricane production benefited from Tedder's work as a temporary civilian in the Ministry of Aircraft Production under Lord Beaverbrook. After returning to the RAF in November 1940, his appearance in the Middle East was accidental. Air Marshal O. T. Boyd, formerly of Balloon Command, was taken prisoner by the Italians when the aircraft taking him to the Middle East landed in Sicily because of a navigational error. Selected in Boyd's place, Tedder preferred to take the Takoradi route and the opportunity to see for himself what was being done to hasten Hurricanes to Egypt.

And now here in the desert he was comforted that more Hurricanes would soon be on the way, hopping the trans-Africa stepping-stones by which he had himself reached Cairo. Hard on his arrival Churchill had signalled: 'We are filling up *Furious* again with another, even larger packet of flyables from Takoradi'. They were needed. In the desert, Tedder saw for himself how serious was the damage done to all aircraft and their engines by the desert. Robust though the Hurricane's airframe and Merlin were, they could take only so much. Valves eroded and salt in the air rotted cables. Pilots taking off into great dust clouds and landing in sandstorms were also at risk from faulty control rods and undercarriage legs seizing-up. As Rommel arrived, the Luftwaffe — so much better equipped and crewed than the

Maintenance of desert squadrons was crucial as is evidenced by the terrain over which these No. 73 Squadron aircraft are flying. *(RAF Museum)*

Regia Aeronautica — was to compound the environmental problems of the Desert Air Force and its Hurricanes.

It will be recalled that at the end of October 1940, the Italians had invaded Greece, eliciting Longmore's gesture of Gladiator biplanes. On 6 April 1941, Germany's Airfleet 4 intervened in the Balkans, issuing a challenge which would involve Hurricane squadrons milked from the Middle East for a hopeless task. Yugoslavia was the first victim of the ferocity with which the Luftwaffe and Italian, German, Bulgarian and Hungarian ground forces totalling 45 Divisions launched a combined attack. As the Luftwaffe struck, the Royal Yugoslav Air Force had 38 Hurricanes, comprising 12 Mark Is flown from Brooklands in December 1938, when export sales were still considered important by Hawkers, and 12 more subsquently delivered. The remainder had been built locally under licence. Rolls-Royce had provided the Merlins, though one aircraft was powered experimentally by Daimler Benz. The Yugoslav Hurricanes lasted one week. During the retreat of Greek and British troops, Hurricanes of Nos 33, 80, 112 and No. 208 (Army Co-operation) Squadrons, switched earlier from the desert to replace the Gladiators, covered the fall-back on Athens as best they could. By 19 April only 22 aircraft remained serviceable and on the following afternoon most of No. 208's last 15 aircraft were sent up to combat 100 Ju 88s, Me 109s and 110s in the Piraeus. In the last significant Hurricane action over Greece 14 enemy aircraft were claimed for the loss of five; one of which was piloted by Squadron Leader Marmaduke St. J. Pattle, the 27-year-old South African ace commanding No. 33 Squadron. Officially credited with 24 victories over Greece, including two 110s and a 109 on the day, suffering from exhaustion and flu, he was shot down.

Tidal fighting in North Africa returned this prisoner-of-war Hurricane to its rightful owners at Gambut in January, 1942. *(RAF Museum)*

Pattle's final score was probably more than the official count of 24. Previously, as a Gladiator pilot defending Egypt, he had accounted for more than six Italian aircraft and his true final total may well have been 40. Yet, because 'Pat' Pattle's short career took place over the desert in 1940, and then in Greece, he is not so well remembered as Hurricane contemporaries of the Battle of Britain.

By 22 April replacements from Crete had raised Hurricane strength to about 20, centred on a training airfield at Argos. Of these, only seven survived an attack by Me 110s and they were withdrawn to Crete.

Reflecting in *With Prejudice* on the Balkan intervention, Tedder commented: 'Whether the decision to send forces into Greece was an act of courageous wisdom or one of tragic folly must remain a matter of opinion'. Whichever view is taken it was undoubtedly Quixotic to commit the Hurricane, the fighter for which Longmore signalled so urgently during the Battle of Britain. The Middle East air commander's request, as he put it 'for modern fighters', submitted to Churchill by Sir Archibald Sinclair, the Air Minister, had infuriated Beaverbrook, responsible for aircraft production and replacing Fighter Command's daily losses. Churchill acceded and Hurricanes were despatched, though shortly afterwards members of Longmore's staff very nearly snookered their commander-in-chief. Extraordinarily, they fed the Air Ministry a report from Gladiator pilots that they preferred the biplane. Marshal of the Royal Air Force Lord Douglas of Kirtleside — then an Air Chief Marshal and deputy chief of the air staff — who was present when this opinion was advanced as an argument for not sending Hurricanes to the desert, recalled: 'That was an occasion when I felt that young fighter bloods should be seen and not heard'.

It was not long before Crete went the way of Greece, there simply not being enough Hurricanes to meet the widely dispersed demands in the Middle East and East Africa and now increased by events in Iraq and Syria.

Compared with the desert and Malta, operations in East Africa and Iraq were distractions. Yet successes in each of those regions contained their lessons for the future, particularly that they owed so much to air power and something to the Hawker Hurricane. First, East Africa. The campaign, beginning in November 1940, ended Italian occupation of Abyssinia which had been annexed by Mussolini — Il Duce, the Italian fascist leader — on 5 May 1936. With neat historical timing, Emperor Haile Selassie was restored on 5 May 1941.

At the outset, after an initial setback on the Sudan border, a museum mix of Hardys, Vincents, Wellesleys and Gauntlets bolstered by Gladiators, fared surprisingly well. But it was not until 10 Hurricanes of South Africa's No. 1 Squadron, followed by Hurricanes of No. 2 and No. 3 SAAF Squadrons, joined them that ground forces, including Brigadier W. J. 'Bill' Slim's 10th Indian Brigade, were assured of victory. Special virtues of the campaign were the confidence instilled by the Hurricane in its ground support role and as a menace to enemy airfields; and the indispensability of air drops by transports. Later, Brigadier Orde Wingate, of the Chindits, and Slim, future leader of the 14th Army, were to value each of these in Burma.

The short Iraq campaign was unexpected and certainly one which Wavell, with North Africa, the Balkans and East Africa on his hands, could have done without. The Middle East Command's air resources were already stretched well beyond their reasonable limits when the Iraqi rebel leader, Raschid Ali el-Gailani, laid siege to the RAF camp and airfield at Habbaniya, 50 miles from Baghdad. It had been manned since 1937 in support of a treaty with Iraq and, as Raschid Ali invested it in late April and early May 1941, accommodated No. 4 Flying Training School equipped with old aircraft of which the Fairey Gordons pre-dated the antiques in East Africa. There were also some Airspeed Oxfords. RAF Habbaniya's defiance of Raschid Ali is described vividly in Air Vice-Marshal Tony Dudgeon's *Luck of the Devil*. Although the immediate crisis was over when the Hurricane appeared in Iraq, it was no less welcome. Raschid Ali's subversive activities had been fostered by Germany. Were Iraq to have been occupied, either by force or invitation, then British oil supplies in the Near East would have been cut off and Japan — after entering the war at the end of 1941 — offered the opportunity of joining hands with Germany in the region.

A raid on Habbaniya by three He 111s on 16 May hastened reinforcement and on the next day four Hurricanes and nine Gladiators of No. 94 Squadron flew in from Egypt. They were followed by two more Mark IIs fitted with fixed 44-gallon tanks to give them the range to reach the Heinkel bases. Another four Hurricanes arrived on 21 May, followed shortly afterwards by a tactical reconnaissance aircraft. Of the two long-range Hurricanes one was piloted by Sir Roderic MacRobert, one of three sons of a Scottish baronet, each of whom inherited the title in succession as they were killed. Sir Roderic died as his Hurricane hurtled into the fragments of an Me 110 he had destroyed over Mosul during a raid on the Heinkel base there. His mother paid for three Hurricane IICs as a gift to the nation and they carried the names of Sir Roderic, Sir Alasdair and Sir Iain, and the family crest, into combat in the Middle East. She also donated a Stirling to Bomber Command, appropriately named *MacRobert's Reply*.

The arrival of Hurricanes and a relief column enforced an end to the Iraqi rebellion. Somerset de Chair, an MP who was intelligence officer of Kingcol, the relief column, describing an attack by three light green Heinkel 111 bombers in *The Golden Carpet*, wrote: 'We saw the planes fly in, growing smaller, while the angry Hurricane, kept on duty for the purpose, took off and rushed snarling after them'.

Attention was now drawn to Syria, which, under the influence of the Vichy government in France, was being used by the Luftwaffe to stage aircraft to Iraq. In a short campaign

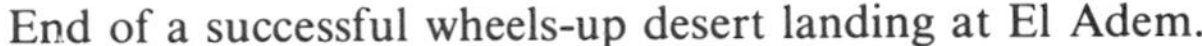
End of a successful wheels-up desert landing at El Adem.

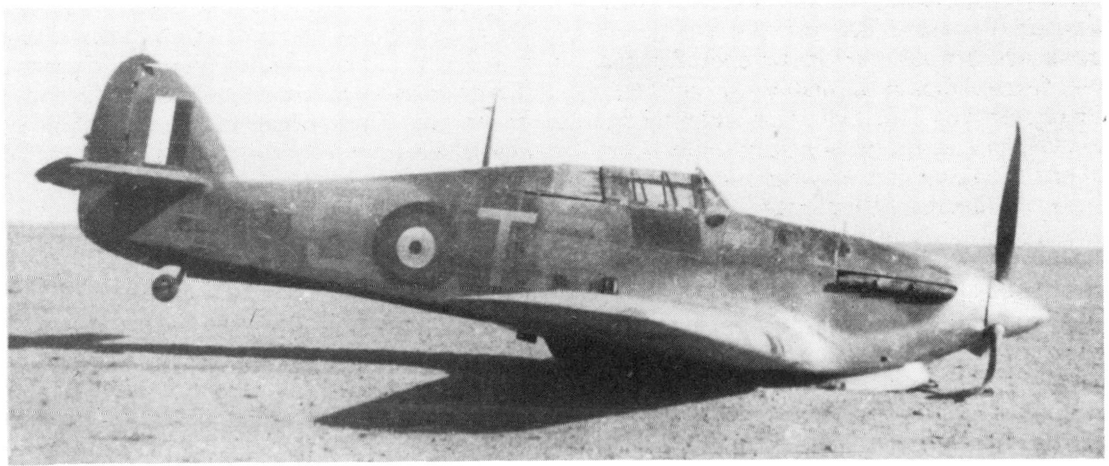

Sir Alasdair, one of three Hurricane IICs presented to the RAF by Lady MacRobert in memory of her three pilot sons killed flying. *(Imperial War Museum)*

Hurricanes of Nos 80, 108 and 260 Squadrons established air superiority leading to Vichy French surrender in Syria and Lebanon.

The desert war became a series of tidal advances and retreats dictated by the resolve and reinforcement of either side. Tobruk and its harbour were twice cut off and isolated by the tide as happened when the overall demands of the campaign in Greece, including the switch of Hurricanes from the desert, underwrote Rommel's drive to the Egyptian border. Yet, if help for Greece weakened British forces in the desert Rommel was himself at risk so long as Malta threatened the short Mediterranean air and sea crossing of the Axis supply route.

In the Spring of 1941, after the Luftwaffe, using Italian bases in Sicily, had assumed responsibility for the reduction of Malta, Hurricane Is defending the island were in a familiar situation; too few and too slow to compete with 109s and Ju 88s based only 60 miles away. Anticipating a field day against Stukas and unescorted Italian bombers, No. 249 Squadron, arriving from the aircraft carrier *Ark Royal* in May 1941, was disappointed at being deprived of easy pickings and much relieved when Mark II replacements with which to combat the stiff German opposition arrived towards the end of June.

Spitfire pilots from home, ferried through the night from Gibraltar in a Sunderland flying-boat to replace lost Hurricane pilots, were shocked on coming ashore as a raid was in progress to see Hurricanes — as Wing Commander P. B. 'Laddie' Lucas was to describe them — 'clapped out' and 'struggling for height'. Lucas recalled that until the first Spitfire arrived in the following March visions of another Crete began to unsettle the new pilots' sleep.

Fortunately, Hitler and Göring, true to their Battle of Britain form of September 1940, awarded Malta and its Hurricane defenders a respite at the critical moment.

As with the let-up on No. 11 Group's airfields so that daylight raids could be concentrated on London, they ordered Fliegerkorps X out of Sicily in preparation for the invasion of Russia. This move, leaving the less determined Italians to resume responsibility for Malta, together with a static period in the desert, eased the reinforcement of the island and the build-up of the air force in the desert in readiness for Operation *Crusader* towards the end of the year — a drive intended to roll back Rommel and relieve the besieged garrison in Tobruk.

'Antiquated' Hurricanes, as pilots posted from Spitfire squadrons thought of them, were flying in defence of Malta as fighters, but in the desert on the eve of *Crusader* in November 1941, Camm's monoplane fighter was gaining a new reputation in the ground attack role. As *Crusader* opened, the Mark II equipped 20 out of 25 Hurricane squadrons in the Middle East, of which 13, including the Fleet Air Arm's shore-based Nos 803 and 806 Squadrons, were involved in that operation.

The Desert Air Force and its Hurricane content had grown and improved beyond measure since the days of 'Collie's Battleship', thanks firstly to trans-Africa staging from Takoradi and secondly to the increasing efficiency of the care and repair organisation.

Operational strengths were sustained by repaired aircraft following the arrival of Air Vice-Marshal G. G. Dawson, renowned for his results at the Ministry of Aircraft Production in 1940. Recommended by Beaverbrook and given his head by Tedder who had admired his trouble-shooting talents as a colleague during the Battle of Britain, Dawson transformed the maintenance and repair organisation.

That *Crusader* got off to a good start on 18 November owed much to Coningham's Hurricanes. It was something of a novelty for the army to find itself supported in the desert by fighter-bombers, even if No. 80 Squadron's Mark Is were a lash-up with four 40 lb bombs under each wing. Together with No. 33 Squadron No. 80 also attacked enemy airfields and army positions. Such unaccustomed support was rendered all the more effective by the work of Nos 208 and 451 Royal Australian Air Force tactical

Rocket projectiles in readiness for arming Hurricanes of the Balkan Air Force — it included No. 351 Squadron of Yugoslavs — supporting Tito and his partisans.
(Imperial War Museum)

reconnaissance squadrons.

When, on 20 November the Tobruk garrison was ordered to break out — by 1 December it would be isolated again — No. 451 Squadron acted as courier, flying in and out of Tobruk with messages. Thanks to the Hurricane, the commander-in-chief, General Sir Claude Auchinleck's generals could monitor enemy movements, No. 2 Photographic Reconnaissance Unit's generally unarmed pale blue Mark Is making high altitude sorties deep into enemy held territory. The pilots' contribution was the more praiseworthy because of their inexperience with the aircraft. After the transition from the vulnerable high-wing maximum speed 216 mph Army Co-operation Lysander to a monoplane fighter, the 'Lizzie' pilots quickly learned, as had the Battle of Britain Poles and so many others, that the tight-turning Hurricane could provide a refuge at low level from 109s.

On 29 November during *Crusader* Flying Officer P. T. Cotton, his aircraft badly shot-up over El Adem airfield, out-turned two 109s until, their ammunition exhausted, they made off. By then Cotton's engine had had enough, enforcing a landing 15 miles from his landing ground. He was rescued and his machine brought in for the attention of Dawson's organisation.

The Hurricane was more vulnerable to the 109 over the desert than over south-east England, tropical filters cutting its speed which was further reduced when bombs were added. Consequently pilots depended on training, airmanship and initiative to counter this handicap.

Operating from the oven desert the Hurricane provided — as also from the cool grass of southern England — a link for the disparate temperaments, talents, services and nationalities of its pilots. At home in 1940 Hurricane squadrons bonded British, Canadian, Polish, Czech and a handful of American volunteers. Similarly in the desert, among others, it created a family of RAF, Fleet Air Arm, Australians and South Africans — and there was also Pilot Officer Lance Wade, a Texan serving in No. 33 Squadron. There was the example on 1 December of pilots of No. 1 South African Air Force and No. 274 Squadrons' 12 aircraft engaging 20 Me 109s and Fiat G50s between them. When Lieutenant Hoffe's glycol tank was hit and set on fire the South African baled out. Flight Lieutenant O. Tracey of No. 274 Squadron landed, picked him up and returned, the South African sitting in his lap.

The South Africans were adept at this cramped form of rescue. In Abyssinia Captain J. Frost of their No. 3 Squadron was rescued by Lieutenant Kershaw. In a double act, Frost, who had destroyed three Italian aircraft that day, held the stick while Kershaw operated flaps and undercarriage. Such Hurricane cameraderie — there were several similar rescues — was not the only parallel with the Battle of Britain. Fire killing or disfiguring and maiming pilots, as with Tom Gleave's 'standard Hurricane burns', was a daily hazard over the desert. In Operation *Crusader* much of the effort of Hurricane pilots was directed at bombing and shooting-up Rommel's motor transport vehicles as he fell back on El Gazala. During one such sortie Nicolson's courage in fighting on in a burning Hurricane in 1940 was matched by Squadron Leader Stephens. His Hurricane ablaze, his feet wounded, after an Italian MC 202 had hit a fuel tank, Michael Stephens prepared to bale out. Then the Macchi sped past. By now the cockpit was a furnace, but the squadron leader resumed flying and shot down the Italian. When he eventually baled out his clothes were on fire. Polish soldiers rescued him and took him into Tobruk. His award did not match Nicolson's VC. He received the DSO.

Crusader recovered Benghazi, the Cyrenaican capital, and pushed the enemy to El Gazala, an Allied advance petering out as in *Battleaxe* against El Agheila where the opposing forces stabilised their positions.

At this point, as with the drain of the Greek campaign a year before, the demands for reinforcement elsewhere weakened the desert effort. Japan had allied itself to the Axis. Hurricanes were required desperately east of Suez.

Following Japan's entry into the war in December 1941 and the resulting threat to India, an even greater onus fell upon Hurricane squadrons defending Malta and Egypt. In May that year it had helped to secure Egypt and prevent the loss of Middle East oil sources. Now, one year later, it would help to frustrate Mussolini's long dreamed of triumphal entry into Cairo and an Axis link-up with its Japanese Ally.

In mid-February 1942, the tidal desert war had carried Rommel's forces back to the El Gazala - Bir Hakim defence line. At this point Auchinleck's problems were compounded by the siphoning-off of Hurricanes and other supplies for the Far East — No. 30 Squadron was ordered to Ceylon — and by the return of Kesselring's Airfleet 2 to the Mediterranean.

On 26 May 1942 a Hurricane pilot of No. 4 SAAF Squadron confirmed that an Axis advance was imminent. He reported Italian troops moving towards Allied positions near El Gazala. Three German divisions were also involved and a battle for Bir Hakim, held by the Free French, raged for ten days. That the Free French brigade stuck out a sustained assault for so long was largely due to the assistance it received from Coningham's fighters which, as their commander put it, had decided 'to adopt the Free French and their fortress'. Hurricanes helped to fight off Luftwaffe attacks, dropped supply canisters and new Hurricane IID tank-busters of No. 6 Squadron tore into Rommel's armour.

The determination with which No. 6 Squadron pressed home its attacks was exemplified in Flight Lieutenant P. Hillier's experience on 15 June. Pulling out after crippling a tank, his aircraft hit the tank, losing tailwheel and part of the rudder. In this attack near Mersa Matruh four IIDs destroyed five lorries and an anti-aircraft gun. Hillier's Hurricane remained airborne justifying yet again Camm's conscious decision to put strength of construction — inherited from the stout Hawker pedigree — before all else. Hillier was credited with nine tank certainties before being killed in an accident in early September while demonstrating to the army how it should be done.

Delay to the Axis advance at Bir Hakim frustrated Rommel's timetable and contributed to the Eighth Army's survival of the ensuing 800-mile, two-week retreat upon El Alamein, its last line of defence before Cairo.

The retreat might so easily have become a disaster. Nose-to-tail convoys heading east, Hurricane airfields and landing grounds abandoned in leapfrogging moves 20 miles ahead of the advancing enemy offered tempting targets for the Luftwaffe. That Auchinleck's troops and so much of their equipment and supplies tumbled to safety behind the El Alamein line owed everything to Tedder's planning and the supply by Dawson's repair organisation of enough Hurricanes for Coningham's pilots to fend off German and Italian fighters and make repeated attacks on the advancing enemy.

Tedder committed every available aircraft, including Hurricanes from operational

Hurricane virtuoso Frank Carey, who rose from Aircraft Apprentice to Group Captain, shot down three Japanese aircraft on the day he was promoted Wing Commander responsible for Nos. 135 and 17 Squadrons. *(Imperial War Museum)*

training units. From the Canal Zone he summoned his Hurricane secret weapon, the IID, as has been described, making its first real impact at Bir Hakim. Hitherto little had been heard of the IID. No. 6 Squadron was in the Canal Zone being re-equipped with IICs — used effectively against ordinary or 'soft-skinned' military vehicles — when it received the first six IIDs in the Middle East.

The IID was a tank-buster and as such the right aircraft in the right place at the right time. Armed with a Vickers Type 'S' 40 mm anti-tank gun under each wing and two Brownings it was employed so destructively against Rommel's armour that it endeared itself to the Eighth Army. Soldiers called it the 'tin-opener'. Wing Commander R. Porteous, commanding No. 6 Squadron, and his pilots, were delighted when no less a personage than Kesselring complimented their work by expressing alarm at the ease with which the tin-opener's 40 mm shells were penetrating tanks. Besides knocking-out tanks, shells were fragmenting inside the armour with the equally desirable effect of lowering tank crews' morale. Porteous learned this from a captured document recording Kesselring's visit to a tank regiment.

If the IID dismayed German tank crews it cheered their British counterparts, suffering the severe disadvantage of inferior tanks and armament, and helped to redress the balance until the Germans received the more heavily armoured Tiger. In being selected as the gun platform for the 40 mm cannon because of its steadiness when opening fire, the Hurricane provided a further testimonial to the strength of Camm's traditional Hawker construction.

In training, 'tin-opener' pilots practised against a captured tank at Shandar in the Canal Zone, diving from 5,000 feet to 20-40 feet before opening fire. Usually rounds were fired a pair at a time. Operationally, No. 6 Squadron, pioneer tank-busters, learned it did not pay to attack tanks unless they were in the open and separated from ground support which included anti-aircraft guns.

For all the success of the tin-opener at Bir Hakim and during the retreat on El Alamein the Eighth Army failed and this was partly due to its inability to co-operate to its best advantage with the air force in the Western Desert.

Command changes had become inevitable and Churchill, visiting Cairo twice in August 1942, while flying to and from Moscow, made them. He replaced Auchinleck with General Sir Harold Alexander from Burma. Lieutenant-General W. Gott was the Prime Minister's first choice to replace General Neil Ritchie as leader of the Eighth Army, but he was killed when an aircraft in which he was passenger was shot down. Churchill then sent for Lieutenant-General B. L. Montgomery. Commending these appointments to the War Cabinet, the Prime Minister commented from Cairo: 'I am sure we were heading for disaster under the former regime'. Montgomery forthwith fostered warm and effective personal working relationships with Tedder and Coningham. Speedily the message spread throughout the Western Desert Air Force — not least the Hurricane squadrons accounting for 22 of the region's 48 fighter and fighter-bomber squadrons — that Monty warmly appreciated their value and knew how to use them.

There had also been a change of command in Malta, where in July 1942, Air Vice-Marshal Keith Park had succeeded Air Marshal Hugh Lloyd. Park's posting contained two ironies. For the second time in two years he was opposed by Kesselring, the Battle of Britain commander of Airfleet 2, who had withdrawn units from North Africa to Sicily to strengthen attempts to obliterate Malta as a base capable of disrupting Rommel's supply routes. The other irony was that the operation of Hurricanes defending the island was all too familiar. Pilots were obliged to climb away from the approaching enemy to gain altitude before returning to engage a raid which was already over Malta. In the run-up to Park's arrival, Malta and its defending Hurricanes had suffered grievously at the hands of the Luftwaffe, the more so after *Crusader* when Hitler had ordered Fliegerkorps II, facing Moscow, back to Sicily, leaving Fliegerkorps X in Crete and the Balkans. Rommel's retreat during *Crusader* had underlined the necessity of reducing Malta.

As a result, Me 109Fs, escorting bombers, had taken an unacceptable toll of Hurricanes of Nos 261, 126 and 185 Squadrons, the Luftwaffe fighters' performance emphasising the obsolescence of the Hurricane in its original fighter role. Malta lost its value as an offensive base and could not itself receive supplies because of the aerial blockade.

It could only be a matter of weeks before the Hurricane was superseded, providing ferry aircraft carriers could fly-off Spitfires within reasonable range. On 7 March 1942, when 15 Spitfires arrived from the carrier *Eagle,* the island had increased its 11 Hurricanes of mid-February to 30. Riches compared with the desperate days of Faith, Hope and Charity, but too few in the face of all that Fliegerkorps II was hurling at it.

Gradually the Hurricane squadrons were re-equipped, 127 more Spitfires flying in by May, thanks largely to *Wasp,* the US aircraft carrier. But in April, the month in which Malta and its people received the George Cross, some 30 Hurricanes carried much of the burden of its defence. Spitfires would soon outnumber Hurricanes, though serviceablility would be a problem. The Spitfire simply did not have the robust operational ground and airborne physique of the Hawker fighter, succumbing to the rough conditions of Malta's airfields. It also suffered badly on the ground from enemy air attacks.

In July, as Park took over, the George Cross island was comparatively calm, some of Airfleet 2 having been transferred to reinforce North Africa, Russia and France. Main responsibility for Malta reverted temporarily to the Italians.

No sooner had Kesselring's aircraft withdrawn than Tedder seized the opportunity to renew air strikes from Malta against enemy cargoes for North Africa, supplemented as Park arrived by submarine operations.

Hurricane's had kept Malta 'afloat'. Now, replaced on the airfields by the Spitfire, the Hurricane, operating as a Fleet Air Arm fighter, helped to protect the ships delivering ammunition, bombs, food and other supplies without which Malta could not survive or sustain Wellington bomber and Beaufort torpedo-bomber operations.

However, Malta's ordeal had been eased but temporarily. Rommel's return to the Egyptian border had provided North African air bases, additional to those in Sardinia and Sicily, for the protection of his supply route, for raiding Malta and harassing Malta-bound convoys.

Enemy air superiority imposed a fearful

This Mark IV, armed with 40 mm cannon flew with No. 6 Squadron in 1944. *(RAF Museum)*

burden on naval efforts to protect shipping. In the spring and summer of 1942 the Sea Hurricane of the Fleet Air Arm was the prime weapon in defence of the convoy routes in 'Bomb Alley'. This was the perilous stretch of sea beyond the range of Malta or North Africa-based fighters. Carrier-borne Sea Hurricanes, assisted by Fulmars, put up a creditable performance despite overwhelming odds — on occasion enemy bomber escorts of more than 100 fighters. Circumstances had necessitated rapid provision of the Hurricane as a naval fighter since the *Glorious* captain's reluctance off Norway in 1940 to receive Squadron Leader Cross and the remains of No. 46 Squadron. Then, carrier captains were horrified at the prospect of Hurricane deck-landings. Now, flown by comparatively inexperienced wartime-trained Fleet Air Arm pilots, the aircraft — predominantly the IBs, adapted from the Mark I — were not merely accepted but heartily welcomed. The view over the nose was an enormous asset for deck-landing, while the Hurricane's quick response to fractional control movements and its stall characteristics were especially commended by pilots.

Serving subsequently in the Pacific, Bomb Alley survivors reflected that the handling and hardiness of the Sea Hurricane, particularly in its IIC variant of 1943, would have been more suitable in the ground attack role than the Spitfire's naval derivative, the Seafire. Meanwhile, in this dangerous and difficult period in the Mediterranean the protectors were as vulnerable as the protected, and not merely to air attack. On 11 August, as if to emphasise the peril from above and below, the carrier *Eagle* was torpedoed and sunk. Of 20 Sea Hurricanes available to Nos 801 and 813 Squadrons, only four — being airborne — survived to land elsewhere.

Between 10 and 19 October Malta endured its last large raids, but now that Spitfires had relieved Hurricanes of the burden of its defence the story returns to the desert where the Hawker machine was still at a premium and where Montgomery, while repelling Rommel's testing jabs, was preparing his renowned El Alamein offensive. In the Western Desert, the Hurricane, joined by Kittyhawks, Tomahawks and Beaufighters, added daily — and nightly — to its reputation, though rather as the reconnaissance eye of the army and as a tank-buster than as a fighter aircraft. Of Tedder's 48 fighter and fighter-bomber squadrons 22 were still so equipped.

Throughout the months preceding the late October early November 1942, Battle of El Alamein, Malta had not received Kesselring's undivided attention. Airfleet 2's Fliegerkorps X, operating from Crete and the Balkans, increased the Hurricane squadrons' responsibilities by appearing over Egypt and attacking airfields in the Canal Zone. No. 73 Squadron was kept particularly busy protecting Cairo by day and night while No. 213 Squadron flew in from Cyprus to help cover the El Alamein line. In July, No. 73 Squadron destroyed 23 enemy aircraft for the loss of six Hurricanes.

Malta's plight and the appearance of the Luftwaffe over Egypt put additional pressure on Montgomery to expedite his offensive. Only occupation of the Cyrenaican bulge into the Mediterranean would provide the RAF with airfields from which to protect convoys sustaining the island. When, on the night of 23 October 1942, Monty opened his offensive, 15 Hurricane squadrons were committed to support it; first among them were the black-painted IIC fighters of No. 73 Squadron. Now the Hurricane, which had suffered so badly as heavily escorted Stukas had cleared the way for rapidly advancing tanks and infantry during the fall of France, was on hand to help turn the tables.

That they could do so was due to the air superiority achieved by the Middle East Air Force. Of this there could be no clearer demonstration than the free rein with which No. 6, the pioneer tank-busting squadron, joined by No. 7 SAAF Squadron, in action from dawn on 23 October, wrought havoc among enemy tanks and transports.

Besides alleviating Malta's distress a successful westward drive by the Eighth Army would also dispel the nightmare of the

This unique Hurricane-made-for-two IIC trainer was delivered to the Persian Air Force in 1947. *(RAF Museum)*

Japanese — by now threatening India — linking up with Axis troops in the Near East. To achieve these objects, with the possible additional bonus of re-opening the Suez Canal passage to India, the Allies hoped to squeeze the enemy between Montgomery advancing west and General Dwight D. Eisenhower pushing east from French North Africa. The instruments of this 2,000-mile pincer were Operation *Supercharge,* Monty's master plan, and Operation *Torch,* launched respectively on 23 October and 8 November 1942. Tedder, recalling this period in *With Prejudice*, wrote: 'We were desperately short of Spitfires and Kittyhawks, so that the brunt had to be borne by Hurricane squadrons, which were quite outclassed. Casualties were heavy and successes against the enemy relatively few'. It was the appearance of the Me 109G that had put the Hurricane so much in the shade as a fighter.

The Monty legend has enhanced the popular misconception that his successes at El Alamein, and thereafter, belonged exclusively to the Eighth Army. But infantry and armour depended on support from Allied land and sea aircraft, among which were biplane Fleet Air Arm Albacores, Wellingtons, Bostons, Baltimores and Mitchells in addition to Spitfires, Kittyhawks and Hurricanes. In this account the spotlight must fall on Coningham's Hurricanes.

Since smashing Axis armour was a prerequisite of an Eighth Army advance, night-fighter Hurricanes of No. 73 Squadron harassed German and Italian armoured divisions on the night of the historic 23/24 October artillery barrage. In the morning IIDs of Nos 6 and 7 SAAF Squadrons followed up, taking out tanks, petrol tankers and a mix of transport vehicles. Above them, No. 208 and No. 40 SAAF Squadrons recced and also spotted for the gunners.

The essence of Montgomery's plan was to break through the enemy's line and pursue such troops and armour as had not been captured or destroyed. Success, Monty reckoned, would depend on hammering Rommel hard on a narrow front and he therefore welcomed an air force proposal to concentrate attacks for this purpose. Desert IIDs spearheaded this operation, the skill and determination of their pilots impelling Tedder to inform Portal, Chief of the Air Staff: 'Hurricanes doing magnificently loyal work, but are of course completely outclassed, and it is hard to tell them they cannot have modern aircraft yet'. It was salutary that towards the end of 1942 a commander-in-chief should repeatedly refer to the Hurricane as 'outclassed', but unhappily some results bore out his opinion. On 25 October six out of 10 IIDs were lost for the claimed destruction of 11 tanks.

Yet as the chase developed spirits were high. Contributing to Chaz Bowyer's *Hurricane at War,* Squadron Leader D. Weston-Burt of No. 6 Squadron wrote: 'On 3 November we were let loose along with all the other squadrons to play havoc as much as possible with the now retreating German and Italian forces. There was no quarter'. Weston-Burt recalled one bus spewing forth 'several dozen Italians which we gleefully and callously mowed down as they ran for their lives across the coverless desert'.

The relentless nature of the Hurricane's part in Monty's victory is further demonstrated by the bold enterprise on 13 November of landing Nos 213 and 238 Squadrons, complete with ground staff, 150 miles behind the retreating enemy. In three days the 36 IICs destroyed or damaged almost 300 vehicles before being withdrawn.

On an altogether different scale the Axis forces retreating before the Eighth Army were threatened in the rear from 8 November by Allied forces landing in French North Africa. Even before the lesson of Dieppe, Churchill and the British chiefs of staff had been concerned that an attempted cross-Channel invasion of France might fail. Landings in Morocco and Algeria were agreed with the Americans as an alternative aimed at relieving enemy pressure on our Russian Ally. It would not be the Second Front in the West for which Stalin so consistently pressed but it was the best they could offer in the circumstances. It also held the merit of being Roosevelt's own 'commanding idea', as Churchill tactfully reminded the US President.

In *Torch,* the western arm of the giant pincer, the Hurricane was prominent from the outset, 18 IICs of the 'Fighting Cocks', No. 43 Squadron, making an early-morning flight from Gibraltar to the Algiers airfield of Maison Blanche. Sea Hurricanes, operating from offshore, were also vital to Torch, reporting on 10 November enemy occupation of Tunisia in an attempt to counter the pincer peril.

Ashore, British commandos welcomed the support of the Sea Hurricanes and were not unduly surprised that the familiar roundels had been replaced by United States white stars. They themselves had been landed in American uniforms as part of an effort not to draw fire from the Vichy French, expected to be less hostile to the Americans than to the British.

The escort carrier *Avenger's* Nos 802 and 883 Squadrons provided fairly unchallenged cover in the area of Algiers. Oran was covered by Nos 804 and 891 Squadrons from *Dasher* and No. 800 from *Biter,* also escort carriers. These squadrons encountered French Dewoitine D520s. In covering the invasion the Fleet Air Arm lost 11 Sea Hurricanes, but after two days the French abandoned opposition, paying the price in the German invasion of unoccupied France.

Meanwhile, swift Axis occupation of next-door Tunisia — unresisted by the French — necessitated another landing east of the existing Algerian invasion and on 11 November *Avenger's* Sea Hurricanes covered troops landing at Bougie. Shortly afterwards *Avenger* was torpedoed by a U-boat.

Now the race was on from east and west to reach Tunis. In the west No. 43 Squadron was busy escorting Dakota-loads of US troops. Unfortunately for Eisenhower the Germans and Italians had snatched the initiative by reinforcing Tunisia from the sea, and the western pincer arm stopped in the Tunisian border mud. Winter had set in and it was almost the end of February 1943 before campaigning could continue. Not that the poor conditions deterred the Hurricane squadrons, the sturdy Hawker construction living up to a reputation which had built and built since that winter of 1939-40 in the mire of the French airfields.

If the eastern pincer had got bogged down, the 2,000 mile gap had closed considerably since the *Torch* landings, the Eighth Army advancing 1,400 miles in three months, driving Rommel back to the Mareth Line on the eastern border of Tunisia. By 23 January 1943, when Monty's troops entered Tripoli, clearance of Cyrenaica had deprived the Luftwaffe of bases from which to harass Malta-bound convoys and menace the island. The Hurricane had helped the Eighth Army every mile of its way and stayed with it, No. 40 SAAF's recce aircraft and No. 73's night-fighters moving immediately into Tripolitanian airfields.

With fighting now taking place in Tunisia, Rommel sought to savage Allied supplies but improving weather enabled No. 225 Squadron to prove itself every bit as adept at ground attack as had the Hurribombers in the Western Desert. Equally, No. 241, operating with No. 225, frustrated German efforts to the north where General von Arnim attempted unsuccessfully to interrupt Allied communications.

Montgomery now needed to get through or round the Mareth Line, a desert version of the Maginot Line originally devised by France, to warn off the Italians. After repelling a desperate attack by Rommel on 6 March at Medenine he faced a second threat from German armour in the south, a flank policed by 2,000 Free French colonial troops whom General Leclerc had led in a 'Beau Geste' march across the Sahara from around Lake Chad. Leclerc's men were poorly equipped and Monty called in the IIDs of No. 6 Squadron. Nineteen Hurricanes landed at an advanced strip which, disconcertingly, was being shelled from enemy positions. By now, in response to Tedder's familiar complaint that the Hurricane was outclassed, Spitfires were escorting the IIDs. the combination forced the German armour to retire, a remarkable achievement for an air strike by Hurricanes unassisted on the ground.

Command of the Western Desert Air Force was now vested in Harry Broadhurst, the fighter pilot who in 1940 had arrived at Hornchurch in his private Hurricane to lead a wing of Spitfires. An Air Vice-Marshal, Broadhurst had succeeded Coningham, elevated to lead the Tactical Air Force which included Broadhurst's desert squadrons.

After the threat from the south had been removed, the IIDs and Hurribombers tore holes in the Mareth Line, allowing Monty's Eighth Army to move forward. On 8 April 1943, the pincers closed.

Chapter 10
East of Suez

'They gripped the Japanese air power and repelled its offensive . . .' Lieutenant-Colonel Frank Owen

Japan's entry into the war created an urgent demand for the Hurricane in the Far East. On 10 December 1941, following the 7 December Japanese attack on Pearl Harbour, lack of air cover resulted in the loss off Malaya of the Royal Navy's new battleship, *Prince of Wales* and an elderly battle-cruiser, *Repulse*, sunk by torpedo aircraft and bombers operating from Saigon.

On land, after invading northern Malaya, troops of General Yamashita's 25th Army had very soon advanced to within 100 miles of the causeway linking the Malayan peninsula to Singapore island. Four defending squadrons of the obsolescent tubby American Brewster Buffalo monoplane fighter and its predominantly Hart biplane-trained Australian and New Zealand pilots were swiftly overwhelmed. The aircraft's performance had provided a mockery of Air Chief Marshal Sir Robert Brooke-Popham's earlier declaration that the Buffalo was 'quite good enough for Malaya.' Commander-in-chief Far East as the Japanese invaded Malaya, this was the self-same Brooke-Popham who, responsible for the Air Defence of Great Britain in 1934, had opposed eight guns for the future Hawker Hurricane as 'going a bit far'. Eight-gun Hurricanes, mostly old Mark 1s, did not arrive until early January — when Brooke-Popham had been replaced by Lieutenant-General Sir Henry Pownall — and even then they were landed at Singapore, 51 of them, in crates. They were accompanied by 24 pilots. The Hurricane's absence hitherto owed more to priority for Fighter Command, the Soviet Union, the Middle East and the Fleet Air Arm than to Brooke-Popham's previous confidence in the Buffalo.

The Hurricanes and their pilots were handicapped from the start. The aircraft had been destined for the desert. Their air filters cost them 30 mph. The pilots were operationally inexperienced and lacked the affinity of membership of a squadron which has worked up and fought as a unit. On paper they belonged to No. 232 Squadron, but the squadron was an administrative formality rather than the close-knit family of fighter pilots which ideally it should have been.

Although they were too few and too late to affect the outcome, the Hurricanes inspired hope in Singapore among military and civilians that the daily raiders would be driven off. Air Vice-Marshal Paul Maltby, the last air commander before surrender, recalled '. . . it was confidently expected that the Hurricanes would sweep the Japanese from the sky.' At the start such optimism was not unfounded. On 20 January 1942, their first day in action, pilots of one Hurricane flight claimed eight of a raid by 27 Japanese bombers. Pilots of the second flight were less fortunate, exchanging losses of three with 350 mph naval Zero enemy fighters. Encounter with the Zero underlined the extent to which the Hurricane was handicapped by its desert filter and by a Japanese preference for operating below the Hurricane's best altitude of 20,000 feet. The pilots' difficulties in attempting to defend Singapore against up to as many as 127 daylight raiders escorted by fighters were heightened by the absence of radar. Located up-country it had been 'taken out' during the rapid Japanese advance or dismantled.

Six days after the Hurricanes' first action they joined Buffaloes covering an attack by 12 obsolete biplane Vickers Vildebeest torpedo-bombers on a Japanese landing at Endau on Malaya's east coast. Linking with troops already ashore on the west coast, this force prevented further defence of the peninsula. By 28 January when Singapore was under day and night attack and awaited invasion, only 21 of the 51 Hurricanes were operationally fit. The Japanese had destroyed 17 and 13 needed repair. With the island's airfields under air attack and vulnerable to shellfire from Johore at the tip of the peninsula, resistance by fighter aircraft was almost over.

At this point Hurricane reinforcements delivered at Takoradi in West Africa by the aircraft transport *Athene,* ferried across Africa and taxied perilously between telegraph poles on a curving desert road to the aircraft carrier *Indomitable* at Port Sudan, were flying in.

The experience of Sergeant Pilot Terence Kelly of No. 258 Squadron, who landed at Singapore's Seletar airfield on the evening of 29 January, typifies their predicament. Early next morning, together with Pilot Officer Bruce McAlister 'the gentlest, the best liked, the quietest of New Zealanders,' Kelly strolled across the airfield to the sandbagged bays where his aircraft was being serviced. The ground crew had problems. The Hurricane was new to them. Their tools were wrong. There were no spares, nor was there any glycol coolant for the Merlin. Moreover the six .303 Brownings arming each wing, caked in grease for the sea passage, would be inoperable until they had been stripped down, cleaned and reassembled; and yet these were the least of their worries, as Kelly explained in *Hurricane over the Jungle*. At about half past nine, anticipating the routine morning air raid, the airmen downed tools and hastened in the accumulating heat to the rubber trees fringing the airfield. McAlister told Kelly to draw his revolver and, threatening to shoot, ordered the groundcrew to resume work. There were no bombs that morning and on 31 January the Hurricanes were operational from Tenghah airfield. McAlister was shot down and killed.

Kelly's and McAlister's aircraft were two out of 13 of No. 258 Squadron's Hurricanes which had flown in from Sumatra after passage from Port Sudan in *Indomitable.*

Another 32 IIAs and IIBs had flown to and remained in Sumatra, where they would soon be joined by any Singapore survivors of Nos 232 and 258 Squadrons. Meanwhile the dwindling Hurricanes, down to 10, and six Buffaloes, covered the evacuation to Sumatra as best they could. By 9 February only seven Hurricanes remained, operating with ever increasing difficulty from soft, boggy ground at Kallang airfield, constructed on reclaimed land by the sea.

On 10 February the seven Hurricanes still operational were ordered to Sumatra. On 15 February Singapore surrendered. The Japanese were under no illusion how fortunate they had been that the Hurricane was so late on the scene. Colonel Tsuji of Yamashita's staff noted that they presented 'a serious challenge'. In *Singapore: The Japanese Version* he wrote that until their arrival 'our mobile corps had been advancing on the paved roads in broad daylight taking no precautions against enemy raids.' When Hurricanes were overhead, he admitted, roads had to be cleared of troops and motorised convoys.

Sumatra, then Java, soon joined Malaya and Singapore on the list of Japan's rapid occupation of South-East Asia. In these islands the Hurricane, poorly supported and out-numbered proved little more than a temporary irritant. Pilots and groundcrew contended with even worse conditions in the Dutch East Indies. Camm's robust construction, which had refused to succumb in the Arctic Circle or Western Desert, received its toughest test. Several failed to survive landings on what passed for airfields, particularly P 1 and P 2 north and south of Palembang, the Sumatran capital, where every landing was a confrontation between the aircraft's tubular construction and undercarriage and rough-hewn jungle clearings. The enemy soon ended such problems at P 1 by dropping paratroops nearby; their task was simplified by the absence of serviceable fighters, which were away escorting an attack by Blenheims and

Hudsons on an approaching Japanese convoy. Not that Air Commodore Stanley Vincent, commanding No. 220 Group, embracing the remants of Nos 232 and 258 Squadrons, was unaware of the peril of leaving an airfield undefended. As might have been expected of Northolt's station commander in No. 11 Group during the Battle of Britain, he had protested at orders from headquarters in Java to provide every serviceable Hurricane for the raid.

But P 2, as yet undetected by the Japanese and concealed in the jungle just south of Palembang, remained. From P 2, Hurricanes, as in their brief appearance before the Singapore surrender, gave the enemy a short sharp shock. In low-level attacks they raked bargeloads of troops, but only to temporary avail. Palembang fell and Vincent's six remaining Hurricanes flew to Java.

On paper Java was comparatively well off for Hurricanes. In addition to the Sumatra six, 24 Mark Is destined for Singapore had been diverted to the Dutch Air Force, and 40 crated IIAs or IIBs, of which 17 had been hastened to Sumatra, had arrived in the aircraft transport *Athene.* Following an RAF reshuffle, some of Nos 232 and 258 Squadrons' pilots were teamed up with ground crew of the newly arrived Nos 242 and 605 Squadrons — which had no pilots — providing between 20 and 30 serviceable Hurricanes.

Losses in Sumatra of Hurricanes on the ground, notably those unserviceable or self-destroyed at P 1, had created a surplus of

One of a batch of 1,205 Mark IIs and Mark IVs built at Kingston and King's Langley for the Middle East and Far East.

pilots and there was resentment at the handing over of Hurricanes to the Dutch whose pilots were not so combat skilled. In the event the Dutch made a creditable effort, their aircraft accounting for 30 of the enemy, destroyed or damaged, against an overall loss of 20. By 9 March, when the Dutch surrendered, No. 242 Squadron, down to its last two Hurricanes, destroyed them.

A glance at the globe recalls how immense were the areas of the then British and Dutch possessions when Japan entered the war. While retreats and surrenders had been taking place in Malaya, Singapore and the Dutch East Indies, another uneven contest, particularly in terms of air cover, was fought in Burma. There, too, swift Japanese success was hastened by a shortage of Hurricanes and inadequate radar. Indeed, as the Japanese invaded from Siam, now Thailand, and bombed the capital Rangoon for the first time on 23 December 1941, air defence of Burma was the responsibility of Brooke-Popham's 'quite good enough' Buffalo and Colonel Claire Chennault's Curtiss P-40 Tomahawk 'Flying Tigers', 24 of which, belonging to the American Volunteer Group in China, had been detached by Generalissimo Chiang Kai-shek to help defend Rangoon. The Hurricane did not appear until 30 crated Mark Is, diverted from Singapore, had been assembled.

After the loss in late January of three advanced airfields at Mergui, Tavoy and Moulmein in Tenasserim, the long coastal strip forefinger of Burma pointing south, Hurricanes of No. 17 Squadron, joined by No. 135 Squadron, operated from Mingaladon with No. 67's Buffaloes and Tomahawks. Lacking early warning, the pilots were obliged to adopt the all too familiar tactic of making a climbing retreat to gain sufficient altitude from which to fight. Considerable losses were inflicted on the enemy — estimated at 60 for the loss of 22 Hurricanes — but Japanese troops entered Rangoon and the capital fell on 7 March.

The RAF's tightest corners extracted the best from the Hurricane and its pilots. Sometimes they produced or developed, as with Pattle over Greece, an outstanding ace. Rangoon was no exception. Frank Carey had joined in the 1930s as an aircraft apprentice, becoming a rigger and fitter in No. 43 Squadron, to which he returned in 1935, after flying training, as a Sergeant Pilot. Weaned on the biplane Fury, Squadron Leader Carey had flown Hurricanes since No. 43's re-equipment in 1938 when he was a contemporary of the bullient Caesar Hull, killed in the Battle of Britain, John Simpson and others of the squadron's 'names'. When he sailed as leader of the newly formed No. 135 Squadron for the Far East on 6 December 1941 — 24 hours before Pearl Harbour — Carey had accumulated an almost unrivalled experience of the Hurricane. His squadron, despatched to stiffen a peaceful Burma's meagre air defence, stumbled into the retreat on India. On 26 February, the day he was promoted Wing Commander responsible for two Hurricane squadrons, Nos 135 and 17, the former aircraft apprentice shot down three Nakajima Ki 43 'Oscars'. As with Pattle there is no certainty about Carey's final tally which was probably more than the 24 generally quoted.

Japanese occupation of Rangoon enforced the withdrawal of the remaining 20 or so Hurricanes and a handful of Buffaloes and Tomahawks to a paddy field improvised as a landing ground at Zigon, which was to prove as hazardous as P 2 in Sumatra. Each landing on this dirt strip was a gamble. Tailwheels were particularly vulnerable and were replaced by bamboo skids. One Hurricane is thought to have fought with a bamboo longeron substituting in the fuselage for one of Camm's stout steel tubes.

Inevitably, Zigon became untenable. Hurricane remnants of Nos 135 and 67 Squadrons escaped to Akyab along the west coast of Burma. No 17's Hurricanes and the Tomahawks regrouped at Magwe, north of Rangoon and convenient for the defence of central Burma. But time was running out for the Hurricane as the retreat on India accelerated and it was the watchfulness on 20 March of a lone Hurricane from Magwe on reconnaissance over Mingaledon that

After the rush production of 1940, and as the Hurricane appeared in increasing numbers in the Far East, its construction became just one of many important war tasks for women on the assembly lines. *(British Aerospace)*

initiated the beginning of the end. Its pilot's report of numerous enemy aircraft on the airfield — possibly as man as 50 — inspired 'Burwing' at Magwe to rally its depleted reserves for a hard hitting raid on Mingaledon. On 21 March nine Blenheims, escorted by 10 Hurricanes, destroyed 16 aircraft on the ground, the Hurricanes accounting for more fighters attempting to intercept. It was a magnificent performance for such a run-down force and it stirred the enemy into swift and decisive revenge. Capable of operating in far greater numbers, the Japanese attacked Magwe in waves totalling more than 200 aircraft. Afterwards only 11 Hurricanes were serviceable. These joined 'Akwing' at Akyab which then suffered a similar fate. Shortly, what remained of Nos 67, 135 and 17 Squadrons dispersed to India and China. For eight weeks their pilots had not missed a day at two minutes' readiness; an ordeal in any circumstances, a torment in tropical Burma.

The fall of Rangoon, the retreat from Burma and the occupation of the Andaman islands in the Indian Ocean rendered Ceylon (now Sri Lanka) distinctly vulnerable; and thus another priority for the provision of Hurricanes. By the end of March some 50-60 serviceable Hurricanes were the star performers of an assortment of Blenheims, Catalina flying-boats and Fleet Air Arm Fulmars and Albacores, Some of the Hurricanes operated from an improvised base on Colombo racecourse. Early in March, 22 Mark IIBs of No. 30 Squadron and 20 of No. 261 Squadron had flown in from *Indomitable*. Embarked at Port Sudan on 25 February and destined for the Dutch East Indies the two squadrons had been diverted. On 22 March, 14 aircraft, a mix of Mark Is and IIBs of No. 258 Squadron, arrived from India.

Although the Japanese did not land and attempt to occupy Ceylon, the Pearl Harbour carrier force under Vice-Admiral Nagumo sank the cruisers *Dorsetshire* and *Cornwall* on Easter Sunday, 5 April, and the carrier *Hermes* and Australian destroyer *Vampire* on 9 April. Hermes was 60 miles from Ceylon where the Hurricanes were otherwise engaged. The remainder and major part of Admiral Sir James Somerville's fleet, discounting an imminent attack on Ceylon, had steamed to the Maldives 600 miles distant. In the Easter Sunday raid the Japanese carrier pilots had divided their attentions between the warships and targets on Ceylon where they obliged No. 30 Squadron, operating from the coastal airfield at Ratmalana, to scramble as the bombs were falling. Robbed of the advantage which efficient radar could have provided they were set upon by the carrier Zeros already overhead. Eight Hurricanes were lost. No. 258 Squadron at least managed to make an undisturbed take-off because the Japanese had not rumbled the new role of the racecourse. Even so they fared disastrously in combat, losing nine aircraft for one Zero and five dive-bombers.

On 9 April it was No. 261's turn to offer itself at the port of Trincomalee for what was becoming an almost ritual slaughter. Better served by radar than No. 30 at Ratmalana, 16 aircraft climbed before the raid began but 10 were lost to the Japanese fighter pilots or in crash-landings. Fortunately, an unusually high percentage of pilots survived Hurricane losses in defence of Ceylon.

That Nagumo's carriers now withdrew owed more to their need in the Pacific than to a few outclassed Hurricanes, but they had helped to prevent Ceylon becoming another Japanese walkover.

Paddy field dirt strips, the P 2 jungle clearing, Colombo racecourse . . . the Hurricane operated from some unusual, not to say exotic 'runways' in the Far East, but pilots of No. 17 Squadron, assisting No. 79 Squadron in the defence of Calcutta in late 1942 and early 1943 could justly claim first prize for the unusual. Their runway was the Red Road alongside the Maidan (park) running parallel with Chowringhee, the Bengal capital's celebrated main street. It was as if in 1940 Hurricanes had taken off in defence of London from Piccadilly and alongside Green Park.

The summer and autumn in Calcutta, other than the sharply reversed climatic conditions, had been reminiscent of the phoney war period of the winter of 1939-40 in France. The Japanese, heavily committed in the Pacific and in China, were hard pressed to reinforce Burma after their victories. Little happened, and the Hurricane pilots, learning to live with prickly heat, all the more irritating in the scratchy wicker chairs of their base at the Grand Hotel, became part of the hotel furniture and of Calcutta's ever-increasing military population.

Their lot was briefly enlivened before Christmas 1942, when the enemy launched a series of night raids. Strategically ineffective, the raids nevertheless terrified the city's masses and practised the Grand Hotel pilots who bagged their first raider on 23 December. Shortly, radar-equipped Beaufighters took over and released Hurricanes from defending Calcutta for their more suitable tactical role.

Among the advantages of an ensuing respite — assisted by the wet April to September monsoon season — was the opportunity to reinforce an air force which had taken such hard knocks from Malaya and Singapore to Ceylon and the eastern borders of India. Hurricanes headed the list and from mid-1942 more than 50 were arriving every week.

The availability of 44-gallon tanks improved the range of the fighter-bombers in the squadrons forming or re-forming for ground support, the value of which had been increasingly appreciated since determined efforts in December and the New Year to hit back at the Japanese in Burma.

Hurricanes supported an abortive push to recover Akyab, one of their bases after the fall of Rangoon, a campaign known as the First Arakan — it being in that coastal strip of Burma. Troops of the 14th Indian Division may not have achieved their objectives — they failed in March before Japanese bunkers at Donbaik — but it was not for lack of recce and ground attack support. Several squadrons, particularly No. 615, displayed remarkable versatility, switching from low-level strafing of troops, bridges, railway and river traffic to fighting in defence of their jungle landing strips. There were numerous individual successes, among them the feat of Flight Lieutenant Storey, an Australian pilot of No. 135 Squadron, in destroying three Oscars in the vicinity of Akyab. Wing Commander Carey further enhanced his Hurricane reputation in defence of Chittagong, managing together with Flying Officer R. Grey to trick two Zeros into flying into a hill. Four Hurricane squadrons, often flying a total of 150 sorties a day, went some way towards offsetting reverses on the ground.

For four years the Hurricane had served as a ubiquitous and versatile fighter. It had predominated in the Battle of Britain and in the Middle East and Hurricanes that had survived the sinkings in the convoys were operated in Russia in ever-increasing numbers. At sea it had bridged the gap between Fulmar and Seafire. Now in Burma it was to support Lieutenant-General 'Uncle Bill' Slim's 14th Army in operations which defeated the Japanese before two atomic bombs induced Emperor Hirohito's surrender. The Hurricane was a prime instrument in turning *Defeat into Victory,* to quote the title of Slim's account of the 'Forgotten War'. As Frank Owen, editor-in-chief of *SEAC*, the daily newspaper of South-East Asia Command, wrote contemporarily of the Hurricanes' role at the outset: 'They gripped the Japanese air power and repelled its offensive . . .' Their part in First Arakan has been described. Concurrently, Brigadier Orde Wingate's Chindits began to operate amid the Japanese deep in the Burma jungle. Wingate was a specialist in guerrilla warfare and, it will be recalled, a fellow soldier of Slim in East Africa. He recognised the vulnerability of enemy troops dependent, as he expressed it, 'on a Line of Communication winding through the jungle'. He asked to be supplied 'like Father Christmas down the chimney.' Dakotas made the drops. Hurricanes escorted them. Wingate's introductory Chindit raid was not cost-effective in terms of lives and sickness but, as Dieppe was to *Torch,* and later to D-Day in the West, the venture was to future operations — under, as it happened, the supreme

General Slim used the Hurricane as artillery in Burma. Here IIBs go in at low level against Japanese positions. *(Imperial War Museum)*

command of Admiral Lord Louis Mountbatten, deviser of Dieppe.

In the context of the Hurricane which, if under-armed had performed so resolutely at Dieppe, its support of Wingate underlined the aircraft's continuing indispensability in the Far East as an escort and ground attack fighter-bomber.

But now the monsoon season of 1943 slowed or bogged down operations that summer and, as in the previous year, respite enabled further reinforcement and training for the task ahead. In November, after the rains, Mountbatten arrived as Supreme Allied Commander — 'Supremo' — of the new South-East Asia Command. It characterised the Supremo's style that henceforth monsoon respites, equally beneficial to the enemy, were out. Within days Mountbatten opened his rounds of visits and told Hurricane squadrons, among others, 'We are not going to quit fighting when the monsoon comes, like drawing stumps at a cricket match when it rains . . . The Japs don't expect us to fight on. They will be surprised and caught on the wrong foot.' Later he confirmed in orders: 'We shall march, fight and fly through the monsoon.' Frank Owen commented: 'Flying around the front himself in the monsoon months he must have sometimes wondered why he ever thought of this idea.'

At Christmas 1943, the next monsoon was a distant menace but the arrival of Spitfire 5Cs, all too rare east of Suez, to re-equip Nos 136, 607, and 615 Squadrons was enough of a hint that serious business lay ahead. Yet the Hurricane, nearing the end of its first-line career, still had much to offer. Burma would

Inspection of a wing after the attack reveals the damage. *(Imperial War Museum)*

provide the stormy backdrop for the last act, a virtuoso performance by IIBs, IICs, IIDs and Mark IV fighter-bombers.

Before moving forward with the 14th Army and the Hurricane squadrons which supported its thrust to defeat the Japanese in Burma after the 1944 monsoon, a pause to record that American GIs had also come to welcome the assistance of the British fighter aircraft. In mid-May on the northern front Merrill's Marauders, part of General 'Vinegar' Joe Stilwell's mostly Chinese force, under the United States Brigadier-General F. D. Merrill, had endured a long and arduous march to capture a valuable airfield near Myitkyina. Ground attack Hurricanes supported them.

Inevitably, an account of the career of one type of aircraft will give an impression of predominance in campaigns in which it served. In Burma, as Wingate had recognised early on, distances and the terrain bestowed exceptional responsibility on the RAF and the Indian Air Force as it also received Hurricanes. It would, however, distort the picture not to credit the indispensable effort of the US Air Force, centred on its magnificent transport contribution. Nevertheless, because mountains, forest and jungle limited heavy artillery and armour, Hurricane fighter cover, recce, bomber and transport escort, and ground attack operations, were the sharp end of an offensive in which air superiority was the decisive element. Crucial engagements of 1944 and 1945 and the Hurricane's part in them bear this out.

Early in 1944 military moves by each side produced several such instances. In the south, as part of a fresh attempt to recover the Arakan, part of the 7th Indian Division was cut off and an assortment of staff officers and clerks held out at Sinzweya until relieved in what became known as the 'Admin Box'. Hurricanes enabled their rescue by escorting Dakota supply drops and supporting the desperate struggle on the ground with low-level attacks. The Arakan drive had been intended as a preliminary diversion for moves in the north but, surprising Slim, the Japanese took the initiative. Proclaiming a 'March on Delhi' — more a propaganda slogan than an Imperial directive — they broke into India on the Imphal plain where in 29 March Squadron Leader Arjan Singh in a Hurricane of No. 1 Squadron, Indian Air Force, saw them coming. The reaction of the Indian squadron and Nos 28, 34 and 42 Squadrons, delayed a deteriorating situation.

Nevertheless, by 6 April 1944, the Japanese, establishing themselves on a vital hill, posed a threat to the airfield at Palel south of Imphal. Hurribombers, hurling themselves at the enemy at tree-top height, swayed a ferocious battle in favour of British and Indian troops. The resolve with which pilots pressed home attacks, particularly those of No. 42 Squadron's Mark IV fighter-bombers, was steeled by their fears for Palel whence the Hurricanes operated from shelters dug into a hillside.

Further north at Kohima on the road linking Imphal with the 14th Army's base at Dimapur a hard — at times hand-to-hand — fight developed. Here, Hurribombers of Nos 11, 34, 42 and 113 Squadrons, belonging to the former Northolt station commander Vincent's No. 221 Group, harried the enemy until relief was at hand between 18 and 20 April.

To the south, the Imphal fighting continued and, true to the Supremo's insistence, the coming of the monsoon failed to ground the Hurricanes. 'Over Imphal,' Frank Owen reported, 'the weather did its worst.' Dust at times restricted pilots' visibility to less than a mile before giving way to the monsoon's sheets of rain. Enormous banks of cumulo-nimbus cloud towered to 30,000 feet. Dakotas and heavy bombers were hurled into spins or tossed to heights at which aircrew suffered loss of oxygen. The smaller, lighter Hurricanes sought to operate below the 1,000 feet cloud level, their pilots regarding the monsoon as more dangerous than encounters with enemy aircraft. Sometimes it beat them to a target, as when the rains destroyed a bridge before the Hurricanes arrived for a low-level attack. In remaining operational under such adverse conditions British and Indian Hurricane squadrons enabled an official Despatch to state drily: 'The enemy's efforts to deploy in the Imphal plain in May 1944, were decisively defeated by Hurricane attacks at short intervals on any concentration reported by ground troops through our Army Support Control operating at a high standard of efficiency.'

Co-operation between army and air force, so refined in the desert between Montgomery and Coningham, was similarly effective in Burma. As the Hurricane had helped to spearhead the advance from El Alamein and beyond the Mareth Line, so it also hastened Slim's victory. Co-operation extended far beyond pinpoint bombing and strafing enemy positions obstructing advance. It gratified Slim that air force officers, sometimes Hurricane pilots, adopted the practice of accompanying troops and observing at close hand targets of a forthcoming raid. He wrote: 'Talked-in by air force officers with the forward troops, our fighters would place their cannon shells and rockets within a hundred yards of our men, and by dummy runs keep down the enemy's heads for the last infantry rush.'

Such precision attacks were in addition to routine sorties in search of Japanese positions. Somewhat akin to the activities of taxis plying for hire, such operations were designated 'Cab Rank'.

Between them, Slim's troops, advancing from Kohima to Imphal, and the air force, primarily Hurricane squadrons, defeated Mutagachi's 15th Army. Thereafter, the pursuit of the Japanese continued through the rains of the summer of 1944 and into the Kabaw Valley, otherwise known as the Valley of Death, a malarial trap. However, the Hurricanes got the better of the mosquito. Smoke-laying canisters were loaded with DDT and the aircraft sanitised the road of advance. Another arm of Slim's drive south followed the Tiddim Road and here too Hurricane squadrons were intimately involved, bombing and strafing the way forward for the troops, contending not only with the enemy but also with the monsoon.

A Hurricane IIc refuelling somewhere in India. Believed to be from No. 67 Squadron, RAF based at Alipore/Amarada Road, late 1943/early 1944. *(Paddy Porter Collection)*

As they ascended the horrific seven-mile 'Chocolate Staircase' before Tiddim, with its 38 hairpin bends, the men of the 'Forgotten Army' blessed No. 221 Group's pilots helping them up and through this winding mudbath. Even without the mud the Chocolate Staircase was so-named because 'viewed from below', as Frank Owen described it at the time, 'the short-terraced lengths as they march upward appear as a series of golden brown steps carved out of the purple jungle'.

It staggered the Japanese that ground and air operations continued with such intensity during the monsoon and they admired the readiness of Hurricane squadrons to conduct routine sorties through the supposedly unflyable.

Slim, never in doubt about their contribution, was to record: 'Throughout the whole of this monsoon the fighters of Air Marshal Vincent's 221 Group flew over our troops every single day. I do not think such devotion has ever been equalled'. For their part the pilots were modest about their achievements, conscious always of the real privations of the 14th Army. A flight lieutenant noted: 'It is the proud boast of the pilots that they have never failed to give prompt aid when called upon by their comrades fighting on the ground . . . Today the army has come to look upon the Hurribomber as an extremely adaptable artillery arm, hitting the enemy at long range or within a few yards of the British front line, whichever hurt him most'.

With the lifting of the rains the worst of the terrain lay behind the troops and their supporting Hurricanes. The road to Mandalay and onward to Rangoon promised the easier passage of the plain, though Japanese readiness to fight to the death assured rough going on the ground and in the air alike. There was, however, one important consolation for the Hurricane squadrons. The advance enabled them to move their bases into Burma and on 2 November 1944 No. 11 Squadron was operating from Tamu in the Valley of Death.

The Axis defeated in North Africa, Malta's siege raised, the Allied 6 June invasion of Normandy over, more attention and expertise were available to the Forgotten Front. Park's arrival towards the end of February 1945, to command Mountbatten's air arm, and the fact that a pilot of the distinction of the bomber and Pathfinder VC, Group Captain Leonard Cheshire, should be flying a Hurricane recce over Akyab symbolised the recognition now accorded to South-East Asia Command. Leigh-Mallory, whose No. 12 Group had not always protected Park's No. 11 Group airfields as conscientiously as might have been expected, and first choice for the SEAC appointment, had been killed on the way out. Some saw the justice in Park, who had sent up the Hurricane so sparingly in the early part of the Battle of Britain, receiving the satisfaction of overseeing its success in Burma before bowing out to the Spitfire and Thunderbolt.

Park and some of his pilots of 1940 had come a long way on the humped back of the Hurricane. For example, Frank Carey, the former aircraft apprentice was now a Group Captain and head of the Gunnery and Tactics School at Calcutta. Pilots over Burma were credited with hearing his voice in combat, so compelling were his lectures.

During the remainder of the campaign the RAF further refined its close support of ground forces, such Hurricanes as had not been replaced participating decisively. The resolve of Nos 34, 42, 60 and 113 Squadrons, and also of the bombers, in the reduction of strongly fortified positions at Gangaw far south of the Valley of Death, moved Slim to credit their capture to the airmen.

Nor was Uncle Bill thinking only of the pilots. Recognising that Hurricane operations depended first on groundcrew, Slim paid tribute to 'the mechanics stripped to the waist who laboured in the sun by day and the glare of headlights by night to service the planes'. He recognised the dedication with which 'they identified themselves utterly with the troops ahead, having the pride and bearing of fighting men, for they were one with them'. Wherever he went, especially during the critical crossing of the Irrawaddy, the 14th Army commander heard praise of the

Hurricanes, some of whose pilots were flying five or six sorties a day; pressures reminiscent to Park because they were comparable to those of August and September 1940, and even harder on the machine on account of terrain and climate. Proudly, Park wrote: 'The armies advanced on the wings of the air force;' and while, of course the Hurricane's contribution was uppermost in his mind, he embraced the entire air effort in that appraisal. 'Strike. Support. Supply. Strangle', was the war-cry of the Allied squadrons.

Generally, Burma was not a tank war. Mountains, jungle and monsoon inhibited armour and, given transport problems, there was not all that much around. However, fearful of the consequences of the establishment of a 14th Army bridgehead on their side of the Irrawaddy, the Japanese had scraped together a few tanks. This much was known, but just how the tanks were winkled out and destroyed was the highlight on 17 February of Hurricane support of the crossing and of the bridgehead at Myinmu; a classic example of co-operation between army and air force, Hurricanes flying from jungle air strips within eight miles of the Irrawaddy.

Searching carefully, Flight Lieutenants Farquharson and Ballard of No. 20 Squadron saw tracks but no armour. Odd, they thought, until they rumbled a camouflaged hut. A call to the squadron summoned reinforcement and in went the tin-openers, ripping off hut roofs and blazing 40 mm cannon shells at Japanese tanks within. Twelve were destroyed. The delighted troops congratulated the squadron: 'Nippon Hardware Corporation has gone bust . . . Tanks, repeat tanks, a million.'

Closing on Rangoon in their push south from Pegu and also on the Prome Road, troops were disappointed to learn that the capital had been re-occupied from the sea on 3 May. But soldiers and the airmen who had helped to push the enemy south were thankful because, as they arrived in Rangoon, down came the rain. The monsoon had broken two weeks early, as if to remind the 14th Army and its supporting squadrons how fortunate they were that this campaign was all but over.

As preparations began for Operation *Zipper,* the expected bloody return to Malaya and Singapore, only 11 Hurricane squadrons remained — Nos 17, 10 and 28 and eight of the

The Hurricane reaches the end of the line — and takes its battle honours into retirement as a member of the Battle of Britain Flight. *(British Aerospace)*

Indian Air Force. Nuclear bombs on Hiroshima and Nagasaki, resulting in formal Japanese surrender on 2 September, rendered the Hurricane and, in its way the monsoon, redundant. It was perhaps fitting that Camm's monoplane fighter, which Bulman had flown for the first time at Brooklands on a damp November day in 1935, should complete its Second World War career almost 10 years afterwards — in a downpour.

Duty done, the Hurricane, outclassed as a fighter so early in its career, as Tedder was so ready to remind the air staff, did not linger in RAF squadron service. The tin-openers, No. 6 Squadron, the last RAF squadron to fly Hurricanes after operating in Palestine were re-equipped in Cyprus with Tempests in the New Year of 1947.

If an account of the Hurricane's career is to be reasonably comprehensive it cannot dwell on any single role or location. Nevertheless, some emphasis has been laid here on the beginning and the end of the aircraft's operational life — the Battle of Britain and Burma. Neither Park, formerly of No. 11 Group and thus the Hurricane's principal employer in 1940, nor Slim, commander of the 14th Army, united as it happened in the last act by the accidental death of Leigh-Mallory, were in any doubt about the value of its contribution.

For all this, just as Burma remains the Forgotten Front there was no official 40th anniversary commemoration last year (1985) — the Hurricane, overshadowed by the Spitfire, is in some measure the forgotten fighter.

Possibly the publicity attaching to the Spitfire was pre-ordained by good looks and its vital statistics, an Adonis against a hunchback, and by the disparate characters and careers of Mitchell and Camm: Mitchell, a Schneider Trophy winner and large screen legend, aged only 42 when he died on 11 June 1937, before the flight of the first production Spitfire; Camm, creator of a pedigree of stout biplanes, perhaps more of a decision-maker than a scientist, knighted in 1953, and who died in his 73rd year on 6 March 1973; Camm, who consciously stayed with the thicker, fabric-covered wing for the prototype.

Such factors, its speed and a media fascination for the Spitfire have stationed the Hurricane in its shadow where, doubtless, it will remain. It is hoped, however, that this account will redress some of the balance and recall that without Sopwith, the 100th anniversary of whose birth is due in 1988, Spriggs, Sigrist — and of course Harry Hawker — the Hawker Hurricane could not have happened.

He tested the first Hurricane and now George Bulman flies the "Last of the Many", a IIC completed in August 1944 at Hawkers' King's Langley works. *(Flight)*

Appendix 1

Leading Particulars, Geometric Data and Performance

THE HAWKER F.36/34 HURRICANE PROTOTYPE

The following leading particulars refer to K5083 at the time of its evaluation by the Aeroplane & Armament Experimental Establishment, Martlesham Heath, in February 1936.

POWERPLANT:
Rolls-Royce Merlin C, No. 19. Engine develops 1,025 bhp at 3,000 rpm at 11,000 ft at +6 lb/sq in boost, and 905 bhp at 2,400 rpm at 9,800 ft. Propeller: Watts two-blade right-hand wooden Type Z33. Diameter 11 ft 6 in Weight 96.5 lb. **Note:** Other Merlin Cs were also fitted in K5083, but were rated differently.

GEOMETRIC DATA:
Wing span 40 ft 0 in. Overall length 31 ft 6 in. Maximum height (propeller vertical) 13 ft 6 in.

LOADINGS:
Wing loading at Aircraft Normal Loaded Weight (5,672 lb), 22 lb/sq ft. Power loading (take-off at 5,672 lb), 5·5 lb/bhp.

WEIGHTS:
Aircraft Tare Weight (with 18 gallons of coolant) 4,129 lb. Pilot and parachute 200 lb. Armament ballast 400 lb. Instruments 52 lb. Fuel (107.5 gallons at 7.7 lb/gallon) 828 lb. Oil (7·0 gallons at 9 lb/gallon) 63 lb. *Aircraft Normal Loaded Weight* 5,672 lb.

PERFORMANCE:

(a) **Stalling Speeds** (sea level)
Wheels and flaps up: 70 mph IAS.
Wheels and flaps down: 57 mph IAS.

(b) Airfield Performance (Grass surface)
Take-off ground run, 265 yards; time, 11½ seconds.
Distance to 50 ft, 430 yards.
Landing ground run, using flaps and brakes, 220 yards.
Distance from 50 ft, using flaps and brakes, 475 yards.

THE HAWKER HURRICANE MARK I

The following leading particulars refer to production Hurricane Mark Is fitted with either fabric- or metal-covered wings, and with Watts, Rotol or de Havilland propellers.

POWERPLANT:
(Early aircraft) Rolls-Royce Merlin II. Engine develops 1,030 bhp at 3,000 rpm at 16,250 ft at +6¼ lb/sq in boost, and 990 bhp at 2,600 rpm at 12,250 ft at +6¼ lb/sq in boost. Propeller: Watts two-blade right-hand wooden Type Z38. Diameter 11 ft 3 in Weight 79 lb.

(Late aircraft) Rolls-Royce Merlin III. Engine develops 1,029 bhp at 3,000 rpm at 16,250 ft at +6¾ lb/sq in boost, and 971 bhp at 12,250 ft at +5.9 lb/sq in boost. Propeller: Rotol three-blade constant-speed right-hand Type RMS7. Pitch range 35° Diameter, 10 ft 9 in. Also fitted with de Havilland two-position propeller.

GEOMETRIC DATA:
Wing span 40 ft 0 in. Overall length 31 ft 4 in. Maximum height (Watts propeller, blades vertical) 13 ft 2 in (Rotol propeller, one blade vertical), 12 ft 11½ in.

WING:
Root chord, 8 ft 1 in. Tip chord 3 ft 11¼ in. Gross wing area 258.0 sq ft. Aspect ratio, 6.2. Wing incidence +2°. Dihedral 3·5° on Datum. Sweepback 3° on front spar. Ailerons: Span 7 ft 9 in. Root chord 1 ft 7¼ in. Tip chord 10½ in. Area (both) 19.64 sq ft. Movement 22° up, 21° down. Landing flaps: Centre section span (each) 4 ft 6¾ in. Out-board section span (each) 6 ft 4 in. Chord (constant) 1 ft 2¾ in. Total area 25.11 sq ft. Movement 80° down.

TAIL:
Tailplane: Span 11 ft 0 in. Chord 4 ft 2 in. Area 19·6 sq ft. Incidence 1·5°.

Elevators (including tabs): Span, 11 ft 0 in. Area 13.65 sq ft. Movement 28·5° up, 25·5° down. Elevator tab range 23° up and down.

Fin and rudder: Fin height 3 ft 1⅞ in. Maximum fin chord 3 ft 7 in. Fin area 8·82 sq ft. Rudder height (early aircraft), 5 ft 11¼ in (modified aircraft), 5 ft 5⅜ in. Rudder area (early aircraft 12·68 sq ft (modified aircraft) 13·06 sq ft. Rudder movement 28° left and right.

UNDERCARRIAGE:
Inwards retracting mainwheels and fixed tailwheel. Track 7 ft 7 in. Main wheels 800 mm x 10 inch, on Vickers oleo pneumatic legs with Dunlop pneumatic brakes. Ground angle 10° 19′. Airscrew ground clearance (static, thrust line horizontal), 11 in.

LOADINGS:
Wing loading at Aircraft Normal Loaded Weight (6,218 lb), 24·1 lb/sq ft. Power loading (take-off at 6,218 lb) 6·0 lb/bhp.

DATUM POINT:
21·2 inches below thrust line and 28 inches forward of the wing leading edge extended to centreline.

CENTRE OF GRAVITY:
C.G. at Normal Loaded Weight 57·3 inches aft of Datum point. C.G. limits, 54·9—58·7 inches aft of Datum point.

STRUCTURE:
Fuselage. Braced structure of steel tubular longerons with steel and duralumin cross tubes; fishplate joints with bolts and tubular rivets; spruce stringers. Metal sheet-covered front fuselage and cockpit, fabric-covered rear fuselage.

Wings. (Late aircraft) Centresection of two high tensile steel spars, braced as Warren truss with girders and diagonal tubes. Outer wings: two tapered dumb-bell spars, braced as Warren truss and metal covered. Early aircraft had fabric-covered wings. Aileron (all production machines) were fabric-covered.

WEIGHTS:

(a) **Merlin II Version.** Aircraft Tare Weight (with 18 gallons of coolant) 4,743 lb. Pilot and parachute 200 lb. 8 Browning guns and accessories 212 lb. Case and link chutes 9 lb. Ammunition and boxes (2,660 rounds) 202 lb. Instruments and gunsight 79·5 lb. G.45 camera 9 lb. Pyrotechnics 48·5 lb. Oxygen equipment 15 lb. First Aid 3 lb. Radio 57 lb. Fuel (77 gallons at 7·5 lb/gallon) 577 lb. Oil (7·0 gallons at 9 lb/gallon) 63 lb. *Aircraft Normal Loaded Weight* 6,218 lb.

(b) **Merlin III Version.** Aircraft Tare Weight (with 18 gallons of coolant), 4,982 lb with Rotol propeller; 5,034 lb with D.H. 2-position propeller. Equipment and fuel as (a) above. *Aircraft Normal Loaded Weight* 6,447 lb with Rotol propeller; 6,499 lb with D.H. 2-position propeller.

(c) **Mark I Overload.** (Tropical aircraft, Rotol propeller, two 44-gallon fixed ferry tanks and full ammunition). *Aircraft Overload Weight* 7,490lb.

(d) **Sea Hurricanes.** Normal Loaded Weights. Mk. IA 6,589 lb. Mk. IB 7,410 lb. Mk. IC 7,605 lb. Tropical Mk. IC, 8,210 lb.

PERFORMANCE:

(a) **Range** (aircraft flying at optimum range speed, 190 mph TAS, mean flying weight 5,830 lb, mean ICAN altitude 15,000 feet).
Mk. I (Merlin II with wooden propeller), 525 statute miles maximum or 440 miles with 20 minute reserve.

Mk. I (Merlin III with Rotol propeller), 505 statute miles maximum or 425 miles with 20 minute reserve.
Mk. I (tropical, Merlin III with Rotol propeller), 460 statute miles maximum or 380 miles with 20 minute reserve.
Mk. I (tropical, Merlin III with Rotol propeller and two 44-gallon ferry tanks), 935 statute miles maximum or 860 miles with 20 minute reserve.

(b) **Stalling Speeds** (sea level)
Clean aircraft, wheels and flaps up: 72-80 mph IAS.
Clean aircraft, wheels and flaps down: 60-75 mph IAS.

(c) **Aerobatics.** The following are the recommended minimum speeds:
270 mph IAS for a loop,
210 mph IAS for a roll,
290 mph IAS for a half roll off a loop and 300 mph IAS for an upward roll.

(d) **Service Ceiling**
Mark I with Merlin II and wooden propeller, 33,400 feet.
Mark I with Merlin III and Rotol propeller, 34,200 feet.
Mark I (tropical) with Merlin III and Rotol propeller, 32,100 feet.

(e) **Airfield Performance** (Grass surface)
Take-off ground run (wooden propeller), 370 yards.
Distance to 50 ft (wooden propeller), 580 yards.
Take-off ground run (Rotol propeller), 350 yards.
Distance to 50 ft (Rotol propeller), 540 yards.
Landing ground run using brakes (either propeller), 205 yards.
Distance from 50 ft using brakes (either propeller 7,420 yards.

THE HAWKER HURRICANE MARK II

The following leading particulars refer to the Hurricane Marks IIA Series 2, IIB, IIC, IID and, unless stated to the contrary, the Hurricane IIA Series 1 and the Sea Hurricane Mark IIC (or "hooked Hurricane II").

POWERPLANT:
Rolls-Royce Merlin XX. Engine develops 1,260 bhp at 3,000 rpm at 11,750 feet in MS gear, and 1,160 bhp at 3,000 rpm at 20,750 feet in S-gear. Sea level take-off power 1,300 bhp at 3,000 rpm. Propeller: Either three-blade Rotol R.S.5/2 with Schwartz blades or Rotol R.S.5/3 with Jablo blades. Gear ratio 0·42. Airscrew diameter 11 ft 3 in.

GEOMETRIC DATA:
Wing span 40 ft 0 in. Overall length 32 ft 2¼ in. Maximum height (one airscrew blade vertical, tailwheel on ground) 13 ft 1in.

WING:
Root chord 8 ft 0¼ in. Tip chord 3 ft 11¼ in. Gross wing area 257·6 sq ft. Aspect ratio 6·2. Wing incidence +2°. Dihedral 3·5° on datum. Sweepback 3° on front spar.

Ailerons: Span 7 ft 8¾ in. Root chord 1 ft 7¼ in. Tip chord 10½ in. Area (each) 9·8 sq ft. Movement 22° up, 21° down. Landing flaps: Centresection span (each) 4 ft 6¾. Outboard section span (each) 6 ft 4 in. Chord (constant) 1 ft 2¾ in. Total area 25·11 sq ft. Movement 80° down.

TAIL:
Tailplane: Span 11 ft 0 in. Chord 4 ft 2½ in. Area 19·8 sq ft. Incidence 1·5°.

Elevators (including tabs): Span 11 ft 0 in. Area 13·65 sq ft. Movement 28·5° up, 25·5° down. Elevator tab range 23° up and down.

Fin and Rudder: Fin height 3 ft 2⅜ in. Maximum fin chord 3 ft 6¾ in. Fin area 8·79 sq ft. Rudder height 6 ft 5½ in. Maximum rudder chord 2 ft 3⅜ in. Rudder area 13·05 sq ft. Rudder movement 28° left and right.

UNDERCARRIAGE:
Track 7 ft 10 ins. Ground angle 10° 19′. Airscrew ground clearance (thrust line horizontal) 11 in. Wing loading at 7,200 lb, 28·0 lb/sq ft.

DATUM POINT:
21·6 inches below thrust line and 30 inches forward of wing leading edge extended to centreline.

CENTRE OF GRAVITY:
C.G. at Tare Weight 9·9 inches above and 55·8 inches aft of Datum Point. C.G. at Normal Loaded Weight 9·45 inches above and 59·5 inches aft of Datum Point. C.G. limits: 57-60 inches aft of Datum Point.

WEIGHTS:

(a) **Mark IIB (Temperate)**—Measured on aircraft Z3067 (14/3/41). Aircraft Tare Weight (with 18 gallons of coolant) 5,467 lb. Pilot and Parachute 200 lb. 12 Browning guns and accessories 318 lb. Case and link chutes 14 lb. Ammunition and boxes (3,990 rounds) 302 lb. Gunsight 17 lb. G.45 camera 9 lb. Pyrotechnics 18 lb. Oxygen equipment 15 lb. First Aid 3 lb. T.R.1133 radio 79 lb. R.3002 radio 24 lb. Fuel (main 69 gallons) 497 lb. Fuel (reserve 28 gallons) 202 lb. Oil (7·5 gallons) 68 lb. *Aircraft Normal Loaded Weight* 7,233 lb.

(b) **Mark IIB (Tropical)**—Measured on aircraft V7480 (23/1/41). Aircraft Tare Weight (with 18 gallons of coolant) 5,594 lb. Pilot and Parachute 200 lb. 12 Browning guns and accessories 295 lb. Case and link chutes 14 lb. Ammunition and boxes (3,900 rounds) 302 lb. Gunsight 18 lb. G.45 camera 9 lb. Pyrotechnics 26 lb. Oxygen equipment 15 lb. First Aid 3 lb. Desert equipment 50 lb. T.R.1133 radio 79 lb. R.3002 radio 24 lb. Fuel (main 69 gallons) 497 lb. Fuel (reserve 28 gallons) 202 lb. Oil (7·5 gallons) 68 lb. *Aircraft Normal Loaded Weight* 7,396 lb.

(Equipped with 44-gallon auxiliary (ferry or combat) drop tanks: Normal Ferry Weight 7,594 lb; Overload Combat Weight 7,896 lb.

(c) **Mark IIC (Temperate)**—Measured on aircraft Z2891 (14/3/41). Aircraft Tare Weight (with 18 gallons of coolant) 5,658 lb. Pilot and Parachute 200 lb. Four 20-mm guns 425 lb. Ammunition boxes and belt feeds (364 rounds) 327 lb. Gunsight 17 lb. G.45 camera 9 lb. Pyrotechnics 18 lb. Oxygen equipment 15 lb. First Aid 3 lb. T.R.1133 radio 79 lb. R.3002 radio 24 lb. Fuel (main 69 gallons) 497 lb. Fuel (reserve 28 gallons) 202 lb. Oil (7·5 gallons) 68 lb. *Aircraft Normal Loaded Weight* 7,544 lb.

(Equipped with 44-gallon auxiliary (ferry or combat) drop tanks: Normal Ferry Weight 7,619 lb; Overload Combat Weight 8,044 lb).

(d) **Mark IIC (Tropical)**—Aircraft Tare Weight 5,785 lb. *Aircraft Normal Loaded Weight* 7,707 lb.

(Equipped with 44-gallon auxiliary (ferry or combat) drop tanks: Normal Ferry Weight 7,782 lb. Overload Combat Weight 8,207 lb.

(e) **Mark IID (Tropical)**—Measured on aircraft BP173/G (28/7/42). Aircraft Tare Weight (with 18 gallons of coolant) 5,550 lb. Pilot and Parachute 200 lb. Two Vickers "S" 40-mm guns and two Browning guns 893 lb. Ammunition (660 rounds of ·303-in and 30 rounds of 40-mm) 230 lb. Gunsight (gyro) 54 lb. G.45 camera 9 lb. Pyrotechnics 26 lb. Oxygen equipment 15 lb. First Aid 3 lb. T.R.1133 radio 79 lb. R.3002 radio 24 lb. Fuel (main 69 gallons) 497 lb. Fuel (reserve 28 gallons) 202 lb. Oil (7·5 gallons) 68 lb. *Aircraft Normal Loaded Weight* 7,850 lb.

(f) **Sea Hurricane Mark IIC (Temperate)**—Aircraft Tare Weight (with 18 gallons of coolant) 5,738 lb. Pilot and Parachute 200 lb. Four 20-mm guns 425 lb. Ammunition boxes and belt feeds (364 rounds) 327 lb. Gunsight (gyro) 54 lb. Oxygen equipment 15 lb. Naval radio 92 lb. Fuel (main 69 gallons) 497 lb. Fuel (reserve) 28 gallons) 202 lb. Oil (7·5 gallons) 68 lb. *Aircraft Normal Loaded Weight* 7,618 lb. (Tropical Aircraft Loaded Weight 8,278 lb).

(g) **Mark II Maximum Ferry Overload Weight**—(Tropical Mark IIC, carrying back and front armour, full ammunition and two 90-gallon ferry tanks) 9,145 lb.

PERFORMANCE:

(a) **Range** (aircraft flying at optimum range speeds, 16,000 feet mean I.C.A.N. altitude, no fuel reserves).

	Optimum Range Speed T.A.S. (m.p.h.)	*Range (statute miles)*		
		Clean Aircraft	*Two 44-Gallon Tanks*	*Two 90-Gallon Tanks*
Mark IIA	177	468	946	1,090
Mark IIA (Trop.)	185	440	900	1,015
Mark IIB	177	465	935	1,080
Mark IIB (Trop.)	185	436	880	1,010
Mark IIC	178	460	920	1,086
Mark IIC (Trop.)	188	426	908	1,022
Mark IID	186	420	895	1,020
Mark IID (Trop.)	192	404	870	995
Sea Hurricane IIC	180	452	908	1,062
Ditto (Trop.)	190	415	895	998

(b) **Stalling Speeds** (sea level)
Clean aircraft, wheels and flaps up, 75-85 mph I.A.S.
Aircraft with stores, wheels and flaps up 80-90 mph I.A.S.
Clean aircraft, wheels and flaps down, 60-75 mph I.A.S.
Aircraft with stores, wheels and flaps down 65-80 mph I.A.S.
At the stall one wing tends to drop sharply, with flaps either up or down.

(c) **Fuel Consumption** Weak Mixture—values in Gallons/Hour.

Boost lb/sq in	*MS Gear 8,000–20,000 feet*			*S Gear 14,000–30,000 feet*		
	2,650 rpm	*2,300 rpm*	*2,000 rpm*	*2,650 rpm*	*2,300 rpm*	*2,000 rpm*
+4	56	50	46	57	51	47
+2	52	46	42	53	47	43
0	47	42	38	48	43	39
—2	42	37	34	43	39	35
—4	37	33	30	38	34	31

Rich Mixture—values in Gallons/Hour.

Boost lb/sq in	*Engine speed rpm*	*Fuel Consumption gallons/hour*
+12	3,000	115
+ 9	3,000	100
+ 9	2,850	95
+ 7	2,650	80

(d) **Aerobatics.** The following are the recommended minimum speeds,
28 mph I.A.S. for a loop,
220 mph I.A.S. for a roll,
300 mph I.A.S. for a half roll off loop and 300 mph I.A.S. for an upward roll.

(e) **Service Ceiling** (rate of climb, 100 ft/min).
Mark IIA 36,300 feet; Mark IIB 36,000 feet; Mark IIB (tropical) 33,600 feet; Mark IIC 35,600 feet; Mark IIC (tropical) 33,200 feet; Mark IID (tropical) 29,100 feet.

THE PERSIAN HURRICANE MARK IIC TWO-SEAT FIGHTER TRAINER

POWERPLANT:

Rolls-Royce Merlin 22. Engine develops 1,435 bhp at 3,000 rpm at 11,000 feet at +16 lb/sq in boost in S-Gear, and 1,460 bhp at 3,000 rpm at 6,250 feet at +14 lb/sq in boost in M-Gear; take-off power 1,390 bhp at 3,000 rpm at +14 lb/sq in boost. Propeller three-blade Rotol R.S.5/11.

WEIGHTS:

Aircraft Tare Weight 5,505 lb. Crew (two) and Parachute 400 lb. Guns, ammunition, boxes and feeds 810 lb. Service equipment 645 lb. Fuel (total 97 gallons) 699 lb. Oil (9 gallons) 81 lb. *Aircraft Normal Loaded Weight* 8,140 lb.

PERFORMANCE:

(Standard atmospheric conditions)
Maximum speed: 320 mph T.A.S. at 21,500 feet.
Normal Cruising speed: 275 mph T.A.S. at 20,000 feet.
Stalling speed, wheels and flaps down: 70 mph I.A.S.
Normal range: 640 statute miles at optimum range speed.
Range with 44-gallon tanks: 1,100 statute miles.
Initial rate of climb: 2,780 feet/minute.
Time to 20,000 feet 10·0 minutes.
Service Ceiling (rate of climb, 100 ft/min): 36,000 feet.
Take-off ground run: 250 yards in 5 kt headwind.

THE HAWKER HURRICANE MARK IV

The Mark IV Hurricane as similar in most respects to the Mark IIC, being distributed in the same production line and using the same assembly jigs. The provision of universal "low attack" wings and attachment points, together with additional armour protection, resulted in greater weights and therefore reduced performance figures. The following figures are therefore quoted for the Hurricane IV with two Vickers 40-mm anti-tank guns for ease of comparison with the Hurricane IID.

WEIGHTS:

Mark IV (Tropical)—Measured on aircraft KZ198. Aircraft Tare Weight (with 18 gallons of coolant) 6,150 lb. Pilot and Parachute 200 lb. Two Vickers "S" 40-mm guns and two Browning guns 905 lb. Ammunition 230 lb. Equipment 210 lb. Fuel (main 69 gallons) 497 lb. Fuel (reserve 28 gallons) 202 lb. Oil (7·5 gallons) 68 lb. *Aircraft Normal Loaded Weight* 8,462 lb.

Appendix 2

Notes on Individual Aircraft, Production Details and Service Allocation

THE HAWKER F.36/34 HURRICANE PROTOTYPE:

One prototype K5083, developed and designed to Air Ministry Specification F.36/34 and ordered under Contract No. 357483/34. Powered by Rolls-Royce Merlin 'C', first flown on 6 November 1935 by Flt. Lt. P. W. S. Bulman at Brooklands. Armament of eight Browning guns not fitted until 1937. Trials at Brooklands, Martlesham Heath and Farnborough 1935-37.

THE HAWKER HURRICANE MARK I (HAWKER-BUILT):

First production batch of 600 aircraft, L1547-L2146, developed to Production Specification 15/36, and ordered under Contract No. 527112/36, dated 3 June 1936. First flight by L1547, 12 October 1937. Deliveries commenced (to No. 111 (Fighter) Squadron, Northolt) 15 December 1937; deliveries of batch completed 6 October 1939. Average rate of production, about one aircraft per day. Rolls-Royce Merlin II engines and Watts wooden propellers fitted initially; many later replaced by Merlin IIIs and Rotol or de Havilland variable pitch propellers. Eight ·303-in Browning gun armament. Fabric-covered wings fitted to almost all aircraft, but later aircraft were sometimes repaired using metal stressed-skin wings.

No. 1 (F) Squadron, Vassincourt, France, 10/39:
L1671, L1673, L1676-L1682 (shot down enemy aircraft, 2/4/40), L1686-L1694, L1842-L1844, L1855, L1905, L1925, L1927, L1959-L1979 (initial issue), L2061 (replacement).

No. 3 (F) Squadron, Biggin Hill, 1938-39:
L1565-L1573 (initial issue), L1576-L1580, L1582, L1586-L1588, L1631, L1917, L1923, L1924, L1926, L1928 (crashed during Squadron's first night flying, 29/8/39; pilot safe), L1932-L1940, L1962, L1973.

No. 29 (F) Squadron:
L2080-L2084, L2086-L2091, L2092 (damaged by enemy action and repaired by Rollasons, 1940).

No. 32 (F) Squadron, Biggin Hill, 2/40:
L1596, L1647, L1655, L1658-L1668 (initial issue), L1670, L1672, L1674, L1675, L1835, L1836, L1841, L1972, L2049, L2050, L2063.

No. 43 (F) Squadron:
L1704, L1723, L1725-L1739 (initial issue), L1744, L1824, L1825, L1847, L1849, L1955, L2066 (replacement).

No. 46 (F) Squadron, Digby, 9/39:
L1791-L1797, L1801-L1807, L1813-L1817 (initial issue), L1853 (P/O McGregor shot down Ju 88 over Tjelbotn, Norway, 28/5/40), L1854, L1857, L1892, L2071.

No. 56 (F) Squadron, 1938-1939:
L1553, L1584, L1590-L1595, L1597-L1603, L1605, L1606 (later G-AFKX, see Trials Aircraft below), L1607-L1611 (initial issue); L1645, L1742 (replacements); L1828-L1830, L1972, L1980-L1992, L1998-L2006 (second issue).

No. 73 (F) Squadron, Caen, France, 9/39:
L1633, L1657, L1826, L1827, L1864; Le Mans, 6/40: L2047, L2076.

No. 74 (F) Squadron, temporary charge, 1939:
L1581.

No. 79 (F) Squadron, Biggin Hill, 1939, and Merville, France, 1940:
L1697-L1701, L1705, L1707 (Paris Aero Show 1938), L1709, L1712, L1714--L1716, L1718-L1722, L1781, L1782, L1784, L1845, L1846, L2140.

No. 85 (F) Squadron, Air Component, France, 1939:
L1604, L1632, L1634-L1637, L1639-L1644, L1648-L1651, L1653, L1656, L1765, L1773-L1775, L1778, L1779, L1833, L1834.

No. 87 (F) Squadron:
L1612-L1630, L1646, L1743, L1744, L1776, L1777, L1831, L1832.

No. 111 (F) Squadron, Northolt, 1938:
L1548-L1561, L1563, L1564: Northolt, 1939: L1581, L1583, L1584, L1589, L1607 (comparative evaluation with Boulton & Paul Defiant, October 1939), L1638, L1654, L1694, L1720, L1730, L1740, L1741, L1748, L1774, L1820, L1821, L1822 (F/O Ferris shot down four Bf 110s (confirmed), 18/5/40, near Dunkirk), L1823 (last Hurricane with Watts wooden propeller disposed of by Squadron, 1/7/40), L1830 (crashed, 24/4/40), L1973 (F/O Dutton destroyed He 111K 8/3/40), L2001, L2051 (shot down by Bf 109E, 18/5/40).

No. 151 (F) Squadron, 1940:
L1724, L1745-L1749, L1753-L1758, L1764, L1766-L1769, L1798, L1799, L1850.

No. 213 (F) Squadron, Wittering, 1940:
L1770-L1772, L1780, L1782-L1790, L1800, L1808-L1812, L1818, L1819, L1851, L1852, L2060, L2062.

No. 501 Squadron, AAF, Tangmere, 1/40:
L1659, L1636, L1866-L1872, L1874-L1876, L1910, L1911, L1949, L1953, L2037, L2038, L2039, L2045, L2046, L2052-L2056, L2124.

No. 504 Squadron, Debden and Martlesham Heath, 4/40:
L1639, L1836, L1911-L1913, L1915, L1916, L1942-L1948, L1950-L1952, L1954, L1956, L1957; Filton and Exeter 12/40: L1583 (with L1913, intercepted raid on London 15/9/40.

No. 605 Squadron, AAF, Tangmere, 1/40:
L2012-L2014, L2018, L2058, L2059, L2061; Drem, 8/40: L2103, L2117, L2118, L2119-L2122.

No. 610 Squadron, AAF:
L2115, L2117-L2123.

No. 616 Squadron, AAF:
L2098, L2101, L2103.

Other RAF Flying Units:
L1683, L1684 (Northolt Stn. Flt.); L17421 (No. 5 (P) AFU, 1942); L1747 (No. 9 (P) AFU 1942); L1873 (No. 23 (Training) Group for Central Flying School, Upavon); L1895-L1897 (Advanced Training Pool, Andover, April 1939); L2006-L2011 (No.11 Group, Andover); L2098 (No. 55 OCU, Aston Down, 11/40); L1910, L2006 (No. 56 OTU, Sutton Bridge 11/40), L2057 (No. 71 OTU); L2064, L2069, L2070, L2072-L2075 (No. 11 Group Pool, Andover, 8/39).

Delivered into Reserve with Maintenance Units: L1652 (crashed, 1938, killing John Hindmarsh) Hawker Test Pilot; aircraft to No. 4 Disposal MU); L1596 (also to No. 4 MU); No. 5 MU, Kemble: L1856, L2037-L2039, L2045, L2046, L2051, L2065, L2067, L2068, L2116, L2141-L2143, L2145; No. 8 MU: L1685, L1889, L1891, L1892, L1894, L1898-L1916, L1921, L1922, L1925, L1927, L1929-L1931; No. 10 MU, Little Rissington: L2015-L2017, L2019, L2024, L2025, L2027-L2030, L2048 (later to Poland; see below); No. 20 MU: L2146; No. 27 MU L2047, L2049, L2050, L2057; Packing Depot, Sealand: L1585.

Aircraft for South Africa; delivered via No. 36 MU, 11/38:
L1708, L1710, L1711.

Aircraft for Yugoslavia; deliveries commenced 15/12/38. (Yugoslavian nos. in brackets):
L1751 (1-205), L1752 (2-206), L1837 (3-291), L1838 (4-292), L1839 (5-293), L1840 (6-294), L1858 (7-312), L1859 (8-313), L1860 (9-314), L1861 (10-315), L1862 (11-316), L1863 (11-316), L1863 (12-317). Total 12 aircraft.

Aircraft for Rumania; deliveries commenced 28/8/39:
L2077, L2078, L2085, L2093-L2097, L2104, L2112-L2114. Total 12 aircraft.

Aircraft for Canada; deliveries commenced, 10/38. (RCAF nos. in brackets):
L1759 (310), L1760 (311), L1761 (312), L1762 (313), L1763 (314), L1878 (315), L1879 (316), L1880 (317), L1881 (318), L1882 (319), L1883 (320), L1884 (312; returned to UK and developed into Hillson FH40 Slip-wing Hurricane), L1885 (322), L1886 (323), L1887 (324), L1888 (325), L1890 (326), L2021 (327), L2022 (328), L2023 (329), L1848 delivered as pattern aircraft, 2/3/39; L2144 delivered as sample material for proposed Canadian production, 28/9/39. Total 22 aircraft.

Aircraft for Belgium; deliveries commenced, 4/39. (Belgian nos. brackets):
L1918 (1), L1919 (2), L1920 (3), L1993 (4), L1994 (5), L1995 (6), L1996 (7), L1997 (8), L2040 (9), L2041 (10), L2042 (11), L2043 (12), L2044 (13), L2105 (14), L2106 (15), L2107 (16), L2108 (17), L2109 (18), L2110 (19), L2111 (20). Total of 20 aircraft exported, of which 15 reached operational service. At least two other (licence-built) aircraft were completed (under Contract No. B.655029/37) before German invasion of 1940.

Aircraft for Poland.
One aircraft, L2048, shipped 24/7/39.

Aircraft for Persia.
One aircraft, L2079 (252), shipped 1939.

Aircraft for Turkey:
Fifteen machines L2125-L2139; deliveries commenced 14/9/39; completed (6/10/39).

Exhibition aircraft:
L1575 (Glasgow Exhibition, 5/38); L1941 (Nottingham Exhibition, 5/39); L1592 (exhibited in Science Museum from 1955; reconditioned by HAL, 1961).

Trials aircraft:
L1547 (performance and handling trials HAL); L1562, L1574 (trials, Martlesham Heath 1939); L1582 (experimental colour schemes, HAL); L1606 (from No. 56 Squadron to HAL for modification and re-registration as G-AFKX); L1638 (hydraulic trials, HAL); L1669 (first tropical aircraft; to Rolls-Royce, thence to Middle East for trials); L1695 (A & AEE propeller trials); L1696 (A & AEE slotted wing trials) L1702 (RAE trials); L1713 (trials with RAE 1938, and Rolls-Royce 1939); L1717 (RAE trials); L1750 (trials with extra armour and two 20-mm guns under wings); L1856 (Merlin XII test bed; later to No. 5 MU as standard); L1887 (first with metal stressed skin wings).

THE HAWKER HURRICANE MARK I (HAWKER-BUILT)

First production batch of 300 aircraft built by Hawker Aircraft Ltd., Kingston and Brooklands, under Contract No. 751458/38, during 1939-40. First 80 aircraft built with fabric-covered wings (some of these were later repaired using metal wings); all remainder were built with metal wings. Rolls-Royce Merlin III engines driving Rotol or de Havilland variable-pitch propellers. *N2318-N2367, N2380-N2409, N2422-N2441, N2453-N2502, N2520-N2559, N2582-N2631, N2645-N2729. Deliveries commenced 29/9/39; completed 1/5/40. Average rate of production, about two aircraft per day.*

No. 1 (F) Squadron, Vassincourt, France, 3/40:
N2326, N2334, N2358, N2380-N2382, N2386.

No. 32 (F) Squadron, Biggin Hill, 1940:
N2406 (P/O Blackford destroyed Bf 109E, 22/5/40), N2409, N2459 (P/O Grice destroyed Bf 109E, 22/5/40), N2460, N2461 (F/L Crossley destroyed Bf 109E), 22/5/40, and another 20/7/40), N2462-N2464, N2524, N2527 (P/O Daw destroyed Bf 109E 22/5/40), N2532 (S/L Worrall damaged 3 Bf 109Es 20/7/40), N2582 (P/O Humpherson destroyed Bf 109E), 22/5/40), N2583, N2657, N2670 (shot down over North Foreland, 20/7/40), N2727.

No. 43 (F) Squadron, Wick, 1940:
N2618.

No. 46 (F) Squadron, Bardufoss, Norway, 1940:
N2543, N2633.

No. 56 (F) Squadron, 1940:
N2386, N2398, N2399, N2400, N2402, N2423, N2428-N2432, N2434, N2437, N2439-N2441, N2468, N2478-N2480, N2522, N2523, N2550, N2553, N2617, N2659, N2664-N2668, N2712.

No. 79 (F) Squadron, 1940:
N2671.

No. 111 (F) Squadron, Drem and Wick, 1939-40:
N2340 (S/L H. Broadhurst, DFC, AFC, destroyed He 111K 29/11/39; first victory of the Squadron), N2482, N2549.

No. 145 (F) Squadron, 1940:
N2583, N2601, N2604, N2610, N2614, N2700, N2701, N2711, N2713.

No. 208 (AC) Squadron, El Khanka, Egypt, 10/41:
N2626.

No. 249 (F) Squadron:
N2440 (in action over Brooklands 4/9/40).

No. 253 (F) Squadron:
N2588 (in action over Brooklands 4/9/40).

No. 274 (F) Squadron, Middle East 1940:
N2498, N2499, N2624 (semi-tropicalised Mark I's).

No. 501 Squadron, AAF, France 1940:
N2329, N2549.

No. 504 Squadron, AAF, Martlesham Heath, 4/40:
N2471, N2705; Filton and Exeter 12/40: N2481, N2669.

No. 605 Squadron, AAF Tangmere, 1/40:
N2349, N2352.

Aircraft shipped to Poland, 9/39, but later diverted to the Middle East:
N2322-N2324, N2327, N2349, N2392-N2395.

Aircraft for Yugoslavia:
12 aircraft shipped during February and March 1940: N2718-N2729.

Aircraft damaged in action, 1940, and repaired by Rollasons:
N2328, N2427, N2586, N2590, N2704.

No. 56 OTU, 11/40:
N2365, N2463, N2469.

No. 59 OTU, 12/43:
N2455, N2471, N2555.

No. 71 OTU, 1941:
N2483, N2674.

Other aircraft:
N2318 (Rolls-Royce engine trials); N2359 (No. 6 OTU); N2365 (No. 9 (P) AFU); N2422 (first production aircraft with metal wings); N2460 (No. 1510 Flt.); N2488 (No. 6 OTU); N2520 (No. 55 OTU); N2541 (de-icing trials, HAL, 1940); N2599 (later converted to Sea Hurricane Mk. IA); N2646 (hydraulic trials, HAL, 1940), N2530 (work commenced under W/O 7522 and C/N 29838/39 to convert this aircraft to a two-seater trainer, but cancelled 10/1/40); N2625, N2626 (at Takoradi, 11/40, *en route* for Middle East).

THE HAWKER HURRICANE MARK I (GLOSTER-BUILT):

First production batch of 500 aircraft built by Gloster Aircraft Co., Ltd., Brockworth, during 1939-40 under Contract No. 962371/38/C.23a. Rolls-Royce Merlin III engines and DH or Rotol propellers. First flight, 20th October 1939. *P2535-P2584, P2614-P2653, P2672-P2701, P2713-P2732, P2751-P2770, P2792-P2836, P2854-P2888, P2900-P2924, P2946-P2995, P3020-P3069, P3080-P3124, P3140-P3179, P3200-P3234, P3250-P3264.*

No. (F) Squadron, Vassincourt, France 3/40:
P2546, P2548. Northolt 7/40: P2571, P2649, P2686, P2751, P2877, P2980, P3042, P3043, P3044 (missing, 3/9/40), P3047 (shot down, 15/8/40), P3105, P3167, P3169, P3170, P3172 (shot down, 11/8/40), P3229.

No. 3 (F) Squadron, Croydon, 1940:
P3143 ("Z").

No. 6 (F) Squadron, Helwan, 2/42:
P3067.

No. 32 (F) Squadron, Biggin Hill, 5/40:
P2755 (F/L Jeff destroyed Bf 109, 22/5/40), P3112 (F/O Humpherson destroyed Ju 87, 20/7/40), P3200, P3214, P3219.

No. 43 (F) Squadron:
P3140.

No. 46 (F) Squadron, Digby, 1940:
P3024 P3026, P3030, P3031, P3052, P3053, P3062-P3064, P3066, P3067, P3114.

No. 56 (F) Squadron, 1940:
P2556, P2677, P2692, P2822, 2857 ("H"), P2863, P2866, P2882, P2910, P2922, P2970, P2985, P3028, P3055, P3123, P3152.

No. 73 (F) Squadron, Le Mans, France 6/40:
P2559 ("D"), P2571 ("X"), P2579 ("J"), Debden and Hornchurch, 10/40): P2815, P2975, P2984, P3034; Sidi Haneish, 1/41: P2640.

No. 79 (F) Squadron, 1940:
P3122.

No. 80 (F) Squadron:
P2864.

No. 85 (F) Squadron, 1940:
P3119 ("X"), P3124 ("L").

No. 87 (F) Squadron, 1940:
P2798 ("A"), P2829 ("G"), P2865 ("X"), P2875-P2877, P2881.

No. 111 (F) Squadron, North Weald and Hawkinge, 1940:
P2806, P2884, P2885 (shot down, 5/6/40), P2886 (shot down 13/3/41), P2888, P2958 (crashed on take-off, Hawkinge, 14/7/40), P2979, P3029, P3044, P3046, P3054, P3105, P3106.

No. 116 (F) Squadron, 1940:
P3212.

No. 145 (F) Squadron, 1940:
P3143 ("Z").

No. 151 (F) Squadron, 1940:
P3065 ("G").

No. 208 (AC) Squadron, Burg El Arab, 1942:
P2638, (Tropical PR Mark I, shot down by three Bf 109F's 24/7/42).

No. 239 (F) Squadron:
P2949, P2956.

No. 245 (F) Squadron, 1940:
P2884, P3165, P3152.

No. 249 (F) Squadron, 1940:
P2863 (in action over Brooklands, 4/9/40).

No. 253 (F) Squadron, 1940:
P2692, P2865, P2883, P3032 (in action over Brooklands, 4/9/40), P3213.

No. 257 (F) Squadron, North Weald, 11/40:
P2835 (P/O Mortimer destroyed BR20, 11/11/40), P2960, P3049; Northolt: P2981 (missing, 8/8/40).

No. 274 (F) Squadron. Sidi Haneish, 11/40:
P2638-P2641, P2643, P2651.

No. 303 (Polish) Squadron, RAF, 1940:
P3069 ("C").

No. 401 Squadron, RCAF:
P3080 ("C").

No. 402 Squadron, RCAF:
P3021 ("X").

No. 501 Squadron, AAF, Anglure, France, 5/40:
P2714 ("F"), P2760 ("B"), P2768 ("E"); Battle of Britain, 7/40: P2485, P2691, P3040, P3041, P3082, P3083 ("E"), P3084, P3141 ("W").

No. 504 Squadron, AAF, Hendon. Following aircraft intercepted raid on London, 15/9/40:
P2725 (Sgt. Holmes rammed He 111K over Victoria Station), P2908, P2987.

No. 527 Squadron:
P2992 ("P").

No. 601 Squadron, AAF, 1940:
P2573, P2673 ("N").

No. 607 Squadron, AAF, 1940:
P2874 ("F"), P2879, P2901.

No. 615 Squadron, AAF, 1940:
P2564, P2578.

No. 680 (PR) Squadron, Middle East, 1943:
P2915 (used for communications).

No. 55 OTU:
P2881, P2887, P3146.

No. 59 OTU:
P2630, P2679, P2877, P3089, P3095.

No. 4 (C) FPP (Ferry Pool), 1940:
P2640, P2641, P2948, P2987.

Tropical Mark I's to Middle East, via Takoradi, 1940:
P2638-P2641, P2643, P2651.

Conversions to Mark II Series 1 (1940; subsequent identities in brackets):
P2682 (DG641), P2829 (DR355), P2835 (DR353), P2863 (DR368), P2904 (DR357), P2908 (DR369), P2975 (DR372), P3023 (DR342), P3103 (DR340), P3106 (DR370), P3151 (DR350).

Other Aircraft:
P2068 (No. 9 (P) AFU and No. 9 FTS. 8/41), P2617 (No. 9 FTS, 8/41), P2968 (supplied to Eire as 107, 2/44), P2972, P3090 (later converted to Sea Hurricane Mark IA); P3178, P3218 (No. 5 (P) AFU); P3250 (No. 71 OTU).

THE HAWKER HURRICANE MARK I (GLOSTER-BUILT).

Second production batch of 100 aircraft built by Gloster Aircraft Co. Ltd., Brockworth, during 1940, under Contract No. 19773/39/C.23a. Rolls-Royce Merlin III engines and DH or Rotol propellers. *R4074-R4123, R4171-R4200, R4213-R4232.*

No. 32 (F) Squadron, Biggin Hill, 1940:
R4081.

No. 43 (F) Squadron, 1940:
R4107-R4110.

No. 87 (F) Squadron, 1940:
R4228 ("X").

No. 111 (F) Squadron, Croydon, 8/40:
R4086, R4115, R4118, R4183 (shot down, pilot safe, 15/8/40), R4188, R4193, R4195, R4226.

No. 249 (F) Squadron, 9/40:
R4229 (in action over Brooklands, 4/9/40.

No. 257 (F) Squadron, Northolt, 8/40:
R4088, R4094 (missing 8/8/40), R4189; North Weald, 10/40: R4188 (Sgt. Lucas destroyed Fiat CR42, 11/11/40), R4190, R4195.

No. 504 Squadron, AAF, 10/40:
R4178.

Conversions to Mark II Series 1 (1940; subsequent identities in brackets):
R4081 (DR358), R4091 (DR373), R4218 (BV155; served with No. 73 (F) Squadron, at El Adem, 2/42).

THE HAWKER HURRICANE MARK I AND II (GLOSTER-BUILT).

Third (main) production batch of 1,700 aircraft built by Gloster Aircraft Co., Ltd., Brockworth, during 1940-41, under Contract No. 857/30/40/C.23a.

Part 1. 500 HURRICANE MARK I's. Rolls-Royce Merlin III engines. *V6533-V6582, V6600-V6649, V6665-V6704, V6722-V6761, V6776-V6825, V6840-V6889, V6913-V6952, V6979-V7028, V7042-V7081, V7099-V7138, V7156-V7195.*

No. 1 (F) Squadron, Kenley, 1941:
V6932, V6933, V6997.

No. 32 (F) Squadron, Acklington, 10/40:
V6724.

No. 46 (F) Squadron, Sherburn-in-Elmet, 4/41:
V6818, V7075.

No. 56 (F) Squadron, 1941:
V6534, V6944, V7100, V7105, V7176 ("P"), V7179.

No. 71 (F) Squadron, 1941:
V6814 ("C"), V6919 ("T").

No. 73 (F) Squadron, Debden and Hornchurch, 10/40:
V6677, V6738, V6857 (shot down, 11/10/40).

No. 85 (F) Squadron, 12/40:
V6611 ("U"), V6672 ("U"), V6730 ("O"), V7074.

No. 87 (F) Squadron, 1/41:
V6915 ("P"), V6960 ("E").

No. 111 (F) Squadron, 8/40:
V6538, V6539, V6562, V6606, V6613, V6696, V6701, V6868, V6984, V6985.

No. 249 (F) Squadron, aircraft in action over Brooklands, 4/9/40:
V6559, V6610 (crashed 7/9/40), V6614, V6625, V6635.

No. 253 (F) Squadron:
V6637 (in action over Brooklands, 4/9/40).

No. 257 (F) Squadron, North Weald, 11/40:
V6558, V6604, V6671, V6680 (P/O Kay destroyed BR20, 11/11/40), V6722 ("P"), V6802, V6864 (P/O North destroyed BR20, 11/11/40), V6873 ("O"), V7076, V7137 ("G"), V7167 ("H"), V7186 (crashed, 1/1/41).

No. 310 (Czech) Squadron, RAF:
V6737 ("R").

No. 501 Squadron, AAF, 1940:
V6799 ("X").

No. 504 Squadron, AAF, Filton and Exeter, 12/40:
V6695, V6700, V6731, V6732, V6750, V6819.

No. 601 Squadron, AAF, 1/41:
V6808 ("D").

No. 680 (PR) Squadron, Middle East, 1943:
V6738, V6747 (used for communications).

No. 41 OTU:
V6741 (Sea Hurricane Mk.IC).

No. 55 OTU:
V6573, V6728, V7137.

No. 59 OTU:
V6613, V6637, V6680, V6728, V6877, V6913, V6918, V6997, V7075, V7180.

Conversions to Mark IIA Series 1 (1940; subsequent identities in brackets):
V6535 (DG630; to No. 208 (AC) Squadron, Burg-el-Arab, 11/42); V6538 (DR371); V6546 (DR374); V6582 (DG639); V6602 (DG638); V6735 (DR352); V6757 (DG619); V6785 (BV157); V6790 (BV196); V6853 (DG643); V6861 (DG650); V6914 (BV165); V6915 (DR351); V6929 (DG647); V6936 (DR360); V6942 (DR391); V6950 (DG624); V6959 (DG627); V6999 (DG648); V7006 (DR347); V7018 (DR392): V7021 (DR394); V7169 (DR339.

Other Aircraft:
V6552 (later converted to Mark I trainer; armament removed); V6557 (trials at TRE, Malvern); V6700, V6801, V6802, V7049 (converted to Sea Hurricane Mk.IA's); V6757, V6813, V7103 (tropical Mk.I's to No. 71 OTU, North Africa); V6784, V7168 (No. 5 (P) AFU); V6940 (No. 9 (P) AFU); V6796 (No. 15 (P) AFU); V7173 (supplied to Eire, 12/43, as 109).

PART 2. 200 HURRICANE MARK I's.

Rolls-Royce Merlin III engines. *W9100-W9159, W9170-W9209, W9215-W9244, W9260-W9279, W9290-W9329, W9340-W9359.*

No. (F) Squadron, Kenley, 1941:
W9151, W9181.

No. 46 (F) Squadron, Sherburn-in-Elmet, 1941:
W9110, W9244, W9301, W9324.

No. 73 (F) Squadron, Bu Amoud, 1941:
W9197, W9198, W9231, W9268, W9293 (in action over Mersa Metruh, 5/41).

No. 87 (F) Squadron, 1941:
W9154 ("D"), W9173 ("V"), W9196 ("B").

No. 111 (F) Squadron, 2/41:
W9112, W9114, W9117, W9179, W9308.

No. 208 (AC) Squadron, Middle East detachments, 1942:
W9267 (trop. Tac R Mk. I, Tmimi, 1/42), W9300 (trop. Tac R Mk. I, Msus, 1/42), W9328 (trop. Tac R Mk. I, Antelat, 1/42), W9354 (trop. Tac R Mk. I, Bu Amoud, 5/42).

No. 213 (F) Squadron, Famagusta, Cyprus, 6/41:
W9238, W9265, W9270 ("A"), W9274, W9290 ("B"), W9291, W9309, W9349 ("E"), W9350.

No. 257 (F) Squadron, 1941:
W9130 ("K"), W9281, W9306.

No. 274 (F) Squadron, 1941:
W9197, W9269, W9296.

No. 335 (Hellenic) Squadron, RAF, Middle East, 1942:
W9155, W9290.

No. 680 (PR) Squadron, Middle East, 1943:
W9225, W9242 (used for communications).

No. 2 PRU, Middle East, 1941:
W9116 (3-camera PR Mk. I; missing over Benghazi, 3/10/41); W9353 (identical to and replacement for W9116).

No. 1413 Met. Flt., Lydda, 1944:
W9155 (converted to Met. (Trop.) Mk. I).

No. 55 OTU:
W9196.

No. 59 OTU:
W9112, W9177, W9202, W9342.

Conversions to Mark II Series I (1941; subsequent identities in brackets): W9191 (DR345), W9265 (DR356).

Other Aircraft:
W9185 (No. 71 OTU, North Africa); W9313 (converted to Sea Hurricane Mk. IA); W9314 (trial installation of four 20-mm gun armament, A & AEE, 1/41).

PART 3. 519 HURRICANE MARK I's

Rolls-Royce Merlin III engines. *Z4022-Z4071, Z4085-Z4119, Z4161-Z4205, Z4223-Z4272, Z4308-Z4327, Z4347-Z4391, Z4415-Z4434, Z4482-Z4516, Z4532-Z4581, Z4603-Z4652, Z4686-Z4720, Z4760-Z4809, Z4832-Z4865.*

No. 6 (F) Squadron, Helwan, 1/42:
Z4350.

No. 43 (F) Squadron, 1941:
Z4515 ("U"), Z4609 ("T"), Z4842 ("L").

No. 73 (F) Squadron, Mersa Matruh, 1941:
Z4173, Z4190 (missing, Tobruk, 26/6/41), Z4238, Z4366, Z4491, Z4630, Z4697, Z4773.

No. 95 (MR) Squadron, Freetown, West Africa, (Squadron Fighter Flt.):
Z4257 (collided with Douglas DC-2, 7/9/42).

No. 98 (B) Squadron, Kaldadarnes, Iceland, 7/41:
Z4607 (crashed 23/9/41), Z4617, Z4631, Z4639, Z4702.

No. 208 (AC) Squadron, El Khanka, Egypt, 10/41; trop. Tac R Mk. I's:
Z4063, Z4231 (3-camera PR Mk. I), Z4252, Z4486, Z4489, Z4539, Z4544, Z4555, Z4616, Z4772 (long range aircraft; abandoned at LG134, near Sollum, 10/41), Z4775 (long range aircraft operating from Gaza and Ramleh, 6/41), Z4864.

No. 213 (F) Squadron, Famagusta, Cyprus, 6/41:
Z4089 ("U"), Z4095 ("W"), Z4163 ("M"), Z4203, Z4205 (crashed 29/12/41), Z4225, Z4242 ("X"), Z4361 ("B"), Z4367 ("G"), Z4374 ("Y").

No. 267 Squadron, Heliopolis, 4/42:
Z4700.

No. 274 (F) Squadron, Western Desert, 1941:
Z4097.

No. 335 (Hellenic) Squadron, RAF, Middle East, 1942:
Z4007 (Fuqa, 10/42), Z4233 (Bardia, 2/42), Z4494, Z4604 (Aqir, Palestine; crashed, 15/11/41, but repaired), Z4652 (missing, 14/3/42), Z4809.

No. 451 Squadron, RCAF, Middle East, 1941:
Z4231 (3-camera, trop. PR Mk. I).

No. 680 (PR) Squadron, Cyprus, 1944:
Z4064 (used for communications).

No. 2 PRU, Middle East, 1941:
Z4182 (trop. PR Mk. I).

No. 1423 Flt., Reykjavik, Iceland, 8/41:
Z4607 (crashed 23/9/41), Z4617, Z4631, Z4639, Z4702.

No. 71 OTU, North Africa:
Z4093, Z4102, Z4113, Z4266, Z4380, Z4425, Z4491, Z4837, Z4855.

Other Aircraft:
Z4037 (supplied to Eire, 7/43, as 106); Z4576 (trials with modified oil system, GAC); Z4646 (trials with modified filter fairing GAC and A & AEE); Z4770 (tests with various spinners); Z4809 (tests with various paint schemes, RAE); Z4838 (night flying equipment tests, Boscombe Down and RAE).

PART 4. 481 HURRICANE MARK IIA SERIES 2's AND MARK IIB's

(Total of 140 Mk. IIA's and 341 Mk. IIB's). Rolls-Royce Merlin XX engines driving Rotol or DH 3-blade variable pitch propellers. ***Z4866-Z4876, Z4920-Z4969, Z4987-Z5006, Z5038-Z5087, Z5117-Z5161, Z5202-Z5236, Z5252-Z5271, Z5302-Z5351, Z5376-Z5395, Z5434-Z5483, Z5529-Z5563, Z5580-Z5629, Z5649-Z5693.***

No. 43 (F) Squadron, 1941:
Z4999, Z5203.

No. 63 (F) Squadron, 1941:
Z4967 ("O").

No. 73 (F) Squadron, 1942:
Z5312 (trop. Mk. IIB; shot down, El Adem, 8/2/42).

No. 81 (F) Squadron, Vaenga, North Russia, 1941:
Z5122, Z5157, Z5207, Z5208, Z5209, Z5228, Z5252, Z5349.

No. 128 (F) Squadron, 1942:
Z4967 ("D").

No. 134 (F) Squadron, Vaenga, North Russia, 1941:
Z5529.

No. 208 (AC) Squadron, Middle East, 1942:
Z4950 (missing 7/9/42), Z4954, Z4958.

No. 213 (F) Squadron:
Z5004 ("A"), Z5005 ("B").

No. 257 (F) Squadron, 1941; Mk. IIB's:
Z5044, Z5045, Z5050 ("T"), Z5083.

No. 274 (F) Squadron, 1941:
Z4944 ("L"), Z4954 ("V"), Z4955 ("P"), Z5087 ("N"), Z5337 ("O"), Z5674.

No. 335 (Hellenic) Squadron, RAF Fuqa, 10/42:
Z5314 (trop. Mk. IIB).

No. 605 Squadron, AAF, 1941:
Z4969.

No. 680 (PR) Squadron, Cyprus, 1944:
Z5132 (trop. PR Mk. II—high altitude aircraft).

No. 2 PRU, Middle East, 1942:
Z5132 (trop. PR Mk. II).

No. 71 OTU, North Africa:
Z4924, Z4933, Z4964, Z5207, Z5261.

Aircraft despatched to Russia, 1941-42 (other than those with Nos. 81 and 134 Squadrons):
Z5159, Z5210-Z5213, Z5227 (FE-53), Z5236, Z5259, Z5262, Z5263, Z5480.

Other Aircraft:
Z4866 (performance and handling trials, GAC and A & AEE); Z4867, Z4922, Z4931, Z5440 (later converted to Sea Hurricane Mks. IA and IB); Z4993, Z5390 (miscellaneous trials, RAE, 1942-43).

THE HAWKER HURRICANE MARK IIA, IIB AND IIC (GLOSTER-BUILT)

Fourth production batch of 449 aircraft built by Gloster Aircraft Co. Ltd., Brockworth, during 1941-42. Rolls-Royce Merlin XX engines. ***BG674-BG723, BG737-BG771, BG783-***

BG832, BG844-BG888, BG901-BG920, BG933-BG977, BG990-BG999, BH115-BH154, BH167-BH201, BH215-BH264, BH277-BH296, BH312-BH360. **About 400 of these aircraft were scheduled for despatch to Russia; most of the remainder were sent to the Middle East as replacement aircraft.**

No. 73 (F) Squadron, Middle East, 1942; trop. NF Mk. IIC's:
BG750, BG751 (S/L Ward destroyed He 111K, 9/2/42); BG867, BG877, BG902.

No. 208 (AC) Squadron, North Africa, 1942; trop. Tac R Mk. IIA's:
BG691, BG785, BG992, BG998 (missing Qattara Depression, 29/8/42).

No. 335 (Hellenic) Squadron, RAF, Middle East, 10/42:
BG859

No. 607 Squadron, AAF, Manston, 2/42:
BG946.

THE HAWKER HURRICANE MARK I, (HAWKER BUILT)

Third production batch of 500 aircraft (plus 30 replacements), built by Hawker Aircraft Ltd., Kingston, Brooklands and Langley, under Contract No. 962371/38. Rolls-Royce Merlin III engines. Metal-covered wings. ***P3265-P3279, P3300-P3324, P3345-P3364, P3380-P3429, P3448-P3492, P3515-P3554, P3574-P3623, P3640-P3684, P3700-P3739, P3755-P3789, P3802-P3836, P3854-P3903, P3092-P3944, P3960-P3984.*** **Replacement machines:** ***P8809-P8818, R2680-R2689, T9519-T9538, W6667-W6670.*** **Deliveries commenced, 21/2/40; completed, 20/7/40. Average rate of production, about 3 aircraft per day.**

No. 1 (F) Squadron, Northolt, 7/40:
P3276 (destroyed Bf 109E over Tonbridge, 1/9/40), P3318, P3395 (destroyed Bf 109E over Tonbridge, 1/9/40), P3396, P3405, P3406 (destroyed Bf 109E over Tonbridge, 1/9/40, P3471 (shot down, 19/7/40), P3653, P3678, P3782 (missing 3/9/40); P3886 (Kenley, 1/41).

No. 6 (F) Squadron, 1941:
P3967.

No. 17 (F) Squadron, Martlesham Heath, 8/40:
P3468, P3482.

No. 32 (F) Squadron, Acklington, 10/40:
P3351, P3460.

No. 43 (F) Squadron, Wick, 1940:
P3468, P3531 (shot down off Shoreham, 19/7/40), P3964, P3971.

No. 46 (F) Squadron, Sherburn-in-Elmet, 4/41:
P3309, P3597, R2684.

No. 56 (F) Squadron, 1940:
P3356, P3384, P3399, P3421, P3473, P3474, P3478, P3479, P3515, P3547, P3554, P3579, P3587, P3612, P3702, P3784, P3787, P3855,P3866, P3870, P3874, P3879, P3902.

No. 73 (F) Squadron, Gaye and Le Mans, France, 6/40:
P3351, P3456; Tobruk, 8/41: T9536.

No. 85 (F) Squadron, 1940:
P3407, P3408.

No. 87 (F) Squadron, 1940:
P3593 ("O"), P3755 ("Z").

No. 111 (F) Squadron, North Weald, 6/40:
P3399, P3459, P3470, P3524, P3548, P3595, P3663, P3671 (missing, (10/7/40), P3942, P3943, P3944 (missing, 15/8/40).

No. 208 (AC) Squadron, El Khanka, Egypt, 11/41:
P3270, P3826 (2-camera Tac R Mk. I, Gambut, 1/41), T9536 (abandoned on LG134, near Sollum, 18/10/41; recaptured 5/42).

No. 249 (F) Squadron, Boscombe Down, 8/40:
P3525, P3576 (shot down by Bf 110 over Southampton, 16/8/40, Bf 110 also destroyed and Hurricane pilot, F/L Nicholson, wounded, awarded VC), P3579, P3594, P3616 (shot down in above combat, 16/8/40; pilot, P/O King, killed).

No. 253 (F) Squadron, 9/40:
R2686 (in action over Brooklands, 4/9/40).

No. 257 (F) Squadron, Northolt, 8/40:
P3412, P3578 (shot down, 3/9/40), P3642, P3643, P3704, P3705 ("B"), P3706, P3707, P3708 (P/O Henderson shot down (but safe) after destroying two Bf 110s near Clacton, 31/8/40, P3709, P3775, P3893.

No. 274 (F) Squadron, Sidi Haneish, 11/40:
P3729, P3821, P3822, P3977, P3980.

No. 501 Squadron, AAF, 7/40:
P3397, P3411, P3582, P3604, P3646, P3679, P3803, P3808, P3901.

No. 504 Squadron, AAF, Hendon; following aircraft intercepted raid on London, 15/9/40:
P3388, P3414, P3415, P3614, P3774.

Aircraft damaged in action:
P3405, P3451, P3489, P3521, P3530, P3780, P3786 (repaired by Rollasons, 1940); P3829 (repaired by Glosters); P3924 (repaired by de Havillands).

Other Aircraft:
P3265 (performance trials, Brooklands, 1940); P3269 (prototype Hurricane Mk. II with Merlin XX; tests with rear view hood, Brookland, 1941; delivered as ground instruction machine, No. 3 S of TT, 12/10/42); P3345 (tests with various paint schemes until 25/5/40); P3416 P3898 (No. 9 (P) AFU. P3416 was supplied to Eire, 12/43, as 108); 3462 (tests with long range fuel tanks); P3463, P3524, P3886 (No. 59 OTU); P3458, P3549 (No. 55 OTU); P3620 (later converted to Sea Hurricane Mk. IA by General Aircraft Ltd.); P3641 (radio trials, TRE, Malvern, 1941); P3705, P3723, P3977 (trop. Mk. I's; No. 103 MU, North Africa); P3715 (No. 17 (P) AFU); P3720 (shipped to Iran as No. 252); P3736 (fuel consumption trials, HAL); P3811 (trial 12-gun wing; also used for airscrew trials); P3820, P3823 (engine handling trials, HAL); P3830 (trials to improve rearward vision, HAL); P3923 (propeller handling trials, HAL); P3967, P3970 (trop. Mk. I's; Ferry Pool, Takoradi, 1940); P3702, P3715, P3881 (No. 4 (C) FPP (Ferry Pool), June 1940).

THE HAWKER HURRICANE MARK I (HAWKER-BUILT)

Fourth production batch of 500 aircraft, built by Hawker Aircraft Ltd., Kingston, Langley and Brooklands, during 1940-41, under Contract No. 62305/39. Rolls-Royce Merlin III engines. *V7200-V7209, V7221-V7260, V7276-V7318, V7337-V7386, V7400-V7446, V7461-V7510, V7533-V7572, V7588-V7627, V7644-V7690, V7705-V7737, V7741-V7780, V7795-V7838, V7851-V7862, AS987-AS990.* Deliveries commenced, 2/7/40; completed 5/2/41. Average rate of production, approximately 4 aircraft per day.

No. 1 (F) Squadron, North Weald, 9/40:
V7256 (destroyed Bf 109E over Tonbridge 1/9/40), V7258, V7301, V7302, V7376, V7377, V7379; Wittering, 10/40: V7464; Kenley, 1/41: V7534.

No. 32 (F) Squadron, Acklington, 10/40:
V7425.

No. 43 (F) Squadron, 8/40:
V7257.

No. 46 (F) Squadron, Digby, 1/41:
V7232, V7443 (missing from combat over Calais, 10/2/41); Sherburn-in-Elmet, 4/41: V7603.

No. 56 (F) Squadron, 1940:
V7315, V7340, V7342, V7352.

No. 73 (F) Squadron, Debden and Hornchurch, 10/40:
V7501, V7502; Sidi Haneish and Bu Amoud, 3/41: V7353 (S/Lt. Littolff destroyed Bf 109E over Tobruk harbour, 22/4/41); V7372, V7491, V7492, V7545, V7546, V7550, V7559, V7561, V7716, V7757, V7822; Mersa Matruh, 5/41: AS987, AS990.

No. 87 (F) Squadron, 1941:
V7646 ("R").

No. 111 (F) Squadron, 10/40:
V7361, V7400.

No. 208 (F) Squadron, Middle East; trop. Tac R Mk. I's:
V7295 (Halfaya, 12/40), V7431 (El Khanka, Egypt, 10/41); V7772 (Tmimi, 1/42).

No. 213 (F) Squadron, Cyprus, 6/41:
AS987.

No. 249 (F) Squadron, 1940:
V7313 (in action over Brooklands, 4/9/40).

No. 257 (F) Squadron, North Weald, 10/40:
V7296 (P/O Pniak destroyed BR20, 11/11/40); V7298 (shot down, 12/10/40); V7351, V7607 (P/O Davey destroyed BR20, 11/11/40); 1:41: V7248, V7667.

No. 274 (F) Squadron, Western Desert, 5/41:
V7354, V7717, V7763, V7820 (shot down at Mersa Matruh, 12/5/41; F/O English missing).

No. 335 (Hellenic) Squadron, RAF, Middle East, 1942:
V7547.

No. 501 Squadron, AAF, 1941:
V7230 ("F"), V7368.

No. 601 Squadron, AAF, 1941:
V7238, V7291, V7411.

No. 2 PRU, Middle East; 2-camera trop. P.R. Mk. I's, engaged in photography of Syria, 6/41; based at Heliopolis, Egypt:
V7423, V7428.

Aircraft delivered to RAF Abbotsinch, 1/2/41:
V7856, V7858-V7862, AS989, AS990 (last Hawker-built Mk. I delivered to RAF).

Other Aircraft:
V7249 (de-icing trials, HAL, 7/40); V7260 (trial installation of four 20-mm. gun armament, 7/40); V7338 (Silloth Stn. Flt.) V7299, V7477, V7482 (at Takoradi, 12/40, *en route* for Middle East); V7366, V7462 (No. 59 OTU 12/43); V7480 (miscellaneous Boscombe Down trials, from 25/3/41); V7504 (converted to catapult aircraft; Speke, 14/3/42); V7540 (supplied to Eire, 7/43, as 105); V7670 (captured intact by Germans, March 1941; recaptured on Gambut airfield later).

THE HAWKER HURRICANE MARK II (HAWKER-BUILT)

Fifth production batch of 1,000 aircraft built by Hawker Aircraft Ltd., Kingston, Langley and Brooklands, during 1940-41, under Contract No. 62305/39. Rolls-Royce Merlin XX engines. *Z2308-Z2357, Z2382-Z2426, Z2446-Z2465, Z2479-Z2528, Z2560-Z2594, Z2624-Z2643, Z2661-Z2705, Z2741-Z2775, Z2791-Z2840, Z2882-Z2931, Z2959-Z2993, Z3017-Z3036, Z3050-Z3099, Z3143-Z3187, Z3221-Z3270, Z3310-Z3359, Z3385-Z3404, Z3431-Z3470, Z3489-Z3523, Z3554-Z3598, Z3642-Z3691, Z3740-Z3784, Z3826-Z3845, Z3885-Z3919, Z3969-Z4018,* Deliveries commenced, 14/1/41; completed, 28/7/41. Average rate of production, 5 aircraft per day.

No. 1 (F) Squadron, Hawkinge (convoy patrols), 3/41; Mk. IIB's:
Z2390, Z2457, Z2482, Z2484, Z2501, Z2628, Z2687, Z2690, Z2746, Z2759, Z2764, Z2802, Z2807, Z2810. Tangmere (Turbinlite and convoy patrols), 7/41; NF Mk. IIC's Z3165, Z3341, Z3355, Z3595, Z3774 (missing from attacks on destroyers in *Scharnhorst* and *Gneisenau* operation, 12/2/42), Z3778 ("Y") Z3826 ("O"), Z3841-Z3844, Z3884 (returned to HAL, Langley, 2/10/41, but crashed on landing), Z3897 ("N"), Z3899 (collided with BD940, 22/11/41, over Isle of Wight), Z3902, Z3903, Z3970 (took part in attack on *Scharnhorst* destroyer escort, 12/2/42), Z3987.

No. 3 (F) Squadron, 1941:
Z2891, Z3025 ("C"), Z3069 ("F"), Z3086 ("P"), Z3894 ("R").

No. 17 (F) Squadron:
Z2801 ("S").

No. 56 (F) Squadron, 1941:
Z2355 ("L"), Z2405, Z2448 ("V"), Z2449 ("M"), Z2572, Z2573, Z2575 ("L"), Z2585, Z2586 ("P"), Z2587, Z2635, Z2636 ("U") Z2664 ("O") Z2674 ("M"), Z2677 ("N"), Z2688 ("S"), Z2697, Z2702, Z2755, Z2763, Z2767, Z2769 ("W").

No. 66 (F) Squadron, 1941:
Z2317 ("L"), Z2318 ("E"), Z2327 ("T").

No. 79 (F) Squadron, 1941; Mk. IIB's:
Z2633, Z2674, Z3151 ("F"), Z3156 ("H"), Z3745 ("B").

No. 81 (F) Squadron, Vaenga, North Russia, 9/41:
Z3746 (Sgt. N. Smith killed in action. 12/9/41), Z4006, Z4010, Z4017, Z4018.

No. 87 (F) Squadron, 1941:
Z3775, Z3778 ("P"), Z3779 ("Y"), Z3915 ("G"), Z3992.

No. 134 (F) Squadron, Vaenga, North Russia, 9/41:
Z3763, Z3768 (FK-49), Z3976, Z3977 (FK-55).

No. 208 (AC) Squadron, Middle East, 1942:
Z2328 (trop. P.R. Mk. IIA; shot down, 28/7/42).

No. 213 (F) Squadron, 1942:
Z3514.

No. 253 (F) Squadron, 1941-42:
Z3171 ("P"), Z3971 (Mk. IIC).

No. 257 (F) Squadron, 2/41; Mk. IIA:
Z2687; 8/41, Mk. IIB's: Z2343, Z2907, Z296, Z3025, Z3164, Z3322, Z3387, Z3380, Z3511, Z3516, Z3744, Z3782; 8/41, Mk. IIC's: Z3051, Z3088.

No. 601 Squadron, AAF, 1941:
Z3257 ("A"), Z3744 ("P").

Aircraft damaged in action and repaired by Rosenfields Ltd.:
Z2484, Z2489, Z2515, Z2565; Repaired by Rollasons: Z2970.

Presentation aircraft:
Z2661-Z2705 (Z2705 — Bahamas), Z2791-Z2840 (Z2840 — McConnell's Squadron), Z2882-Z2931 (Z2899 — McConnell's Squadron).

Boscombe Down Trials Aircraft:
Z2320/G, Z3092/G (RP trials, 4/41); Z2326 (Rolls-Royce BF and Vickers "S" 40-mm guns 1941-42); Z2346 (cockpit heating trials); Z2461 (hood jettisoning trials, 9/2/41); Z2885 (four 20-mm Hispano guns, 9/3/41); Z2895 (modified fuel system); Z2905 (TI of 90-gallon ferry tanks on 4-cannon wing, 13/3/41); Z3157 (8-gun tests); Z3451 (miscellaneous trials, 5/41); Z3564 (armament trials, Mk. IIB; 14/6/41); Z3888 (TI's for Mk. IIC, 2/7/41 and 4/1/42).

Other aircraft:
Z2308 (air intake and performance trials, HAL); Z2326 (external store trials, HAL); Z2399 (tests with modified oil cooler, HAL); Z2415 (high altitude trials, HAL, 12/40); Z2457, Z2691 (miscellanous trials, RAE, 1942); Z2589 (company TI's on Mk. IIC wing, HAL, 31/1/41); Z2340 (not delivered; cannibalised for spares); Z2795 (radio trials, TRE, Malvern); Z2832 (force landing in Eire, 1943. Temporarily registered 94 in IAC; returned to RAF, 7/43); Z2903, Z3036, Z3056, Z3058 (Station Flt, Northolt); Z3067 (damaged during tests; delivery delayed until 24/3/41); Z3078 (crashed during delivery, 23/3/41; subsequently repaired); Z3179 (to GAC, 6/4/41), for development flying); Z3249 (damaged during test; delivery delayed until 30/4/41); Z3682 (remnants stored at Waterbeach, 1953, and used for spare parts for LF363); Z3687 (fitted with low-drag AWA wing, 1946-47); Z3919 (RAE trials with RP's); Z3981 (miscellaneous trials, HAL, 7/41-8/41); Z4015 (Mk. IIB, later converted to Sea Hurricane Mk. IC).

THE HAWKER HURRICANE MARK II (HAWKER-BUILT)

Sixth production batch of 1,350 aircraft built by Hawker Aircraft Ltd., Kingston, Langley and Brooklands, during 1941-42. Rolls-Royce Merlin XX engines. *BD696-BD745, BD759-BD793, BD818-BD837, BD855-BD899, BD914-BD963, BD980-BE986, BE105-BE117, BE130-BE174, BE193-BE242, BE274-BE308, BE232-BE372, BE394-BE428, BE468-BE517, BE546-BE590, BE563-BE651, BE667-BE716, BM898-BM936, BE947-BM996, BN103-BN142, BN155-BN189,*

***BN203-BN242, BN265-BN298, BN311-BN337, BN346-BN389, BN399-BN435, BN449-BN497, BN512-BN547, BN559-BN603, BN624-BN654, BN667-BN705, BN719-BN759, BN773-BN802, BN818-BN846, BN859-BN882, BN896-BN940, BN953-BN987*. Deliveries commenced 24/7/41, completed, 18/3/42. Average rate of production, 6 aircraft per day.**

No. 1 (F) Squadron, Tangmere, 2/42. Intruder operations; NF Mk. IIC's:
BD770, BD935, BD937, BD940 (collided with Z3899 over Isle of Wight, 22/11/41), BD945-BD947, BD949, BD950, BD983, BE150, BE215 (in action against *Scharnhorst* and *Gneisenau,* 12/2/42), BD949 (lost), BE670 ("Y"), BN205, BN232, BN373, BN969 ("S").

No. 3 (F) Squadron, Mk. IIC's, 1942:
BD696, BD836, BD860 ("Y"), BD867 ("W"), BD868 ("P"), BD893 ("G"), BD948 ("X"), BD982 ("L"), BE116, BN185 ("B"), BN188 ("A").

No. 6 (F) Squadron, Helwan and El Adem, 6/42; tropical Mk. IID's:
BN677, BN797, BN841, BN842, BN845, BN846, BN860 (in action at Bir Hakim, 6/42).

No. 17 (F) Squadron, Burma; tropical Mk. IIC's:
BN462, BN463.

No. 43 (F) Squadron, Acklington; Turbinlite patrols, 2/42; N.F. Mk. IIC's:
BD715, BD717, BD762, BD863; Tangmere, Intruder N.F. Mk. IIC's: BN229, BN230, BN234, BN235.

No. 73 (F) Squadron, Middle East, 2/42; tropical Mk. IIB's:
BD774, BD782, BD887, BD916, BD920, BD930 ("R"), BD931, BD957 (flown by F/L. Johnston, destroyed Bf 109F, 9/2/42), BE169; tropical N.F. Mk. IIC's: BE231, BE372, BE557, BM967, BM975 ("G"), BN115, BN121 (shot down 17/6/42), BN131, BN155, BN156, BN157 (shot down 17/6/42), BN277 (missing with S/L Ward, 17/6/42); Heliopolis, 6/42, tropical N.F. Mk. IIC's: BN410, BN415, BN538 (shot down over Cairo, 29/8/42; pilot safe); BN560 (missing, 16/6/42), BN649 (missing, 17/6/42).

No. 79 (F) Squadron, Burma; tropical Mk. IIC:
BN596.

No. 80 (F) Squadron, El Alamein, L.G.92, 8/42; tropical Tac R Mk. IIC's:
BE395, BN351, BN355.

No. 81 (F) Squadron, Vaenga, North Russia, 9/41; Mk. IIB's:
BD697, BD792, BD822.

No. 87 (F) Squadron, Mk. IIC:
BE508 ("A").

No. 128 (F) Squadron, Mk. IIC:
BE673 ("M").

No. 134 (F) Squadron, Vaenga, North Russia, 9/41; Mk. IIB:
BD825 (crashed, 27/9/41, with two airmen on tail; both killed).

No. 174 (F) Squadron, N.F. Mk. IIC's:
BE421 ("G"), BE684, BN795 (Mk. IIB; presentation aircraft in memory of S/L John Gillan).

No. 175 (F) Squadron, Warmwell, 1942; Mk. IIB fighter-bombers:
BE417, BE419, BE482 ("T"), BE485, BE486, BE492, BE503, BE650, BE687; attacked and sank three E-boats in English Channel, 15/5/42: BE301, BE478, BE484, BE489, BE667, BE668, BE690.

No. 208 (AC) Squadron, Middle East, 1942; tropical Tac R Mk. IIA's:
BE567 (missing, 24/8/42), BN127 (missing with F/O Eshelby, 2/11/42); tropical P.R. Mk. IIA: BE709 (shot down at Burg-el-Arab, 28/9/42); tropical Tac R Mk. IIC's: BD793, BN156 (missing, 24/8/42).

No. 213 (F) Squadron, Middle East, 1942; tropical Mk. IIC's:
BE200 ("M"), BE340 ("W"), BE355 ("Q"), BE569 ("P"), BE643 ("U"), BE701 ("S"), BE702 ("V"); motor patrols from El Gamil, 6/43: BM966 ("T"), BM974, BN117 ("X"), BN132 ("X"), BN133 ("Y"), BN134 ("Z"),

BN136 ("S"), BN137, BN159 ("J"), BN184 ("W"), BN231 ("Y"), BN285 ("M"), BN286 ("O"), BN354 ("S"), BN368 ("Z").

No. 229 (F) Squadron, Mk. IIC:
BD696.

No. 239 (F) Squadron, Mk. IIC's:
BN373, BN411, BN864, BN966.

No. 242 (F) Squadron, tropical Mk. IIB's:
BE402, BE565.

No. 247 (F) Squadron, Mk. IIC:
BD936 ("S").

No. 335 (Hellenic) Squadron, RAF, Middle East, 10/42:
BE681 (trop. Mk. IIB).

No. 402 Squadron, RCAF, Southend; bomber escorts, 8/41; Mk. IIB's:
BD707, BD712 (missing from Dieppe raid, 19/8/42), BD764, BD765; offensive sweeps, 9/41; Mk. IIB fighter-bombers: BE221, BE417 ("K"), BE419, BE424, BE426, BE470-BE473, BE477 ("S"), BE478, BE479, BE483, BE484, BE485 ("W"), BE486, BE488, BE489, BE492, BE502.

No. 451 Squadron, RAAF, Cyprus and Alexandria, 1942-43; F.R. patrols, tropical Mk. IIC's:
BD779, BN114, BN115, BN290, BN356, BN518 (crashed into sea off Alexandria, 19/5/43; pilot safe); Idku, 1/43: BN404.

No. 601 Squadron, AAF, Mk. IIC:
BD712.

No. 607 Squadron, AAF, Martlesham Heath, 12/41; Mk. IIC's:
BE222, BE394, BE397, BE398, BE400, BE401, BE403-BE405, BE418, BE420-BE423, BE425, BE474-BE476; Manston, 4/42: BM948, BN163.

No. 41 Squadron, SAAF, Aksum and Debarec, Abyssinia, 11/42; tropical Mk. IIB:
BE667.

No. 1413 (Meteorological) Flt., Rayak, Damascus, Aquir and Lydda, 1943-45; Met. Mk. IIC:
BN974.

No. 1414 (Meteorological) Flt., Mogadishu and Eastleigh, East Africa, 1943-45; Met. Mk. IIC:
BN347.

No. 1415 (Meteorological) Flt., Habbaniyah, 1943-45; Met. Mk. IIC:
BE487.

Aircraft shipped to Russia, 1942; Mk. IIB's:
BD709, BD731, BD956, BD959, BE470, BN416, BN471, BN481; Mk. IIC's: BE162 (converted from Mk. IIB), BN428.

Other aircraft:
BD772, BD916, BE157, BE167, BE227, BN837 (tropical Mk. IIB's and IIC's; No. 103 MU, North Africa, 1942): BD787 (later converted to Sea Hurricane Mk. IA); BE173/G (retained by HAL, at Langley for miscellaneous armament trials); BE329, BE494, BN627, BN961 (tropical Mk. IIB's of No. 71 OTU, North Africa, 1943); BE711 (to Rolls-Royce Ltd., for trials, 1942); BN114/G, BN526/G, BN571/G (armament trials at A & AEE from 1942); BN635 (to Field Consolidated Aircraft Services, Hanworth, 5/4/42); BN878 (to TRE, Malvern, for radio trials).

THE HAWKER HURRICANE MARKS II AND IV (HAWKER-BUILT)

Seventh production batch of 1,888 aircraft built by Hawker Aircraft Ltd., Kingston and Langley, during 1942. Contract No. 62305/39B, Parts 1-9. ***BN988-BN992, BP109-BP141, BP154-BP200, BP217-BP245, BP259-BP302, BP316-BP362, BP378-BP416, BP430-BP479, BP493-BP526, BP538-BP566, BP579-BP614, BP628-BP675, BP692-BP711, BP734-BP772, HL544-HL591, HL603-HL634, HL654-HL683, HL698-HL747, HL767-HL809, HL828-HL868, HL879-HL913, HL925-HL941, HL953-HL997, HM110-HM157, HV275-HV317, HV333-HV370, HV396-HV445, HV468-HV516, HV534-HV560, HV577-HV612, VH634-HV674, HV696-HV745, HV768-HV799, HV815-HV858, HV873-HV921, HV943-HV989, HW115-HW146, HW167-HW207, HW229-***

HW278, HW291-HW323, HW345-HW373, HW399-HW444, HW467-HW501, HW533-HW572, HW596-HW624, HW651-HW686, HW713-HW757, HW779-HW808, HW834-HW881. **Deliveries commenced, 17/3/42; completed, 23/11/42. Average rate of production, 8 aircraft per day.**

No. 1 (F) Squadron, Tangmere, 6/42; intruder operations, NF Mk. IIC's:
HL589, HL603 ("I").

No. 6 (F) Squadron, Mersa Metruh, 6/42; tropical Mk. IID's:
BP131, BP137, BP182 ("X"), BP188 ("Z"), BP326, BP550; Heliopolis, 1/43; tropical Mk. IIC's: HM118; Castel Benito, 3/43; tropical Mk. IID's: BP193 ("Z"); following aircraft attacked heavy enemy armoured concentration at Zamlet El Hadid, 10/3/43: HM595, HM597, HM663, HM672, HM876, HW271, HW298, HW303, HW439.

No. 17 (F) Squadron, Burma, 1943; tropical Mk. IIC:
HV798.

No. 30 (F) Squadron, Burma, 1943-44; tropical Mk. IIC's:
BP110, BP510 ("H").

No. 43 (F) Squadron, Tangmere, 7/42; shipping strikes and sweeps; Intruder NF Mk. IIC's:
HL656, HL863 (missing from sweep over Fecamp, 26/7/42); following aircraft took part in combined operations at Dieppe, 19/8/42: BP703, HL560, HL562, HL563. North African landings; Maison Blanche airfield, 9/11/42; sweeps, convoy patrols and escorts; tropical Mk. IIC's: HV399, HV402, HV403, HV406-HV409, HV417, HV536, HV541, HV580, HV740, HV817, HV970; Algiers, 2/43: HW122, HW137, HW197, HW204, HW421.

No. 73 (F) Squadron, Heliopolis, Alexandria and LG 92, El Alamein, 8/42; tropical NF Mk. IIC's:
BP167 (destroyed Ju 88, Burg-El-Arab, 31/8/42); BP175, BP177, BP186, BP287, BP344, BP380, BP398, BP518 (destroyed Ju 88, El Alamein, 31/8/42), BP521, BP566, BP584, HL664, HL707, HL796, HL799, HL801, HL839, HL852, HL956, HM118, HM136, HV299, HV3127, HV400, HV426, HV441, HV516, HV585, HV818.

No. 80 (F) Squadron, LG 92, El Alamein and El Bassar, Palestine, 8-9/42; Tac R and Anti-Tank Support; tropical Tac R Mk. IIC fighter-bombers:
BP337, BP340, BP414.

No. 113 (F) Squadron, Burma, 1943-44; tropical Mk. IIB's:
HW666, HW881 ("X").

No. 174 (F) Squadron, Manston, 1942; Intruder Mk. IIC's:
BP649, BP653, BP657, BP672; 1943, Mk. IIB's: HL705, HL715.

No. 175 (F) Squadron, Warmwell, 8/42; shipping strikes, Mk. IIB fighter-bombers:
HV506, HV555, HV844; Harrowbeer, 10/42: HL723, HL728, HW118, HW140; Stoney Cross and Lasham, 3/43: BP295, HW118, HW140.

No. 176 (F) Squadron, Baigachi, East Bengal, 11/43; tropical NF Mk. IIC:
HW415 ("O").

No. 208 (AC) Squadron, Western Desert, 10/42; tropical Tac R Mk. IIB's:
BP604, BP610 (crashed during low flying, 16/1/43), HL739, HL875; tropical Tac R Mk. IIA's: HL566, HL567, HL591; Rayak and Habbaniyah, 1/43; tropical Tac R Mk. IIC's: BP446, HL678; El Bassa, Palestine, 11/43: HL678, HL830, HL849, HL855.

No. 213 (F) Squadron, El Alamein, 8/42; tropical Mk. IIC's:
BP123 ("S"), BP128 ("W"), BP189 ("S"), BP219, BP231 ("Y"), BP237 ("X"), BP341 ("J"), BP342, BP409, BP462 ("Z"), BP515, BP580, BP581, BP592 (destroyed three Ju 88's over El Alamein, 1/9/42), BP734; El Gamil, 1-6/43; MT convoy patrols: HL609, HL833, HL883 ("W"), HL887, HL941 ("V"), HM131 ("Y"), HV305, HV315, VH440 ("U"), HV468 ("P"), HV474, HV483, HV511, HV539 ("T"), HV587 ("N"), HV609 ("S"), HV712, HV830, HW571, HW800.

No. 237 (F) Squadron, Middle East, 1942; tropical Mk. IIC's:
BP359 ("P"), BP397 ("J"), HL735, HL844, HL851, HL859.

No. 239 (F) Squadron, 1942, Mk. IIC's:
BP359 ("P"), BP389, BP397.

No. 274 (F) Squadron, Western Desert, 1942; tropical Mk. IIA fighter-bomber:
HL795 ("V").

No. 335 (Hellenic) Squadron, RAF, Middle East; tropical Mk. IIB's: in action over Fuqa and Daba, 10/42:
BP279, BP290, BP317; in action over Avacado, 7/43: HL599, HL785, HL834.

No. 451 (F) Squadron, RAAF, Mersa Matruh, 1/43; interception duties, tropical Mk. IIC's:
HL805, HL835, HL965, HV843; Idku, 3/43: BP342, HL611, HV294, HW538, HW404.

No. 527 (Calibration) Squadron, Hornchurch, 10/43; various Mk. II's:
BP672, BP737, HW206, HW207 (used for calibration of East Coast radar, 1944-46; also Continental mobile radar, 1945).

No. 607 Squadron, AAF, Manston, 1942; Channel sweeps with Mk. IIB fighter-bombers:
HL867, HM110, HV428, HV437, HV652, HW270, HW489; Mk. IIC fighter-bomber: HV947.

No. 615 Squadron, AAF, Far East, 1944; tropical Mk. IIC:
HV828.

No. 680 (PR) Squadron, Tocra, Libya, 7-10/44; tropical PR Mk. IIC's:
HV295, HV479, HW663 (used for communications).

No. 1413 (Meteorological) Flt., Lydda, 3/44-10/45; tropical Met. Mk. IIC's:
BP224, BP228, BP391, HL790, HV711.

No. 1414 (Meteorological) Flt., Mogadishu and Eastleigh, East Africa, 9/43-7/45; tropical Met. Mk. IIC's:
HV370, HV500, HV583, HV608, HV780.

No. 1415 (Meteorological) Flt., Habbaniyah, 9/43-11/45; tropical Met. Mk. IIC's:
BP466, BP763, HV609, HV890.

No. 41 Squadron, SAAF, Bu Amoud, 8/43; tropical Mk. IIB fighter-bombers:
HV480, HV490, HV796, HV911.

No. 71 OTU, North Africa, 1942-43; tropical Mk. IIB's:
BP606, HL612, HL628, HL706, HL934, HV369, HV581, HV664, HV673, HV837, HV853, HV854, HV857, HV911, HW659.

Aircraft shipped to Russia (some from the Middle East), 1943; Mk. IIB fighter-bombers:
BP657 (converted from Mk. IIC), HL629, HL992, HL994, HV362, HV364, HV840, HV844, HV880, HW117, HW143, HW233, HW347, HW364, HW471, HW551, HW552, HW557, HW571; Mk. IIC fighter bombers: HL549, HL665 (converted to two-seater by Russians, 1943), HV279, HV287, HV293, HV556, HV593, HW168, HW205, HW300, HW357, HW371, HW406, HW715, HW868, HW872, HW879; tropical Mk. IID: HW686.

Aircraft supplied to Turkey from Middle East stocks, 10-11/42; tropical Mk. IIC's:
HV513, HV551, HV608.

Other aircraft:
BP173 (also BP173/G; built as Mk. IIB and delivered to No. 47 MU, Sealand, 1/4/42; returned to HAL, and modified to Mark IV; thence to A & AEE, 29/7/42 for trials); BP734 (to No. 1 FT Flt, Lyneham, 24/6/42, before despatch to the Middle East); HL673 (later converted to Sea Hurricane (Tropical) Mk. IC); HL706-HL714 (Mk. IIB's to No. FT Flight, Lyneham, 4/6/42. HL707 was badly damaged during delivery but was repaired and re-delivered, 4/7/42; some aircraft were later despatched to the Middle East); HV366 (tropical Mk. IIC used by Cranwell Station Flt., 1942-43); HV559 (tropical Mk. IIB to AFTU, India, 1944); HV722 (No. 231 Group Communications Flight, 1944); HW115 (production oil system check, 9/42); HW182/G (to A & AAE for armament trials, 15/10/42); HW187 (also HW187/G; to A & AEE for armament trials, 12/10/42); HW203

(trials with HAL with drop tanks on universal wings, 9/42); HW566 (tropical Mk. IIB to TSTU, India, 1943-44); HW747 (trials at A & AEE, from 24/12/42).

THE HAWKER HURRICANE MARKS II AND IV (HAWKER-BUILT)

Eighth production batch of 1,200 aircraft built by Hawker Aircraft Ltd., Kingston and Langley, during 1942-43. Contract No. 62305/39C, Parts 1-6. *KW696-KW731, KW745-KW777, KW791-KW832, KW846-KW881, KW893-KW936, KW949-KW982, KX101-KX146, KX162-KX202, KX220-KX261, KX280-KX307, KX321-KX369, KX382-KX425, KX452-KX491, KX521-KX567, KX579-KX621, KX691-KX736, KX749-KX784, KX796-KX838, KX851-KX892, KX922-KX967, KZ111-KZ156, KZ169-KZ201, KZ216-KZ250, KZ266-KZ301, KZ319-KZ356, KZ370-KZ412, KZ424-KZ470, KZ483-KZ526, KZ540-KZ582, KZ597-KZ612.* Also Sea Hurricane Mk. IIC conversions, ***NF668-NF703.*** **Deliveries commenced, 20/11/42; completed 19/4/43. Average rate of production, slightly more than 8 aircraft per day.**

No. 6 (F) Squadron, Grottaglie, Italy, 3/44; tropical Mk. IV's with anti-tank guns:
KW716 ("A"), KX178 ("P"), KX805 ("V"), KX826 ("R"), KX885 ("Z"); 4/44, tropical Mk. IV's with RP's: KZ187 ("X"), KZ188 ("E" and "C"), KZ321 ("N"); detached to Haifa, 12/43; mixed gun and RP armament: KZ240 ("Y"); detached to Fayid, 12/43; mixed gun and RP armament: KZ397.

No. 113 (F) Squadron, Burma, 1944; tropical Mk. IIB fighter-bomber:
KZ279.

No. 137 (F) Squadron, Milfield and Southend, 7/43; Mk. IV's with anti-tank guns and RP's:
KZ399, KZ400, KZ620, KZ655, KZ676, KZ827, KZ829; following aircraft took part in first Mk. IV Rhubarb with anti-tank guns, Belgium, 23/7/43; KW918, KZ827; following aircraft attacked and destroyed the Hansweert lock gates, Holland, 2/9/43, with RP's: KX585, KZ248, KZ396, KZ576 (missing with F/O J. L. De Houx).

No. 164 (F) Squadron, Middle Wallop, 6/43; anti-shipping reconnaissance and sweeps, Mk. IV's:
KX413 ("H"), KX540, KX541, KX702, KZ406; Warmwell, 7/43; anti-shipping reconnaissance, Mk. IV's: KX409, KX536, KX542, KZ193 ("O"): Manston, 8/43; Rhubarbs, Mk. IV's: KX582, KX596, KX879, KZ480; Fairlop, 9—10/43; intruder operations, NF Mk. IV's: KW919, KZ405, KZ552, KZ609.

No. 184 (F) Squadron, Manston, 6—8/43; anti-shipping strikes; Mk. IV's with mixed anti-tank and RP armament:
KX401 ("G"), KX407 ("A"), KZ584 ("W"), KX807 ("Q"), KX884 ("T"), KZ185 ("K"), KZ188 ("E"), KZ189 ("F"), KZ193 ("X"), KZ378 ("V"; missing from attack on shipping off Dutch coast, 28/6/43), KZ554 ("S"), KZ572 ("B"), KZ579 ("Z"), KZ606 ("L"), KZ607 ("F"), KZ611 ("B").

No. 213 (F) Squadron, El Gamil, 6/43; MT convoy patrols, tropical Mk. IIC:
KZ130.

No. 279 (F) Squadron, 1943; Mk. IIC's:
KZ571, KZ576.

No. 283 (F) Squadron, 1943; Mk. IIC:
KW280.

No. 288 Squadron, 1943; Mk. IIC's:
KZ405 ("J"), KZ576 ("P").

No. 335 (Hellenic) Squadron, RAF, Middle East; shipping protection, 10/43, with tropical Mk. IIC's:
KZ130, KZ142, KZ335, KZ435.

No. 451 Squadron, RAAF, Middle East; interception duties at Idku, 3/43, with tropical Mk. IIC's:
KZ115, KZ118, KZ446.

Sea Hurricane Mk. IIC conversions. The following aircraft were delayed for naval conversion at Langley; subsequent registration in brackets:
KW770 (NF668), KW774 (NF671), KW791

(NF669), KW792 (NF670), KW799 (NF672), KW800 (NF673), KW804 (NF674), KW807 (NF677), KW808 (NF675), KW809 (NF678), KW810 (NF676), KW816 (NF679), KW817 (NF680), KW827 (NF681), KW828 (NF682), KW849 (NF683), KW850 (NF684), KW860 (NF685), KW862 (NF686), KW868 (NF687), KW870 (NF688), KW878 (NF689), KW880 (NF690), KW897 (NF691), KW899 (NF692), KW908 (NF693), KW909 (NF694), KW910 (NF695), KW911 (NF696), KW918 (NF697), KW919 (NF698), KW920 (NF699), KW921 (NF700), KW928 (NF701), KW929 (NF702), KW930 (NF703), Delivery, May 1943.

Aircraft shipped to Russia, 1943 (some from Middle East stocks). Mark IIC fighter-bombers:
KW706, KW723, KX113, KX125 (fighter), KX137, KX538 (tropical), KX545 (tropical), KZ234; Mark IID's: KW777 (tropical), KX177 (tropical), KX181 (tropical), KZ301; Mk. IV's: KX813 (fighter), KX865 (anti-tank), KX888 (believed lost at sea); KZ509 (shipped as catapult Sea Hurricane Mk. IIC, but not used on voyage to Russia).

Other aircraft:
KX180 (Mk. IV to A & AEE for RP trials); KX247 (tropical Mk. IV to AFTU India, 1944); KX405 (built as tropical Mk. IV; converted to Mk. V prototype standard with Merlin 32; trials at Langley and A & AEE); KX412 (comparative trials with KX405 with HAL, 2/43); KX700 (training aircraft Mk. IIC; no guns); KX858, KX862 (Mk. IV TI aircraft, A & AEE, 1943); KX877 (built as tropical Mk. IV; spent short time modified to Mk. V standard, HAL and A & AEE, 3/43); KZ138 (tropical Mk. IIb of No. 71 OTU, North Africa, 1944); KZ193 (prototype Hurricane Mk. V; later returned to Mk. IV standard); KZ232 (used for stability trials, HAL and A & AEE, 1943); KZ352 (tropical Mk. IIC to GATU, India, 6/45); KZ466 (performance trials, HAL, 4/43); KZ569 (to TSTU, India, 1944-45).

THE HAWKER HURRICANE MARKS II AND IV (HAWKER-BUILT).

Ninth production bach of 1,205 aircraft built by Hawker Aircraft Ltd., Kingston and Langley, during 1943. Contract No. *62305/39/C Parts 7-12. KZ613-KZ632, KZ646-KZ689, KZ702-KZ750, KZ766-KZ801, KZ817-KZ862, KZ877-KZ920, KZ933-KZ949, LA101-LA144, LB542-LB575, LB588-LB624, LB639-LB687, LB707-LB744, LB769-LB801, LB827-LB862, LB873-LB913, LB927-LB973, LB986-LD131, LD157-LD185, LD199-LD219, LD232-LD266, LD287-LD315, LD334-LD351, LD369-LD416, LD435-LD470, LD487-LD508, LD524-LD539, LD557-LD580, LD594-LD632, LD651-LD695, LD723-LD749, LD772-LD809, LD827-LD866, LD885-LD905, LD931-LD979, LD993-LD999.* Deliveries commenced 18/4/43; completed 29/9/43. Average rate of production, slightly more than 7 aircraft per day.

No. 6 (F) Squadron; tropical Mk. IV's with RP'; Grottaglie, Italy, 4/44:
LB649 ("T"); Falconara, Sardinia, 10/44: LB774 ("E"), LD162 ("B"), LD168 ("N").

No. 28 (F) Squadron, Burma, 1944; tropical Mk. IIB fighter-bomber:
LD172.

No. 113 (F) Squadron, Burma, 1944; tropical Mk. IIB fighter-bombers:
LB551, LD667 ("C").

No. 137 (F) Squadron, Southend, 7/43; Mk. IV's with anti-tank guns and RP's:
KZ620, KZ655, KZ676, KZ827, KZ829; following aircraft took part in first Mk. IV Rhubarb with anti-tank guns, Belgium, 23/7/43: KZ661, KZ662.

No. 164 (F) Squadron, Fairlop, 9-10/43; intruder operations, N.F. Mk. IV's:
KZ708, KZ912.

No. 184 (F) Squadron, Manston, 8/43; anti-shipping strikes; Mk. IV's with mixed anti-tank and RP armamanent:
KZ678 ("D"), KZ703 ("H"), KZ715 ("N"), KZ918.

No. 438 Squadron, RCAF, Hurn, 1944; Mk. IV:
LD973 ("O").

No. 439 Squadron, RCAF, Wellingore and Hurn, 3/44; Mk. IV's:
LD570, LD972 (collided with Thunderbolt fighter, 21/3/44).

No. 451 Squadron, RAAF; interception duties at Idku, 10/43, with Mk. IV's:
LB938, LB939.

No. 607 Squadron, AAF, Far East, 1944; tropical Mk. IIC fighter-bomber:
KZ724 ("S"); tropical Mk. IV fighter-bomber: KZ729.
No. 10 Squadron, IAF, India and Burma, 1944; tropical Mk. IIC:
LB732; tropical Mk. IV's: LB602, LB664.

No. 1344 Flight; tropical Mk. IIC's:
KZ710, LB734.

No. 1415 (Meteorological) Flight, Habbaniyah, 1945; tropical Met. Mk. IIC:
LD109.

Aircraft shipped to Russia, 1943-44; Mk. IIC Fighters:
KZ858, LD205; Mk. IIC fighter-bomber: LB991.

No. 71 OTU, Middle East, 1944:
KZ819 (tropical Mk. IIC), LB675 (tropical Mk. IIB).

No. 73 OTU, 1944; Mk. II target tugs:
LB891, LB893.

Other aircraft:
KZ679 (also as KZ679/G, to A & AEE for RP trials); LB771 (later Ground Instruction Machine 4628M); LD182 (crashed during test, 16/7/43; deposited at Premier Garage, Bath Road, Slough, 13/9/43); LD264, LD438, LD439 (to A & AEE for trials, 23/7/43); LD412 (tropical Mk. IV to GATU, India, 1944); LD621 (damaged in forced landing during flight testing, 25/8/43).

THE HAWKER HURRICANE MARKS II AND IV (HAWKER-BUILT).

Tenth production batch of 1,357 aircraft built by Hawker Aircraft Ltd, Kingston and Langley during 1943-44. Contract No. 62305/39/C, Parts 13-19. LE121-LE146, LE163-LE183, LE201-LE214, LE247-LE273, LE291-LE309, LE334-LE368, LE387-LE405, LE432-LE449, LE456-LE484, LE499-LE535, LE552-LE593, LE617-LE665, LE679-LE713, LE737-LE769m KE784-LE816, LE829-LE867, LE885-LE925, LE938-LE966, LE979-LE999, LF101-LF135, LF153-LF184, LF197-LF237, LF256-LF298, LF313-LF346, LF359-LF405, LF418-LF435, LF451-LF482, LF494-LF516, LF529-LF542, LF559-LF601, LF620-LF660, LF674-LF721, LF737-LF774, MW335-MW373, PG425-PG456, PG469-PG499, PG512-PG554, PG567-PG610, PZ730-PZ778, PZ791-PZ835, PZ848-PZ865. Deliveries commenced, 29/9/43; completed, 24/5/44. Average rate of production, almost 6 aircraft per day.

No. 6 (F) Squadron, Canne, 11/44; Mk. IV's with RP armament:
LE291 (operating from Vis, attacked German HQ at Zegar, Yugoslavia, 18/12/44); LF482 ("C"; RP attack on Risan, Yugoslavia, 21/11/44); LF498 (RP attack on bridge at Spuz, 11/44).

No. 20 (F) Squadron, Burma, 1944; tropical Mk. IID:
LF113.

No. 113 (F) Squadron, Burma, 1944; tropical Mk. IIB fighter-bomber:
LF346 ("F").

No. 247 (F) Squadron:
PG739 ("E"; used for communications).

No. 309 (of Province Ziemia Czerwienska) Squadron. (Polish), RAF:
LF363 (Mk. IIC; last RAF Hurricane on Charge; see below).

No. 288 Squadron, Mk. IIC:
LE836 ("W"; used for communications).

No. 289 Squadron, Mk. IIC's:
LF580 ("W"), LF626 ("N"), LF628 ("S"), LF636 ("Z"), LF757.

No. 501 Squadron, AAF:
PG570 (used for communications).

No. 514 (Combined Operations) Squadron, 1944; Dundonald, Mk. IIC's:
LF428, LF514, LF534.

No. 516 (Combined Operations) Squadron, 1944; Dundonald, Mk. IIC's:
LE999, LF133, LF160, LF165, LF180, LF207, LF534 (hit landing craft at Troon, 18/3/44, during exercises and crashed).

No. 521 (Meteorological Calibration) Squadron, Langham, 11/44; Met. Mk. IIC's:
PZ803, PZ806, PZ818-PZ820.

No. 601 Squadron, AAF, 1945; Mk. IV:
PG440 (used for communications).

No. 650 Squadron, 3/44; Mk. IV:
LE514.

No. 695 Squadron, 1944:
PG751 ("W").

No. 10 Squadron, IAF, India and Burma, 10/44; tropical Mk. IV:
LF497.

GATU, India, 1945; tropical Mk. IIC's:
LE398, LE502, LE815, LF157, LF203; tropical Mk. IV's: LE646, LE993.

No. 41 OTU, 5/45; Mk. IIC's:
LF295, LF296, LF322, LF346, LF363 (see also under Other Aircraft below), LF366, LF368, LF376, LF379, LF386 (to No. 49 MU, 7/45), LF396, LF680, MW363, PG476.

No. 61 OTU, 7/45; Mk. IIC's:
LF293 (tropical), LF366, LF367, LF379, MW366.

Aircraft shipped to Russia, 1944; Mk. IIC fighter-bombers:
LE529; Mk. IV's: LF463, LF470, LF473, LF481, LF509, LF510, LF592, LF595, LF596.

Aircraft sold to Portugal, 1945-46; tropical Mk. IIB fighter-bomber:
LF342; tropical Mk. IIC fighter-bombers: LF133, LF360, LF383, LF422, LF425, LF514, LF564, LF565, LF568, LF570, LF586, LF620, LF699, LF706, LF717, LF757, LF772, MW373, PG521, PG535, PG538, PG543, PG599, PG610, PZ735, PZ738, PZ745, PZ759.

Aircraft sold to Eire, 3/45. IAC Nos. in brackets:
LF541 (116), LF624 (118), PZ796 (120).

Coningsby Station Flight, 1944; Mk. IIC's:
LF374, LF382, LF395.

Waddington Station Flight, 1944; Mk. IIC's:
LF404, LF421.

Empire Central Flying School, Hullavington, 1944; Mk. IIC's:
PG567, PG568, PG571, PG573.

Ground Instruction Machines (subsequent airframe nos. in brackets where known):
LE747 (5496M), LF398 (5415M), LF580 (5402M), LF627 (with No. 5 School of Technical Training); LF674 (5418M), LF680 (with No. 5 School of Technical Training); LF738 (5405M), LF745 (5406M), LF755 (5419M), MW340 (5463M), MW341 (5311M), MW534 (5321M), PG440 (5462M), PG541 (5420M), PG484 (5422M), PG497 (5147M), PG498 (5421M), PG517 (5407M), PG529 (5408M), PG546, PG570 (5464M), PG593, PG604 (5416M).

Other aircraft:
LE353 (Mark IIC; armament later removed and aircraft supplied to No. 231 Communications Flight); LE525 (to A & AEE for trials, 11/43); LE796 (tropical Mk. IIC of D Flight, No. 22 AACU), 1944); LE806 (Mk. IIC; force landed during test; delivery delayed until 19/12/43); LF363 ("F"); Mk. IIC of No. 309 (Polish) Squadron, 2/44; No. 41 OTU, 1945; to Waterbeach Station Flight, 1950-54; Biggin Hill, 1959. Last Hurricane held on RAF Charge; leader of Battle of Britain commemorative "fly-past"; also used in several films); LF422 (trials with Merlin 22

engine at Langley 1/45); LF632 (Mk. II trainer; guns removed); PZ865 (purchased by HAL off Contract, named *The Last of the Many!* Registered G-AMAU and raced by HAL on many occasions, 1945-60).

THE HAWKER HURRICANE MARK II (AUSTIN-BUILT)

One production batch of 300 aircraft built by the Austin Motor Co., Ltd., Longbridge, during 1941. *AP516-AP550, AP564-AP613, AP629-AP648, AP670-AP714, AP732-AP781, AP801-AP825, AP849-AP898, AP912-AP936.* Excepting *AP516-AP518,* this entire batch was scheduled for supply to Russia during 1941-42, for service with the Russian Navy. Although a large proportion in fact sailed by PQ convoy (many aircraft being lost en route due to enemy action), other aircraft were retained for issue to the Royal Air Force, principally as replacements.

No. 208 (AC) Squadron, Western Desert and Habbaniyah, Iraq, 1942; tropical Tac R Mk. IIB's:
AP851, AP852.

No. 312 (Czech) Squadron, RAF, Kenley, 6/41; offensive sweeps, Mk. IIB's:
AP518, AP519.

No. 335 (Hellenic) Squadron, RAF, Middle East, 1942-43:
AP656 (tropical Mk. IIB in action over Fuqa and Daba, 10/42); AP888 (tropical Mk. IIC engaged in shipping protection, Central Mediterranean, 10/43).

No. 607 Squadron, AAF, Manston, 2/42; Channel sweeps, Mk. IIB:
AP896.

No. 1414 (Meteorological) Flt., Mogadishu and Eastleigh, East Africa, 1943-45; tropical Met. Mk. IIC:
AP920.

Other Aircraft:
AP516 (retained by Austins for performance and handling tests); AP517 (production performance and handling checks, HAL and A & AEE, 1941).

THE HAWKER HURRICANE MARK I (CANADIAN-BUILT)

First production batch of 40 aircraft built by the Canadian Car and Foundry Corporation, Canada, during 1939-40. *P5170-P5209.* Rolls-Royce Merlin III engines, DH-Hamilton Hydromatic 3-blade propellers and many other proprietary items despatched from the United Kingdom; completed aircraft shipped to Britain during March-August 1940. Some aircraft retained in Canada.

No. 1 (F) Squadron, Wittering, 9/40:
P5187.

No. 43 (F) Squadron, Tangmere, 8/40:
P5191, P5196.

No. 111 (F) Squadron, Croydon, 8/40:
P5209.

No. 249 (F) Squadron; in action over Brooklands, 4/9/40:
P5206.

No. 253 (F) Squadron; in action over Brooklands, 4/9/40:
P5172, P5179, P5181.

No. 502 Squadron, AAF, 8/40:
P5189 ("M"), P5193 ("O").

No. 56 OTU, Sutton Bridge, 11/40:
P5195.

Other Aircraft:
P5170 (production check trials at RAE, HAL and A & AEE, 3/40-8/40); P5176 (forced landed in Eire, 1942; bought and transferred to IAC as 93); P5183 (later converted to Sea Hurricane Mk. IA; Merchant Ship Fighter Unit, Speke, 1941); P5187 (catapult trials, RAE, 11/40-3/41).

THE HAWKER CANADIAN HURRICANE MARK X.

Second production batch of 340 aircraft built by the Canadian Car and Foundry Corporation, Canada, during 1940-41. *AE958-AE977, AF945-AG344, AG665-AG684.* Packard-built Rolls-Royce Merlin 28 engines driving 3-blade Hamilton Hydromatic

propellers, many without spinners. Approximately the first 100 machines built with eight-gun wings, the remainder with Mk. IIB twelve-gun wings, but many subsequently equipped with four Oerlikon 20-mm guns. Some aircraft were retained in Canada and served with the RCAF, 1940-42.

No. 1 Squadron, RCAF (later No. 401 Squadron), Northolt, 8/40-9/40; all with 8-gun wings:
AE960 ("W"), AE966 ("A"), AE974 ("C"), AF990-AF992, AG108-AG112, AG667 ("L"), AG670.

No. 1 (F) Squadron, Hawkinge, 5/41; 12-gun wings:
AG118, AG216 ("O"); Tangmere, 1942; intruder with 4-cannon wings: AG118.

No. 43 (F) Squadron, Tangmere, 6/42; anti-shipping strikes; 4-cannon wings:
AF961, AG236.

No. 56 (F) Squadron, 2/41; 12-gun wings:
AG196, AG248 ("B").

No. 182 (F) Squadron, 1942; 12-gun wings:
AG159 ("O"), AG232 ("P").

No. 527 (Calibration) Squadron, Hornchurch, 10/43; armament removed:
AG146.

No. 607 Squadron, AAF, Manston, 2/42; daylight sweeps; fighter-bomber with 12-gun wings:
AG338.

No. 680 (PR) Squadron, Communications Flt., Cyprus, 9/43; tropical aircraft, guns removed:
AG513.

No. 1432 (Army Co-operation) Flt., tropical aircraft with 8-gun wings:
AG177 (Oshogbo, Nigeria, crashed 12/12/42); AG276 (Kano, Nigeria, 1942-43).

Other aircraft converted to take 12-gun wings at No. 13 MU, Henlow:
AG277, AG301, AG341, AG344, AG671, AG680.

Aircraft serving with RCAF, Canada (RCAF nos. in brackets):
AG299 (1378), AG310 (1379).

No. 55 OTU, 1941; 8-gun wings:
AG237, AG253, A267.

No. 59 OTU, 1941; 8-gun wings:
AG123, AG212, AG245.

THE HAWKER CANADIAN HURRICANE MARK X.

Third production batch of 149 aircraft built by the Canadian Car and Foundry Corporation, Canada, during 1941. *AM271-AM369, BW835-BW884.* Packard-built Merlin 28 engines. Aircraft built with eight Browning gun wings but many later modified with twelve-gun or four-cannon wings. Some aircraft retained in Canada for service with the RCAF.

No. 1 (F) Squadron, Tangmere, 1942; intruder fighter with 4-cannon wings:
AM280.

No. 43 (F) Squadron, Tangmere, 1942; intruder fighters with 4-cannon wings:
AM311 ("X"), AM315 (took part in Dieppe operation, 19/8/42).

Aircraft converted to take 12-gun wings at No. 13 MU, Henlow:
AM271, AM301, AM302, AM349, AM367, BW870, BW883.

Aircraft shipped to Russia, 1/42:
AM367, BW835, BW851, BW878, BW879.

THE HAWKER CANADIAN HURRICANE MARK XI

Fourth production batch of 150 aircraft built by the Canadian Car and Foundry Corporation, Canada, during 1941-42. *BW885-BX134.* Many aircraft later modified to take 12 Browning guns or 4 Oerlikon or Hispano cannon. Some aircraft retained for service with the RCAF in Canada.

Aircraft converted to take 12-gun wings at No. 13 MU, Henlow:
BW901, BW906, BW907, BW914, BW919,

BW941, BW944, BW948, BW962, BW963, BW967, BX125, BX128, BX133.

Delivered to No. 22 MU, Silloth, with 4-cannon wings for despatch to Russia, 1942:
BW920, BW922, BW926, BW984, BX102, BX108-BX111, BX119-BX124.

THE HAWKER CANADIAN HURRICANE MARK XII

Fifth production batch of 248 aircraft built by the Canadian Car and Foundry Corporation, Canada, during 1942. *JS219-JS371, JS374-JS420* (with 12-gun wings); *JS421-JS468* (most of these aircraft equipped with 4-cannon wings in the United Kingdom, 1943).

No. 59 OTU, 12/43; 12-gun wings:
JS330.

Delivered to No. 22 MU, Silloth and Packing Depot, Sealand, for despatch to Russia; 12-gun wings:
JS220, JS221, JS225, JS227, JS228, JS233, JS240, JS256, JS300, JS391, JS396-JS399, JS405-JS412, JS415, JS419.

Delivered to No. 13 MU, Henlow and Packing Depot, Sealand, for despatch to Russia:
JS219, JS229, JS232, JS235, JS237, JS241, JS257, JS309, JS317.

THE HAWKER CANADIAN HURRICANE MARK XIIA

Sixth production batch of 150 aircraft built by the Canadian Car and Foundry Corporation, Canada, during 1942. Packard-built Rolls-Royce Merlin 29 engines driving 3-blade Hamilton Hydromatic propellers. Most aircraft built initially with 8-gun wings, but some subsequently modified with 12-gun and 4-cannon wings. *PJ660-PJ695, PJ711-PJ758, PJ779-PJ813, PJ842-PJ872.* Most aircraft despatched direct to Russia or to Burma at end of 1943; few sent to the United Kingdom, 1943. Small number was fitted with deck landing equipment for use by the Royal Canadian Navy as the Sea Hurricane Mark XIIA.

The Hurricane Repair Organisation

Having recorded at some length the production and service details of the Hawker Hurricane, some measure of the efforts of the United Kingdom Hurricane Repair Organisation is provided by the accompanying table. The Organisation was based at the Langley Repair Department and the procedure adopted was as follows: The existence of a crashed or damaged Hurricane was notified to the nearest Unit in the complex which, if not already performed by the Service, would inspect the aircraft and categorize the extent of damage. While the aircraft was removed to the Unit for repair, the damage extent would be notified to Hawker Aircraft Ltd., who would issue the necessary drawings and instructions and any proprietary equipment necessary to make the aircraft fully serviceable again. Repair of the 4,500-odd Hurricanes returned to the Royal Air Force involved the issue of early 120,000 drawings in the United Kingdom alone.

Contractor or Unit	*1939*	*1940*	*1941*	*1942*	*1943*	*1944*	*1945*	*Total*
Airtraining (Oxford) Ltd	—	86	136	130	17	—	—	*369*
Airwork Ltd, Renfrew	—	—	1	1	—	—	—	*2*
Austin Motor Co Ltd	—	13	11	—	—	—	—	*24*
CRU No. 1, Cowley	—	128	193	44	—	—	—	*365*
Cunliffe Owen Aircraft Ltd	—	5	2	—	—	—	—	*7*
David Rosenfield Ltd	—	—	—	50	96	34	—	*180*
De Havillands, Hatfield	—	138	12	—	—	—	—	*150*
De Havillands, Witney	—	—	17	90	116	41	—	*264*
Gloster Aircraft Co (Works)	—	15	23	1	—	—	—	*39*
Gloster Aircraft Co (Site)	—	—	1	—	—	—	—	*1*
Hawker Aircraft Ltd (Works)	—	55	106	8	—	—	—	*169*
Hawker Aircraft Ltd (Site)	5	70	381	276	7	—	—	*739*
Helliwells Ltd, Walsall	—	—	26	28	—	—	—	*54*
Henlow, No. 13 MU	—	272	254	205	9	—	—	*740*
Morrison Engineering Ltd	—	—	—	20	62	97	37	*216*
Reid and Sigrist (Site)	—	1	—	—	—	—	—	*1*
Rollasons, Hanworth	—	38	55	87	82	2	—	*264*
Rolls-Royce Ltd	—	147	118	—	—	—	—	*265*
Sealand, No. 30 MU	—	—	2	—	—	—	—	*2*
Scottish Aviation Ltd (Works)	—	4	13	—	—	—	—	*17*
Scottish Aviation Ltd (Site)	—	1	15	—	—	—	—	*16*
Short Bros. Ltd (Works)	—	—	10	9	2	—	—	*21*
Short Bros. Ltd (Site)	—	—	3	3	—	—	—	*6*
Taylorcraft Ltd, Rearsby	—	—	64	175	107	—	—	*346*
43 Group Salvage Units	—	—	—	43	111	107	19	*280*
Annual Totals	5	973	1,443	1,170	609	281	56	*4,537*

Appendix A: "One-off" Hurricane Experiments

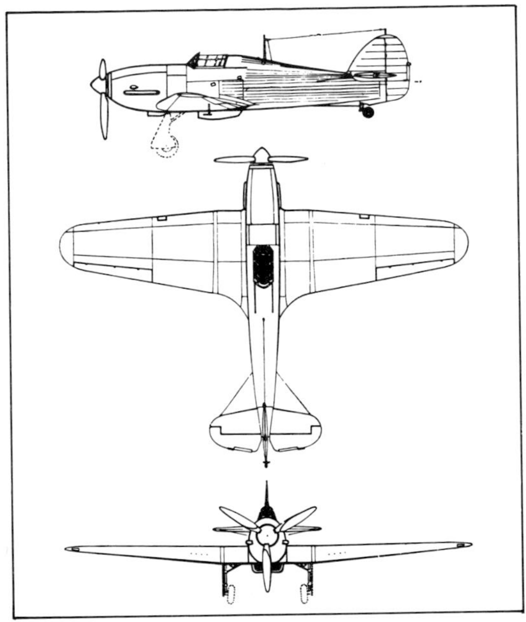

The Yugoslav Hurricane with Daimler-Benz DB601A.

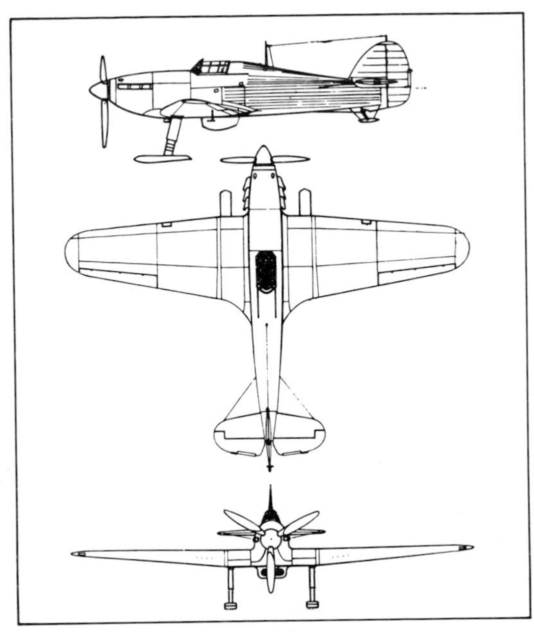

The Canadian Hurricane with fixed ski undercarriage.

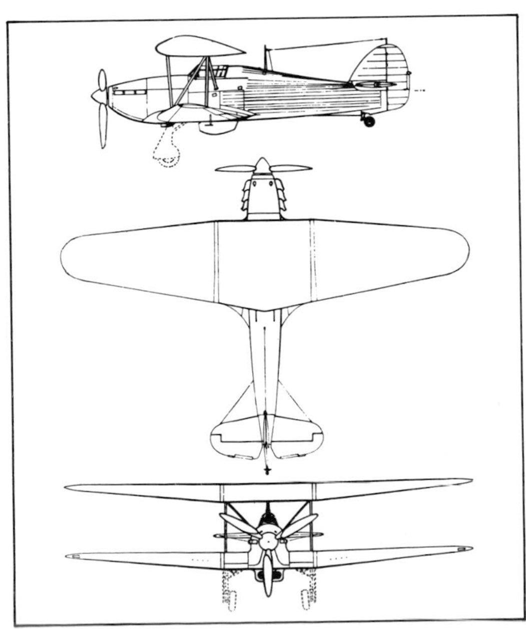

The Hillson FH.40 Hurricane Slip-wing aircraft.

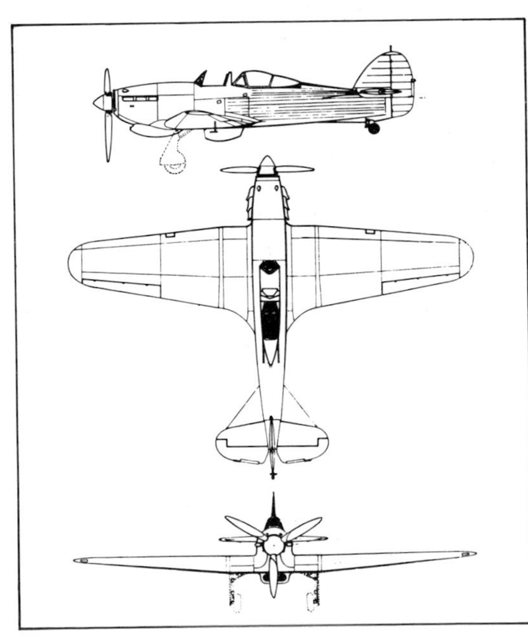

The Persian Hurricane Two-Seater Trainer.

Appendix B: Uncompleted Hurricane Projects

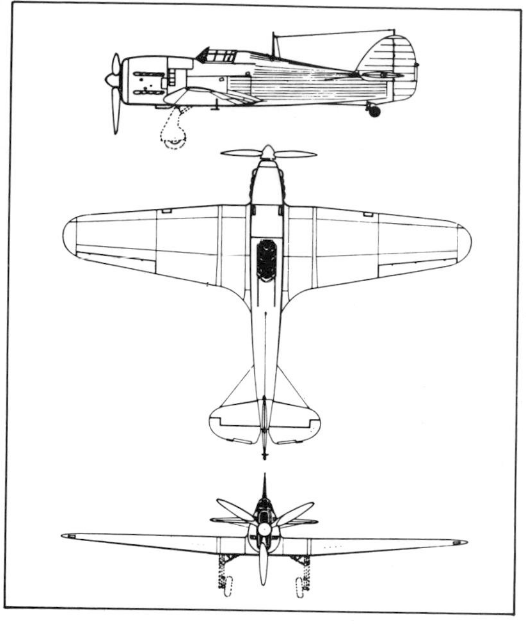

Hurricane project with Napier Dagger engine.

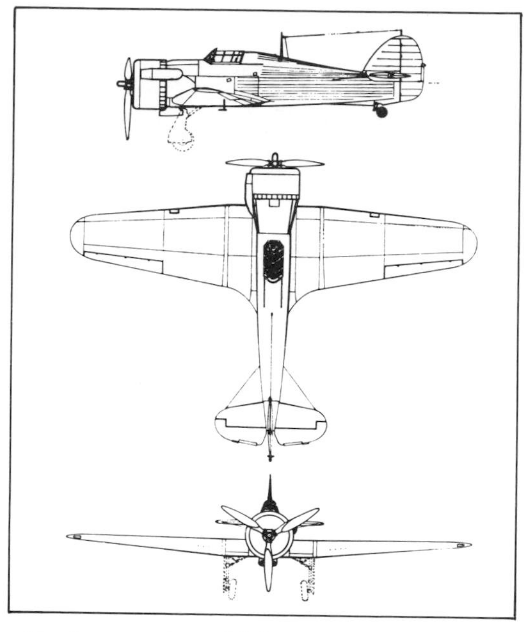

Hurricane project with Bristol Hercules engine.

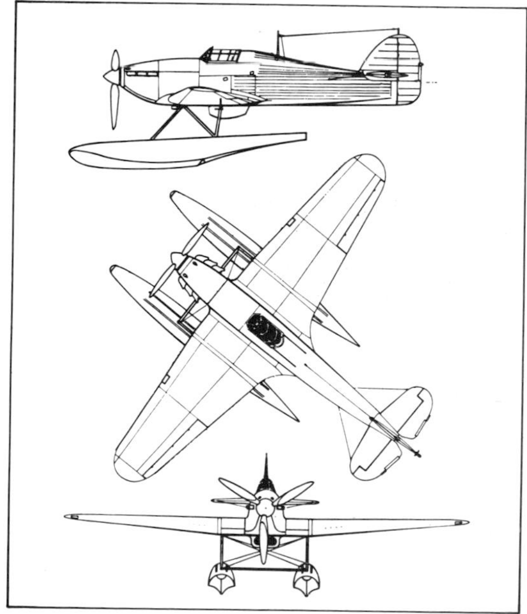

Hurricane with twin-float undercarriage (conversion commenced but not completed).

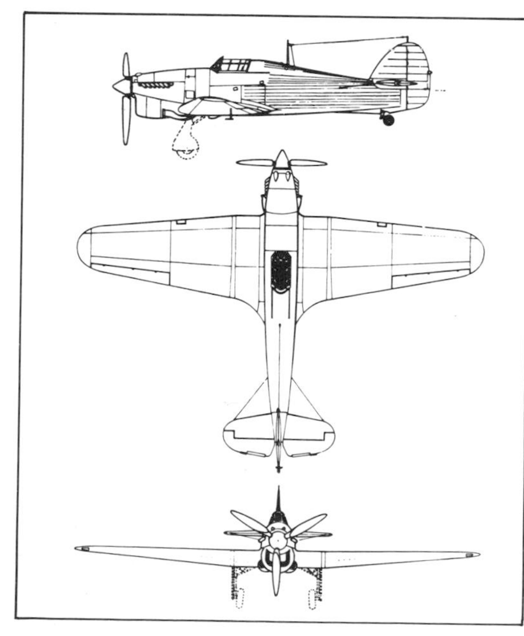

Hurricane project with Rolls-Royce Griffon engine.

Selective Bibliography

Allward, Maurice. *Hurricane Special* (Ian Allan, 1975).
Babington-Smith, Constance. *Testing Time* (Cassell, 1961).
Bader, Group Captain Douglas. *Fight For The Sky* (Collins, 1973).
Barker, Ralph. *Hurricats* (Pelham Books, 1976).
Beedle, J. *43 Squadron* (Beaumont, 1966).
Bishop, Edward. *The Battle of Britain* (Allen & Unwin 1960).
Their Finest Hour (Ballantine Books, 1968).
The Guinea Pig Club (Macmillan, 1963).
Bolitho, Hector. *Combat Report* (B. T. Batsford, 1943).
Bowyer, Chaz. *Hurricane at War* (Ian Allan, 1974).
Brickhill, Paul. *Reach for the Sky, the Story of Douglas Bader* (Collins, 1954).
Churchill, Winston. *The Second World War* (Cassell, 1948-1954).
Collier, Basil. *The Defence of the United Kingdom* (HMSO, 1957).
Collier, Richard. *Eagle Day* (Hodder and Stoughton and J. M. Dent, 1966).
Dean, Sir Maurice. *The Royal Air Force and Two World Wars* (Cassell, 1979).
De Chair, Somerset. *The Golden Carpet* (Faber, 1944).
Douglas-Hamilton, Lord James. *The Air Battle for Malta* (Mainstream, 1981).
Douglas of Kirtleside, Marshal of the RAF Lord, *Years of Command* (Collins, 1966).
Dudgeon, Air Vice-Marshal Tony. *Luck of the Devil* (Airlife, 1985).
Farrier, David. *The Sky is the Limit* (Hutchinson, 1943).
Galland, Adolf. *The First and the Last* (Methuen, 1955).
Gallico, Paul. *The Hurricane Story* (Michael Joseph, 1959).
Grey, G. G. *British Fighter Planes* (Faber, 1941).
Griffith, Flight Lieutenant Hubert. *RAF Wing in Russia* (Hammond, Hammond, 1942).
Hawker, H. M. and Grieve, K. M. *Our Atlantic Attempt* (Metheun, 1919)
Hyde, H. Montgomery. *British Air Policy Between the Wars* (Heineman, 1976).
Jackson, Robert. *Fighter Pilots of World War II* (Arthur Barker, 1976).
Kelly, Terence. *Hurricane Over the Jungle* (Kimber, 1977).
Kinsey, Gordon. *Martlesham Heath.* (Lavenham Press, 1975).
Leasor, James. *Singapore: The Battle That Changed the World.* (Hodder & Stoughton, 1968.
Lloyd, F. H. M. *Hurricane* (Harborough Publicity Co, 1945).
Mason, Francis K. *The Hawker Hurricane* (Macdonald, 1962).
Masters, David. *So Few* (Eyre & Spottiswoode, 1941).
Orange, Vincent. *Sir Keith Park* (Methuen, 1984).
Owen, Lieutenant-Colonel Frank. *The Campaign in Burma* (HMSO, 1946).
Penrose, Harald. *The Pioneering Years, 1903-1914*
The Adventuring Years, 1920-1939 (Putnam, 1973).
Widening Horizons 1930-1934. (HMSO, 1980).
The Ominous Skies, 1935-1939 (HMSO)
Quill, Jeffrey. *Spitfire: A Test Pilot's Story* (John Murray, 1983).

Richards, Denis and Saunders, H. St J. *RAF 1939-1945* (HMSO 1953-1954).
Roskill, Captain S. W. *War At Sea* (HMSO 1954-1961).
Smith, Malcolm. *British Air Strategy Between the Wars* (Oxford, 1984).
Slim, Field Marshal Sir William. *Defeat into Victory* (Cassell, 1956).
Stewart, Adrian. *Hurricane* (William Kimber, 1982).
Tedder, Marshal of the Royal Air Force Lord, *With Prejudice* (Cassell, 1966).
Terraine, John. *The Right of the Line* (Hodder & Stoughton, 1985)
Thetford, Owen. *Aircraft of the RAF since 1918* (Putnam, 1957).
Till, Geoffrey, *Air Power and the Royal Navy* (Janes, 1979).
Townsend, Group Captain Peter. *Duel of Eagles* (Weidenfeld & Nicolson 1970)
Tsuji, Colonel M. *Singapore: The Japanese Version* (Mayflower-Dell 1960; UK, 1966).
Wood, Derek and Dempster, Derek. *The Narrow Margin* (Hutchinson, 1961).
Wragg, David. *Wings Over The Sea* (David & Charles, 1979).
Wright, Robert. *Dowding and the Battle of Britain* (London, 1969).
Wykeham, Peter. *Fighter Command* (Putnam, 1960).

Index